PARENTING AND DISABILITY

Disabled parents' experiences of raising children

Richard Olsen and Harriet Clarke

First published in Great Britain in April 2003 by

The Policy Press
Fourth Floor, Beacon House
Queen's Road
Bristol BS8 1QU
UK

Tel +44 (0)117 331 4054
Fax +44 (0)117 331 4093
e-mail tpp-info@bristol.ac.uk
www.policypress.org.uk

British Library Cataloguing in Publication Data

A catalogue record for this book is available from the British Library

ISBN 1 86134 364 7 paperback

A hardcover version of this book is also available

Richard Olsen is a Research Fellow at the Nuffield Community Care Studies Unit,
University of Leicester and **Harriet Clarke** is a Lecturer in Psychology and Social
Work in the Institute of Applied Social Studies, University of Birmingham.

Cover design by Qube Design Associates, Bristol.
Front cover: photographs supplied by EyeWire and Stone.
Printed and bound in Great Britain by Hobbs the Printers Ltd, Southampton.

Dedicated with love to our parents, Pauline (RO),
Jane and Michael (HC)

Contents

List of tables

Acknowledgements

We gratefully acknowledge the support of the Department of Health in funding this research under the Supporting Parents programme. We would also like to thank the many organisations, and the individuals within them, who supported us throughout this research. They helped in various ways, including giving advice on the design and content of the research, putting us in touch with families directly, and giving us a platform from which to publicise the work. We are particularly indebted to Fairdeal, an advocacy organisation run by disabled people in Leicester and Leicestershire, for their initial support in putting us in touch with disabled parents locally. We would also like to thank the members of our advisory group for their supportive advice throughout the research. They were Jo Bodsworth, Julie Falvi, Debbie Mumford, Jools Potter, Jacqui Sealy, Jackie Shenton, Peter Smith, Roy Taylor, Vince Thacker and Michele Wates. In addition, we would like to thank Trent Focus, a primary care research and development network based at the Universities of Leicester, Nottingham and Sheffield, for their help with recruitment. Furthermore, we would like to acknowledge the helpful support of Sue Moyers, of the University of Bristol, for her help in providing data from the Looking After Children community sample.

We also received a great deal of support from colleagues within the Nuffield Community Care Studies Unit at the University of Leicester. In particular, Gillian Parker and Billie Shepperdson gave us encouragement and support throughout the project, as well as the benefit of their wide experience. We received great support from secretarial colleagues Anne Ablett, Teresa Faulkner and Linda Norman. We also want to express our thanks to Rachel Clarke who worked on the management of the quantitative data in SPSS.

Finally, we would like to thank all the members of those families we interviewed. We hope that this book does full justice to the range and depth of experiences they shared with us.

Terminology

Social research places particular importance on labels and definitions. This is especially so in the areas of disability and family life, where they reflect the assumptions that researchers make about what it is to experience disability, and what it means to be a parent, mother, father, daughter, son, and so on.

In our research, we have conformed to the terminology and definitions of disability preferred by most organisations of disabled people in the UK. For example, we prefer the terms 'disabled people' and 'disabled parents' to 'people with disabilities' and 'parents with disabilities'. These latter terms, still popularly used about (and by) disabled people in North America and elsewhere, locate disability within the bodies (and minds) of disabled people themselves. They do not sit easily with our commitment to a social model of disability that sees the fundamental experience of disability as one of social organisation, access and equality of opportunity. In this book, then, the term 'disabled parent' is used inclusively, not just for those with physical impairments. When we do want to distinguish between the experience of parents with different impairments, we use the terms 'physical impairments', 'sensory impairments' and 'mental health impairments'. The first two terms are commonly accepted ways of describing the impairments of disabled people; however, the latter term is less commonly used, but is chosen to reflect our commitment to include all parents within a social model perspective that differentiates between impairment and disability. In addition, we argue that alternatives serve either to locate the 'problem' in impairments themselves ('mental health problems', 'mental health difficulties') or define people in terms of their service use ('mental health service user', 'mental health system survivor') in a way which would not only be unacceptable for people with physical and sensory impairments, but which does not reflect the lived reality of the people in our study, many of whom had not accessed the mental health 'system' and can hardly therefore be said to be 'users' or 'survivors' of it. In Chapter Six, however, we use the term 'mental distress' in preference to 'mental health impairments'. This reflects our argument that the social model is in need of renewal in order adequately to account for the experiences of parents experiencing mental distress, and that the neat separation of impairment and disability in mental health terms is inappropriate given the multiplicity of causes – physical, biological as well as experiential and social – of mental distress. We acknowledge, however, that adequate terminology that synthesises a social model approach with the particular experiences of people with different impairments is yet to be developed fully; we simply present here the thinking behind the approach we have taken.

We have tried to be consistent in our labelling of family members. The questionnaires that we developed at the outset of our research used the terms 'parent', 'spouse' and 'child' to describe the people in each family that we interviewed. However, in this book we prefer the term 'partner' to spouse when talking about the other parent in two-parent families. By consistent use of the terms 'mother' and 'father', we specify the gender of parents. Similarly, we label children as 'son' or 'daughter'.

When quoting from interviews with family members, we have used codes to indicate the speaker. The following are examples:

Mother (PI), dual-parent family indicates a mother with physical impairments in a dual-parent family.

Father, dual-parent family (mother, MHI) indicates a father in a dual-parent family whose partner or wife has mental health impairments.

Son (14), single-parent family (mother, PI, SI) indicates a 14-year-old son, in a single-parent family, where the mother has both physical and sensory impairments.

When quoting families that took part in Stage Two of the research, each family is denoted by a letter from A to L. This enables the reader to refer to Table 2.5 for more background information on each particular family.

In some families, both parents are disabled. In order to avoid confusion, we do not represent the impairments of partners or children of the disabled parent in the above coding system. If a partner's or child's disability is significant, we elaborate in the text.

Introduction

In recent years, disabled parents have grown increasingly vocal in challenging the barriers that they face in fulfilling their parental role. They, and their organisations, have begun to place issues of importance to disabled parents on national and local policy agendas, often in collaboration with allies in academia and both statutory and voluntary sectors. They have also sought to transform public and professional perceptions of disabled people as the recipients (as opposed to providers) of 'care', which often reflect a deep-seated antipathy to the very idea of disabled people having children. Indeed, we deliberately chose this book's subtitle – *Disabled parents' experiences of raising children* – because of the assumption that would inevitably be made in some quarters of a book entitled *Parenting and disability*: that it must be about disabled children and their (implicitly non-disabled) parents. An important aspect of these attempts to challenge dominant perceptions, and to raise the profile of the parental responsibilities of disabled people, is the development of a literature that views parenting and disability as essentially about equal opportunities. Others, often disabled parents themselves, have already begun this process and we hope that this book makes a contribution to the development of such a literature.

Our book is the result of a research project entitled 'Parenting and disability: the role of formal and informal networks', funded by the Department of Health as part of its Supporting Parents research programme, and carried out at the Nuffield Community Care Studies Unit, University of Leicester, between 1997 and 2000. The Supporting Parents programme followed on from previous research initiatives funded by the Department of Health, which had pointed to the ways in which child protection work, as opposed to family support work, had dominated the post-Children Act environment. Therefore our research, with a 'normative' group of disabled parents (that is, a group not defined by their use of a particular service), was very timely in that it looked at access to support for a group of disabled parents who were not predetermined in some sense as a 'social problem', or already identified as having 'failed' for any reason. This made a research study informed by a social model perspective on disability possible from the outset.

Parenting is simultaneously one of the most private, intimate roles that we undertake and yet is one subject to the greatest public gaze and scrutiny. Its position at the intersection of public and private worlds makes parenting a wonderfully rich subject to research. Indeed, it is also an *enriching* subject to research, and we know that we have a different understanding of parenting, and of disability, in our own lives as a result of carrying out this project and of being flying visitors in the lives of the families we met. The public and private faces of parenting also make for data that are complex, difficult and contingent. They do not make for easy analysis and flat description. This research, and the process of dissemination we are now undertaking, has therefore involved a process whereby the ideas and concepts emerging from the data are continually revisited and subject to critical scrutiny. From the genesis of the original research study in the concerns we had about the construction of the children of some disabled parents as 'young carers', through the process of designing the research tools we would use, to the gathering and analysis of the data, the publication of our report for the Department of Health, and to the delivery of the final typescript for this book, we have been engaged in a continual development of ideas. This development of our ideas is partially in response to the gathering pace of change in the policy and practice backdrop to disability and parenting. This book, then, is more a staging post in the development of our ideas about parenting and disability than a definitive statement.

Chapter One situates parenting and disability within a review of the relevant literature. We argue that disabled parents have been largely invisible in that tradition of social policy research, which has looked at parenting support and at the barriers that particular parents face in bringing up their children. Of course, disabled parents are anything but absent from a much larger research tradition that looks for deficits and pathology in their parenting and for negative consequences for children of having a disabled parent. We also look at the policy context, focusing in particular on the 1989 Children Act and the 1990 NHS and Community Care Act. What role do these Acts play in structuring the response of formal services to disabled parents? And how will their policy and practice legacies (direct payments legislation, the *Framework for the assessment of children in need and their families, fair access to care services*) influence the way in which parents are supported?

Chapter Two is a brief overview of the demographic characteristics of the sample of parents and families who took part in the research. A lengthy discussion of methodological issues was thought unnecessary in the body of the text, although Appendix One discusses these issues in greater depth.

In Chapter Three, we tackle the issue of support, and in particular the barriers that many disabled parents can face in accessing support in raising children. We argue that the support needs of disabled parents are essentially no different to those of all parents. It is more important therefore, to remove the barriers to participation in parenting than it is to establish an inappropriate welfare response aimed at meeting their 'special needs'. We examine access both to formal and informal sources of support, and the interaction between them. Access to support for disabled parents in the context of broader divisions within society, and especially those rooted in social disadvantage and gender, is also discussed. For us, understanding how disability is experienced by parents is intricately bound up with these broader issues.

Chapter Five places disabled parents' experiences of raising their children in a life course perspective. Change – be it in the nature of impairments, the size and structure of the family, the social and economic circumstances of the family, the needs of individuals (parents and children) in the family, and so on – is fundamental to an understanding of parenting and disability. We consider the changing dilemmas and choices faced by disabled parents, from decisions about having children in the first place, through changes to family composition and parental impairment, to their plans for the future.

Chapter Six addresses the importance of seeing parenting and disability as involving sets of relationship between family members, and of promoting parental choice and control in the ways in which family relationships can be maintained. Our emphasis here is on the social experience of disability, one that affects individuals and relationships both within the family and between family members and the outside world. We also discuss the complex ways in which the experiences of impairment and the experiences of disability intersect. We do this in particular with reference to the complex nature of mental health impairments as well as to their origin, in many cases, in social experience. This requires us to re-examine (and renew) our understanding of the social model of disability so that the experiences of those with mental distress can be adequately represented.

Chapter Seven presents our overall conclusions. It also suggests potentially fruitful areas of future research.

ONE

Invisibility and exclusion

Introduction

This chapter provides an overview of the research literature concerning the parenting of disabled people, as well as other issues – or 'problems' – that relate more indirectly to the parenting of disabled people. In addition, this chapter places our research within some of the key legislative and policy frameworks that underpin the relationship between the state, disabled parents, and their children.

This highlights three particularly important issues. First, disabled parents are all too often absent from research agendas that emphasise the social and environmental context in which parenting takes place. We look at their exclusion from the growing body of research that has, in recent years, focused on the provision of parenting support and education services. However, this reflects a much broader invisibility: a search of the literature for the terms 'disabled' and 'parents' yields many studies of childhood disability but fewer about parental disability. Where parental disability is referred to, it is more commonly in the context of elderly, disabled parents, and the role of their adult children in caring for them, reflecting a deeper antipathy to the fact of disabled people having children. This itself reveals the assumption that disabled people are somehow inevitably the recipients of 'care', rather than the providers of it.

Second, excluding disabled parents from mainstream parenting agendas means that studies of disability and parenting have generally involved a search for deficits in parents and/or negative outcomes in their children. Furthermore, they underline the idea that parental impairment – rather than social disablement – is the key variable of interest. The result is a literature that is not only often weak in understanding the importance of economic and social structures in facilitating parenting, but also separates and fragments the study of disability and parenting by looking at the issue in impairment-specific chunks (such as parents with multiple sclerosis, depressed parents, visually impaired parents). It is a literature that is dominated both by clinical, or quasi-clinical, research designs, and by studies of particular 'social problems', again usually involving the welfare of children, which reflect more indirectly on the (quality of) parenting of disabled people. We review one such example – the construction of some disabled parents' children as 'young carers' – in some detail, given the important role it has played in driving forward policy, practice and research agendas in the past decade.

We also look briefly at the place of parenting in the literature and politics of the disability movement itself. The emergence of parenting within the work and writings of the disability movement, and therefore the emergence of the disabled parents' movement itself, is intertwined with the development of an explicitly feminist disability perspective. This particular perspective challenges the marginalisation of issues important to disabled women within and without the disability movement and its literature.

Third, the absence of disabled parents from mainstream parenting support research agendas is consistent with a UK policy and practice framework that, despite trying to incorporate an understanding of the social context in which parenting takes place, remains wedded to the idea that effective parenting rests centrally on the capacities and attributes of individual parents. An example of this is the tension with which parenting capacity is constructed in important policy and practice documents, such as the *Framework for the assessment of children in need and their families* (DoH, DfEE and HO, 2000). This attachment to individual capacity, we argue, is inconsistent with a social model approach to disability that sees parenting as a social role that disabled people can find difficult to access, and one where the support necessary for them to sustain occupation of that role is differentially available.

As its starting point, this chapter looks at recent mainstream research into parenting, and parenting support, in the UK, and at the absence of disabled parents from this research. We contrast this with a review of key issues in the clinical literature on disability and parenting, looking in particular at how the adoption of a medical model approach has led researchers to ask very different questions about the parenting of people with different impairments. This is then followed by a review, not only of the explosion of interest in 'young carers' since the early 1990s, but also of the critique made by authors (ourselves included) arguing for a reorientation of the issue towards one of parental support and independence.

The second half of the chapter situates parenting and disability issues within a broad and complex legislative and policy framework, governing, among other things, the relationship between the state and the family, and the delivery of support for disabled people. It also highlights significant recent developments in the growth of an active disabled parents' movement in the UK, and in a growing recognition of the parenting role of disabled people in policy and practice circles. The chapter ends with a brief discussion of some other key issues, including the importance of gender in research on parenting and the development of inclusive approaches, not only to disability, but to parenting itself.

Disabled parents: invisibility and pathology

Parenting research: where are disabled parents?

Parents – or, more specifically, *parenting* – lie at the heart of many recent UK social policy initiatives. These include initiatives aimed at addressing educational underachievement, promoting social inclusion and reducing levels of juvenile crime and disorder (Lloyd, 1999). This is reflected in government policy and practice in two ways. The first is the long-term aim of reducing the number of children in poverty, through changes in benefits and in taxation systems – for instance, increases in Child Benefit, targeting tax breaks at people with dependent children through the Working Families' Tax Credit, the replacement of the married person's tax allowance with a children's tax credit, and so on. These changes represent an important recognition of the significance of material security to the wellbeing of children and in enabling parents to parent successfully.

In addition to this focus on poverty, however, is a second element of social policy on parenting: the significant expansion of programmes and initiatives collected under the loose umbrella terms 'parenting education', 'parenting support' and 'family support'. The focus of these interventions is extremely varied, from North American-developed behavioural modification programmes (Webster-Stratton, 1999), to a range of voluntary and statutory sector-led services aimed at supporting parents[1]. Furthermore, provision varies in terms of the following:

- preferred format (for instance, group-based versus individual-based);
- provider (from the statutory/voluntary sector, led by health/social care professionals or volunteers, and so on);
- target audience (for example, a universal focus on parents, or specifically aimed at children of a certain age, parents of a certain gender or ethnic group).

There is also now a growing body of descriptive and evaluative work looking at the effectiveness of family and parenting support initiatives[2]. Of particular importance in this body of work are issues of access. For instance, it is widely recognised that existing initiatives have been largely aimed at mothers, and that barriers to the participation of fathers should be addressed (Smith, 1997; Mortley, 1998; Webster-Stratton, 1999). In addition, the accessibility of parent support measures for people from minority ethnic groups has also been called into question (Webster-Stratton, 1999). Other studies highlight the particular support issues for parents in various marginalised groups. For instance, in their review of support programmes for parents of teenagers, Roker and Coleman (1998) report service provision developments that aim to meet the specific needs of gay and lesbian parents, lone parents, parents of adopted children, parents in stepfamilies and parents from travelling communities. What is particularly striking in this agenda is the absence of disabled parents, especially given the inclusion in discussions about service developments of parents of disabled children and parents in rural areas who are said to face additional transport problems (Roker and Coleman, 1998).

This invisibility is illustrated further in other work on the provision of parenting support. For example, in her review of the growing involvement of statutory and voluntary bodies in providing parenting education and training, Smith (1997) discusses the broader context in which parenting takes place. She talks about changes and challenges for parents and parenting in the 1990s, including issues such as sex on TV, the availability of drugs, concern about children and the environment, the impact of geographic mobility on support for parents, the smaller families from which parents themselves come, as well as the increased prevalence of single parenting and reconstituted families. Smith also examines structural factors, such as poverty, poor housing, unemployment and family conflict, and the role they play in exacerbating challenges to parenting. In addition, she invokes developments in the promotion of children's rights, parental responsibility and the legislative framework on children and the family, shifting attitudes towards fathers and fathering, cultural influences on child rearing, the links between parenting, family support and criminal behaviour in young people, and the balance (for women, at least) of work and family life. The invisibility of disabled parents from this panorama is again immediately apparent, despite the importance of most – if not all – of these issues to disabled parents themselves. Even when Smith discusses access issues, she does so in a generic sense, for instance, when discussing whether support groups should levy a charge, whether they take place in 'ambient' surroundings, whether they should be available only to those parents already tied into other support mechanisms, and whether or not they have a crèche available for people with young children. She makes no specific mention of disability in terms of access *barriers*, but, rather, only in terms of the importance of making parents with learning difficulties aware that they can cope with "the demands of the course" (Smith, 1997, p 28).

In sum, then, mainstream parent support provision, and the research literature accompanying it, is bereft of consideration of disabled parents as a group with particular access issues. This is supported by evidence provided by the National Family and Parenting Institute (NFPI) mapping exercise, which reported that only around one in five services made efforts to include disabled parents (Henricson et al, 2001).

Social and family policy research: where are disabled parents?

The past 30 years have been a time of great change in terms of the economic and social context in which families are formed and sustained. These changes include dramatic shifts in the nature of the labour market, the shrinkage of traditional male manual employment, and the expansion of service sector jobs, many of which are filled by women looking to combine work with childcare responsibilities. At the same time, a higher proportion of people are not having children, while those that choose to are having them later in their lives and in smaller numbers (Ferri and Smith, 1996). Children are much more likely to experience parental separation and divorce now than in previous decades. For example, approximately 25,400 couples divorced in 1961, compared to around 155,000 in 1991. Lone-parent families constituted 9% of all families in 1971, but by 1994, this figure had risen to 21% (Oakley et al, 1998). It is currently estimated that around 28% of children will experience the divorce or separation of their parents before they are 16 years of age, although the picture is complicated further by the high level of remarriage and repartnering (Oliver and Sapey, 1999, p 78). Therefore, families are more likely to be smaller and to be 'atypical'; that is, they are increasingly unlikely to conform to the stereotype of two married, co-resident parents, and are increasingly likely to involve unmarried parents, lone parents, step-parents and stepchildren, foster and adoptive parents/children, and even same-sex parents. In addition, the increased demand for flexibility in the labour market means that families are less likely to live within established informal networks, and are more likely to be dispersed from available support (Harding, 1996).

These changes are extremely important in the context of how disabled parents manage the job of rearing children. This is particularly so given the increasing polarisation of wealth and resources over this same time period, which has seen a dramatic increase in the numbers of children living in poverty, as well as the growth in the number of two-wage and no-wage families, and the corresponding decline of the single-wage family (Ferri and Smith, 1996). This polarisation of wealth and the close association, not only between disability and poverty, but also between poverty and single parenthood, constitute an important context to this research. Of further significance is what some authors describe as a shift towards parenting as a consumer *choice*, and away from parenting as a taken-for-granted social function and responsibility (Ferri and Smith, 1996, p 9). This has important implications for the balance between parents and the state in rearing children. While legislation such as the 1989 Children Act seems to offer opportunities for parental support, it must be remembered that it was introduced against the background of a raft of social policies aimed at minimising the role (and responsibility) of the state, and reinforcing the self-reliance of individuals and their families (Harding, 1996). Indeed, it has been argued (Tunstill, 1997) that the ideology underpinning the 1989 Children Act and other family and child welfare policy developments – that is, that children's needs are best met within autonomous, and largely private, (nuclear) families – owes as much to the concerns of 'New Right' authors about the breakdown of society as it does to the aspirations of liberal social policy (see, for example, Morgan, 1995).

This increasing 'privatisation' of child rearing coincides with a greater focus on the qualities required to parent in the first place. Campion (1995) identifies key historical, social and technological developments that have led to a greater willingness to scrutinise the parenting qualifications of various individuals and groups. These include a greater awareness of children's rights; the demands of previously excluded groups (including disabled people) to have and raise children; the increasing divorce rate, which necessarily involves an assessment of who children should subsequently reside with; and advances in fertility treatments that raise moral and ethical dilemmas – for instance, older mothers, lesbian and gay parents, and surrogacy.

However, conventional social policy research and analysis has been almost universally blind to the existence of disabled parents. When disability does get discussed, it is usually in the context of informal caring, and the degree to which broader socioeconomic changes threaten the availability of women as care givers (Harding, 1996). Correspondingly, various pieces of equal opportunities legislation (sex discrimination and equal pay legislation in particular) are often cited (for example, Harding 1996) as significant in shaping debates about family law, parenthood and domestic responsibilities. However, a legislative framework seeking to promote the equal opportunities of disabled people is seldom, if ever, seen as central to debates about parenting and the family. This highlights a broader invisibility of disability and parenting in social and family policy. For example, De'Ath's (1989) review of research concerning children and the family explores issues of step parenting, single parenting, children who run away, and so on, but says nothing about disabled parents.

Finally, research into domestic work – whether carried out by children or parents – has seldom seen illness or disability as an important issue (notwithstanding the 'young carers' debate, which we review later). Research into children's domestic work has generally been informed by a broader, feminist literature about gender and housework (see, for example, Oakley, 1976). Typically, it has focused on gender stereotyping and the choices that (implicitly non-disabled) parents make regarding their children's socialisation (Zill and Peterson, 1982; Bird and Ratcliff, 1990). Consequently, sociological interest in children's contribution to domestic work has overwhelmingly focused on gender and socialisation, with disabled parents once again overlooked (Morrow, 1996).

Substantial changes have taken place in recent decades in the size and shape of families, as well as the economic and social framework in which they are formed and sustained. These changes are as relevant to disabled parents as they are to non-disabled parents; in some cases, such as the increasing polarisation of wealth, the increasing number of families with children in poverty, and the increasingly dispersed nature of informal networks, the changes may be particularly pertinent to disabled parents. However, conventional family policy and research have yet to consider parental disability (as opposed to childhood disability) as a major issue, thereby contributing further to the relative invisibility of disabled parents.

Deficits and (in)capacity in research on parenting and disability

We have already discussed the exclusion of disabled parents from the developing research literature on parenting support. That body of work locates parenting within what might be broadly called an 'equal opportunities' framework, with an emphasis on access and equity with regard to parenting support, and on barriers to support that might exist for particular groups of parents. This is significant: the absence of disabled parents in this literature only serves to isolate them within an even longer tradition of 'clinical' work.

Pathology is the perspective typically adopted by researchers looking at parenting and disability from within clinical disciplines. That is, the (in)capacity of disabled parents, and the search for negative outcomes for children of disabled parents. Studies in this area indicate the degree to which clinical research on parenting and disability has adopted negative and pathologising frames of reference[3].

Physical and sensory impairment and the impact on parenting

Antipathy towards disabled people having children has deep historical roots, finding its most violent expression in the murder of up to 200,000 disabled people in Nazi Germany. This atrocity was fuelled by the adoption of 'eugenicist' theories by mainstream scientific communities in Europe and North America in the first half of the 20th century (Burleigh, 1994), which emphasised the danger to the health of the population as a whole of allowing 'defectives' to reproduce. The strength of such eugenicist thinking was also evident in the subsequent restrictions on the reproductive rights of disabled people (including forced sterilisation) practised in many countries in the second half of the 20th century. This antipathy towards disabled people having children was also apparent in academic publications. For example, less than 30 years ago, one book counselled:

> In a young married couple, who want a child, pregnancy is not inadvisable where multiple sclerosis can be controlled.... [A]n abortion must be seriously considered where coping with the disease, the pregnancy and the family prove to be too much. (Heslinga et al, 1974, p 87)

The same book goes on to suggest that any disabled person's wish to adopt children must be interpreted as fulfilling a need to "brighten up their dreary lives" (Heslinga et al, 1974, p 178). Of course, what is absent from these extreme assertions is *support* (or the lack of it), and the role it plays in enabling disabled people to parent successfully. This forms a recurrent theme in our research.

The ambivalence towards the parenting of disabled people was apparent in research carried out by the Maternity Alliance (Goodman, 1994). This found significant evidence that professionals continue to counsel and pressurise disabled women into avoiding pregnancy, or into choosing abortions on the basis of anticipated difficulties with parenting.

Studies of the 'impact' of parental physical impairments on children inherently pathologise the parenting provided by those parents, since they search for deficits in parenting or family functioning. Studies focusing on the benefits to children of having disabled parents are seldom seen. One exception is a study by Reinelt and Fried (cited in Kelley et al, 1997), in which mothers with multiple sclerosis (MS) described their children as independent, self-sufficient, empathetic, sensitive and helpful, and thought their disability had little negative effect on their children. Despite such success, most mothers in that study reported facing scepticism or discrimination about their parenting capacity from both the medical profession and the general public.

Studies of parenting and physical impairments have also typically adopted an implicitly 'medical' model of disability, with a range of problems in family life, including behavioural problems in children, parental divorce and educational underachievement, inappropriately ascribed to parental impairment. For instance, Jamison and Walker (1992) report the effects of parents' chronic pain on the social and developmental problems in children. However, they neglect to look at the support in managing pain that parents receive (or do not receive), and the disabling response of others to parental pain. As Greer (1985, p 134) argues:

> Since society has often been portrayed as viewing physical disability as bad, it is understandable that parents with disabilities might perceive any misbehaviour on the part of their children as a reflection of themselves.

Researchers have also attached importance to the issue of children's *adjustment* to parental disability (LeClere and Kowalewski, 1994), with a familiar medical model approach to impairment and its direct causal relationship with negative child outcomes. Aside from the shortcomings of this kind of approach, it says little about the 80% of disabled parents, surveyed by the Maternity Alliance (1994), who chose to become parents as disabled people, rather than who became disabled following the birth of their children.

The literature raises two further important issues concerning parents with physical impairments. The first of these is discipline. The assumption is often made that lack of physical mobility will necessarily restrict the ability of parents to discipline their children. This, it is argued, has long-term ramifications, first, with regard to child wellbeing, second, concerning the extra 'burden' placed on non-disabled partners, and finally, for public order. Greer (1985) is critical of such narrow thinking. Not only is the environment in which parents promote the safety and good behaviour of their children often ignored (for instance, the affordability of stair safety-gates, the limited options for moving house that disabled people often have), but such an approach also lacks imagination on the issue of discipline itself. Greer points out that the problem is an overreliance on the physical disciplining of children in our society, and not the physical inability of some disabled parents fully to engage in it.

Second, research into physically disabled parents has placed great emphasis on parenting as a set of *tasks*, from picking up toys and opening cans of baked beans, to changing nappies and engaging in 'rough and tumble' (Heslinga et al, 1974). Consequently, fears about the quality of parenting are essentially fears about the inability of parents with physical impairments to carry out this range of tasks. Within this approach, the research raises such questions as 'Can the parent do the things parents have to do?', 'And if not, what are the effects on the child?' (Greer, 1985). Absent is consideration of the relative accessibility of the environment in which parenting takes place; absent, also, is consideration of the availability of support (whether technological, financial, practical, emotional, and so on) that will compensate for those areas where physical difficulties exist. Disabled parents themselves have led the challenge to this assumption, placing greater emphasis on the *role* of parents in providing love, support, guidance, leadership, organisation, and so on, rather than on the physical tasks associated with parenting:

> [M]any of us find that, even while lying flat on our backs in hospital, we are the ones who have to organise to keep the family together and cared for. (Morris, 1989, p 127)

This conceptual distinction between tasks associated with parenting, and the broader role of 'parent', is an important theme in our research. Much of the substantive material presented hereafter is informed by an approach that emphasises parenting as being essentially more about a role than about a series of discrete physical tasks.

Mental health impairments and the impact on parenting

Research into parenting and mental health has a long history, with interest focused mainly on motherhood, especially in the North American literature (Oyserman et al, 1994; Mowbray et al, 1995; White et al, 1995; Zeitz, 1995). While much clinical research into parenting and disability has involved the search for deficits (as well as for more general negative impacts on children's wellbeing), the focus of the literature has linked parental mental health much more directly with child deprivation, neglect and abuse. The roots of this association can be traced back to early studies of maternal deprivation and to the influence of attachment theory[4] in highlighting the 'dangers' of 'mentally ill' mothers (for a review, see White, 1996). Indeed, a concern that the children of 'mentally ill' parents have a greater likelihood of developing mental health impairments of their own later in life continues to inform current policy and practice. For instance, the current *National strategy for carers* (DoH, 2000a) highlights the risk to children of 'mentally ill' parents of developing mental health impairments of their own.

Of particular significance are a number of popular studies that have shown an apparent overrepresentation of parental mental health impairments in cases of fatal child abuse. For instance, Falkov (1996) found parental 'psychiatric disorder' to be present in 32 of the 100 fatal child abuse cases he studied. Similarly, James (1994) found that out of 30 fatal child abuse cases, six involved parental mental health impairments. However, as Stanley and Penhale (1999) rightly point out, what these studies show is that most child abuse fatalities involve families *without* parental mental health impairments.

The mental health impairments of parents continue to feature prominently in research and policy concerning parenting and the family. For example, the influential Department of Health Child Protection Research Programme of the early 1990s drew attention to the significance of a lack of parental warmth and high levels of criticism as risk factors for child neglect. These were implicitly and explicitly associated with parental (or typically maternal) depression and anxiety (Dartington Social Research Unit, 1995). Parton argues that a key outcome of the child protection research programme was the recognition that:

> with the exception of a few severe assaults and some sexual maltreatment, long-term difficulties for children seldom follow from a single abusive event or incident – rather they are more likely to be a consequence of living in an unfavourable environment, particularly one which is *low in warmth and high in criticism*. (Parton, 1997, p 6, emphasis in original)

Research into the reasons why children enter the care system also shows a strong association with depression and other mental health impairments in parents (Bebbington and Miles, 1989). Similarly, the relationship between child abuse and maternal depression is a well-researched area. Of particular importance here is work of Sheppard (1997, 2002). In one study, in which 116 mothers of children on child protection registers were interviewed, Sheppard found that:

> The really marked difference between families with abused children and those not abused was where maternal depression was present. (1997, p 97)

Sheppard's is an important study, in that it acknowledges the importance of addressing depression among mothers of children on child protection registers. It also acknowledges the disabling effect that child protection proceedings can have on the capacity of parents to fulfil their parenting responsibilities:

> [T]he effects of these [child protection] investigations on women already wracked by the effects of depression may be even more severe, and in some circumstances inhibit the very parenting capacities which practitioners are ultimately attempting to encourage. (Sheppard, 1997, p 105)

Yet, as with much of the research into parenting and disability generally, what evidence there is suggests that one can only understand the impact of mental health impairments on parenting within the context of available support, and the broader socioeconomic disadvantages that face people with mental health impairments. For example, Stanley and Penhale (1999) found that nine out of 13 mothers with severe mental health impairments (whose children were the subjects of child protection proceedings) had no access to a mental health social worker. Furthermore, seven had no access to community psychiatric nurse support. This indicates that, when statutory authorities register child protection concerns in families with parents with mental health impairments, support for parents is often a secondary concern.

This is compounded by the fact that formal services available to people with mental health difficulties have traditionally neglected any parenting responsibilities once people have entered the system of psychiatric services (De Chillo et al, 1987; Cottrell, 1989; Gross, 1989). A study by Coleman and Cassell (1994) found that, while family composition was typically recorded in the case notes of adults admitted to psychiatric hospitals, this usually involved information about the *family of origin* of the patient. This is evidence not only of the way in which disabled people are constructed essentially as *recipients* of care and support, but also of how their impairments are constructed in terms of their own relationship as children to *their* parents and family circumstances. Furthermore, research suggests that the parenting responsibilities of mental health service users will be noted only in those cases where social services are involved. What this indicates is that, for services to take an interest in service users as parents, they need to be identified in some way as 'failing' parents, or as having children 'at risk' (Hawes and Cottrell, 1999). Hawes and Cottrell (1999) point out that no mention is made of childcare in the *Health of the nation outcome scales* (Wing et al, 1996). Similarly, in a survey of one UK health region, Sayce (1999) found that social service records provided no space to note the existence of the children of adult mental health service users; there was space, however, to record information concerning 'carers'.

More recently, researchers have begun to adopt a more holistic approach to the parental responsibilities of mental health service users. For instance, Wang and Goldschmidt (1994) sought the experiences of professional interventions on the part of their sample: newly admitted Danish psychiatric patients with young children. Although a key part of the study remained the presence or otherwise of mental health impairments in the children, this research at least located the 'problem' in terms of the availability of support, and in terms of interventions that might enable and sustain family relationships rather than undermine them. Also, while parenting and mental health remains an overwhelmingly *clinical* research area, the social and support context in which people parent with mental health impairments is receiving more attention (for a review, see Oyserman et al, 1994). In the UK, Carlisle (1998) also reported on two modest projects that were examining the increasing recognition of parental responsibilities of women with mental health impairments, research that continues to highlight the health services' lack of awareness concerning the presence of children in the families of their patients. Researchers are now discussing the close and reciprocal relationship between parenting and mental health, especially in the context of the extra anxiety generated by having to make arrangements for children while being in receipt of inpatient psychiatric treatment (Coleman and Cassell, 1994). Other researchers are focusing on the negative impact that fear of losing one's children can have on mental health (Sayce, 1999).

Another important issue when looking at parenting and mental health is the powerful role that adult psychiatry plays in the UK's child protection system (Appleby and Dickens, 1993; Reder and Lucey, 1995; Reder and Duncan, 1997, 1999). Researchers in this area point to the authority afforded psychiatrists in diagnosing mental illness, and the weight that their diagnoses carry in child protection proceedings. Reder and Duncan argue, for example, that professionals should be aware that, if children are at risk in some way because of parental mental health impairments, then they are at risk "from their parent's behaviour, not from their diagnosis" (1999, p 148). In addition, Reder and Lucey have argued that the individual focus of psychiatric diagnosis and intervention means that "the interpersonal contributions to, or consequences of, the index patient's problems receive comparatively less interest" (1997, p 37). In other words, the medical care that parents with mental health impairments encounter is likely to be focused on their needs as individual patients, and not on their support needs as people with caring responsibilities. The stigma associated with mental health impairments, the often deeply personal and sensitive issues that underpin it, and the importance of confidentiality in medical relationships, make it increasingly likely that parents with mental health impairments will be 'treated' in isolation from their broader family context.

As we have seen, the literature on parenting and mental health has much in common with the wider clinical research literature on parenting and disability. The focus is on the impaired capacity of parents to parent, and on the search for negative long-term outcomes for children of parents with mental health impairments. In addition, parenting and mental health are linked very closely with the risk of neglect and abuse (see, for example, Sheppard, 1997), while the context of available support is generally ignored, both by researchers and by professionals interacting with 'patients' in a clinical setting.

Learning disabilities and the impact on parenting

The origins of research into the parenting of people with learning disabilities lie in eugenics, and in a concern for the quality of the 'population stock' (Booth and Booth, 1993a, 1993b, 1994a, 1994b), as well as a persistent concern with controlling fertility, particularly that of young disabled women (Newbrough, 1985). Indeed, the involuntary sterilisation of disabled people, and people with learning disabilities in particular, has been a common practice throughout most of the 20th century (Gilhool and Gran, 1985; Begum, 1996).

Even progressive campaigners on family planning in the first half of the 20th century were clear about the need for:

> the compulsory sterilisation not only of the insane and feeble minded, but of revolutionaries, half-castes, the deaf, the dumb, the blind and anyone else who might threaten the vigour of the race. (Campion, 1995, p 131)

Several researchers have pointed to the subsequent replacement of a eugenicist agenda primarily by a concern with the likelihood of children inheriting learning disabilities from their parent(s), and secondarily by a focus on risk and on child protection (for a review, see Andron and Tymchuk, 1987). Research adopting a social model perspective on the parenting of people with learning disabilities has shown, however, that these parents are subject to more stringent criteria than non-disabled parents regarding what constitutes 'good enough parenting'. Intelligence Quotient (IQ) has been used as a spurious proxy for the quality of parenting that people with learning disabilities can provide (Dowdney and

Skuse, 1993; Booth and Booth, 1994a), but so too have 'common' aspects of parenting, such as minor childhood injuries and the physical punishment of children, which are more likely to be seen as evidence of poor parenting on the part of learning-disabled parents than of the population of parents as a whole (Andron and Tymchuk, 1987). Furthermore, studies have often focused on single mothers, raising the question as to whether deficits identified are the product of learning disabilities, or of the lack of support available to them as single parents. They have also failed to acknowledge that many parents with learning disabilities will have grown up in institutional settings and may therefore have lacked appropriate parental role models, and will have been excluded from the usual transmission of parenting skills and techniques within families (Gath, 1988).

In addition, there is often an unnecessary link made between the skills lacking in parents with learning disabilities and the quality of parenting they give. For example, the consequence of an inability to read and write may be the failure to respond to official correspondence (concerning immunisation, school events, and so on). This can then be reinterpreted as a problem of parental motivation, rather than the inadequate ways in which the NHS and schools choose to communicate with parents (Booth and Booth, 1993a). Indeed, the views expressed by disabled parents in our study indicate that parents with a wide variety of impairments (and not just learning disabilities) experience this negative reinterpretation of their parenting behaviour in the light of assumptions about parenting (in)capacity. Parents with learning disabilities are also significantly overrepresented in child protection figures. For example, the Social Services Inspectorate (SSI) inspection of services for disabled parents found that child protection concerns had been raised in almost two thirds of cases involving parental learning disabilities, compared to a figure of around 20% for the group of disabled parents as a whole (DoH, 2000b).

In sum, the parenting of people with learning disabilities is conventionally seen as problematic, the common assumption being that not only will children be at significant risk of harm, but that the root cause of the problem is the lack of the skill and good judgement needed for effective parenting. This helps to explain why the issue of baby care dominates the research literature, and perhaps also the decision to take the infants of learning-disabled mothers into care.

The parenting of disabled people as a social problem: the case of 'young carers'

An issue that has thrust the parenting of disabled people into the academic and policy limelight over the past decade or so is one of 'young carers'; that is, children 'caring' for ill and disabled family members (usually their parent or parents). The origins of the research on which this book is based lie partly in our concern with the appropriateness of constructing children of disabled parents in this way. (Indeed, we have devoted Chapter Four to children's involvement in domestic and 'caring' activity.) Our central concern is to explore the factors that lead some disabled parents to require inappropriate levels of assistance from their children. The question to be asked, then, is no longer "How can children labelled 'young carers' best be supported in their 'caring' role?", but rather, "What kind of support do disabled parents need that will enable them not to rely on children for assistance?".

'Young carers' emerged as a new welfare category in the late 1980s and early 1990s. Their arrival was the product of increasing awareness, particularly within the voluntary sector, of the inappropriate roles that some children appeared to be taking on. This was combined with the publication of various academic and non-academic papers, each seeking to do a number of things:

- to estimate the numbers of 'young carers' (Page, 1988; O'Neil and Platt, 1992; Walker, 1996);
- to present qualitative data about the lives of children 'caring' for other family members (Aldridge and Becker, 1993a, 1993b, 1993c, 1994);
- to evaluate the first wave of dedicated 'young carer' support projects (Bilsborrow, 1992; Meredith, 1992; Mahon and Higgins, 1995);
- to raise awareness about this group of children among professionals (Fallon, 1990; Dearden et al, 1994).

Of particular – and continuing – importance was the work of the Young Carer Research Group (YCRG) at Loughborough University, which was instrumental in raising the profile of 'young carers' on policy and practice agendas, and in further developing the research literature on 'young carers' to include more quantitative work on the characteristics of those children to whom existing 'young carer' services provide support (Dearden and Becker, 1995, 1998). More researchers have since begun to publish work on 'young carers', whether from the perspective of a particular local authority (Munoz, 1998), from the perspective of 'ex-young carers' (Frank et al, 1999), or from the perspective of Asian 'young carers' (Shah and Hatton, 1999). More recently, guidelines for good practice with 'young carers' have been produced (Frank, 2002).

The influence of this body of work in shaping the provision of support for children with disabled parents, and in structuring the issue as one of 'children's rights/carer's rights', cannot be overstated. There are now well over 100 dedicated 'young carer' services in the UK, provided by social services departments, and by a range of organisations in the voluntary sector. The place of 'young carers' is also enshrined in legislation (the 1996 Carers Act) and in various policy and practice documents, such as the *National strategy for carers* (DoH, 2000a) and the *Framework for the assessment of children in need and their families* (DoH, DfEE and HO, 2000). In addition, 'young carer' has entered not only the lexicon of welfare professionals, but also that of the public consciousness, with 'young carers' frequently included in popular/populist media occasions such as the *Children of Courage Awards* – some local agencies even run *Young Carer of the Year Awards*.

By the early 1990s, the growing profile of informal carers as a cornerstone of community care policy and practice had already caused disquiet within the disability movement. Concern was expressed that a community care infrastructure, heavily reliant on unpaid informal care, was not consistent with the campaign by the disability movement for control over the way in which personal assistance was provided. Inevitably, then, the growing move to construct the children of some disabled parents as 'young carers' was not well received by disabled parents and their allies, especially given the use of emotive terms such as 'punishment' (Aldridge and Becker, 1993c), 'abuse' (Aldridge and Becker, 1993d) and 'curse' (Siddall, 1994) in describing the experience of 'young carers'. At the same time as the 'young carer' literature was developing, a number of writers began developing what might be called a 'disability perspective'[5]. They challenged the theoretical, empirical and political basis of this growing academic and policy interest in 'young carers'. In particular, they sought to highlight the potential for disempowerment when services take the 'caring' role of children at face value and seek to support children *in* that role, without critical scrutiny of the support that their parents would find helpful in preventing the need for that assistance in the first place. The common purpose of these researchers has been to reframe the issue of 'young carers' as one of parental independence and support, and as one of equal opportunities for disabled people in their parenting role.

More recent publications articulating a children's rights perspective on 'young caring' have adopted a more balanced approach. Terms such as 'holistic support' or 'family-centred support' are increasingly replacing an emphasis on children's rights as 'carers' and the more emotive language highlighted above. For instance, such researchers outline a 'family approach' that acknowledges the significance of the lack of services in generating the need for children to act as 'carers' in the first place, and:

> highlights and promotes the needs of all family members where there is an illness or disability present. (Dearden and Becker, 2001, p 226)

However, this increasingly holistic approach remains based on:

- an understanding of the 'care' needs of disabled parents that is heavily rooted in the medical model of disability;
- an emphasis on parental impairment as the trigger for children's involvement in 'caring' (Aldridge and Becker, 1999);
- a continuing focus on the parenting of disabled people through the lens of 'capacity' (Dearden and Becker, 2001).

An important element of some discussions of 'young caring' is their reference to the evidence for role reversal or role change; that is, where a child takes on responsibility for a parent and/or other members of the family *as if they were the parent.* For example, Handley et al interviewed children of parents with mental health impairments, and found that

> in some of the children's stories there was evidence of 'parentification' and 'adultification'. (2001, pp 225-6)

However, Handley et al do not expand on the possible or expected outcomes from this process. Barnett and Parker (1998) reviewed the literature on parentification, and pointed out that it can often be used in a non-rigorous way, while retaining an assumption of permanence, centrality and pathology. Indeed, Aldridge and Becker have borrowed from the idea of parentification in their later work, but couch it in terms of the interdependence of parents and children in families where children are assisting parents:

> The reciprocal and interdependent nature of the caring relationship enables the family to survive as a unit. It allows young carers and their families to go on living, loving and working together as a family. (Aldridge and Becker, 1999, p 313)

But does theorising the involvement of children in inappropriate 'caring' as one of parentification or role swapping, or even of interdependence, help us address the issue of parental support and the equal opportunities of disabled adults in undertaking parenting with choices, control and independence? In this sense, we reiterate our conceptual distinction between the parenting tasks that parents actually do, and the parenting role itself embedded in relationships of love, protection, support, and so on. The fact that children may get involved in the tasks of parenting should not mean that the parents' role is compromised, especially if policy and practice responses are to underpin parents' choices concerning receipt of assistance.

In summary, then, 'young caring' has been a bone of contention between academics, professionals and disabled people since the creation, over a decade ago, of a service infrastructure aimed at supporting 'young carers'. The influence of the publications and awareness-raising activities of the YCRG has been significant, especially in constructing a particular way of seeing the issues in 'children's rights' terms. From this have emerged policy and legislation rooted in the recognition of the role of children who take on 'caring' roles and in promoting their interests as child 'carers'.

These developments, and the growth of a disability perspective on 'young caring', represent the political and theoretical background of this book. In Appendix One, we outline how the 'young carer' literature – and the challenge of a social model approach – informed the design of this study and of the materials developed for our data collection.

Parenting within the disability movement

So far, we have examined the presence and absence of disabled parents in various contexts and literatures. In this final part, we look briefly at the place of parenting within the disability movement itself. We argue that disabled writers have been slow to recognise the parental responsibilities shared by many disabled people, illustrated by their absence from various studies, including those on the effectiveness of independent living and direct payments schemes (Brindle, 1995), and on the experiences of disabled women using primary-care services (Begum, 1996). This is despite the fact that some of individuals whose stories feature in evaluations of direct payments *happen* to be parents, and are quick to point to the benefits for the whole family of the provision of personal assistance through direct payments (Hasler et al, 1999).

Until quite recently, the only exception to the conspicuous absence of disabled parents from the literature of the disability movement was the work of disabled feminists, and especially that of Morris (1989, 1991, 1992). For her, a disability rights perspective is indistinguishable from a feminist perspective, given the dual oppression of disabled women, on the one hand as disabled, and on the other as women (Morris, 1992). Inevitably, in the construction of a feminist disability perspective, Morris tackles some of the issues we have discussed (the medicalisation of disabled people, eugenics and fertility, the reproductive rights of disabled women, and the way in which impairment is used to deprive disabled women of contact with, and custody of, their children). In addition, her writing highlights the ways in which inadequate housing and social support, as well as physical and attitudinal barriers, can work against disabled women in bringing up their children.

More recently, other disabled authors have developed the themes of motherhood and disability in their writings, either as the product of research with disabled mothers (Wates, 1997) or as personal accounts of motherhood (see especially, Finger, 1990; Mason, 1992; Wates and Jade, 1999). Wates (1997) explores parenting from the perspective of 21 disabled mothers. She examines the tensions that exist for disabled parents, especially when balancing the recognition that there are additional barriers to overcome against the desire to appear 'normal' and to avoid stigmatising intervention from welfare services.

> The association is easily made between being seen as different and being seen as problematic. And so, from a disabled parent's point of view, doing one's best to appear normal may seem like the safest route to a family life free from unwelcome intervention. (Wates, 1997, p 14)

Wates also discusses some of the key theoretical and empirical issues that ought to lie at the heart of parenting and disability research. These include the importance, in terms of the attitudes that disabled people are likely to face when it comes to having children, of having been disabled from birth or childhood, compared to being impaired in adulthood. They also include the importance of visible – as against invisible – impairments (and the way in which visibility shapes disabling encounters), and the contrast between more stable and predictable impairments on the one hand, and progressive impairments on the other (in terms of changing assistance requirements, the capacity of formal services to respond, and so on). Importantly, Wates also locates her analysis in a critique of the assumptions that are made about disabled people as being inevitably the passive *recipients* of care, and therefore implicitly not as carers of other people:

> To be disabled and a parent counters the assumptions of emotional dependence
> and passivity which are often made about disabled people. (Wates, 1997, p 15)

This also echoes the feminist perspective developed by Morris in identifying barriers to participation in parenting as particularly important for disabled women, given dominant social norms that see caring roles in general, and childcaring roles in particular, as an important element of adult, female identity. Barron (1997) makes the same point in her work on the transition of disabled adolescent girls into adulthood:

> Motherhood is in our culture viewed as an essential part of womanhood. It is
> an important part of what constitutes a 'real' woman. (Barron, 1997, p 232)

It is clear that, despite the relatively marginal place of parenting in disability thinking, disabled writers are beginning to assert themselves as parents, and to generate a social model literature on parenting, often informed by a broader feminist perspective[6].

However, significant gaps remain to be filled in this ever-developing literature. Importantly, the more or less explicit association of parenting issues and feminism within the disability movement's work on parenting is significant, yet leaves a theoretical and empirical space for exploring disability and fatherhood. (Issues of gender, disability and parenting are discussed later in this book.) It is also important to acknowledge the importance of inclusiveness in the development of the parenting and disability literature. The disability movement has been active in debating the adequacy of the social model in fully encapsulating the experiences of people with learning disabilities, people with mental health impairments, and so on (for instance, Beresford, 2000). However, while the mainstream literature on parenting is beginning to acknowledge diversity in terms of parenting (for example, gay and lesbian parents, adoptive and foster parents), work on parenting from the disability movement has yet to broaden its horizons to incorporate fully such diversity.

Summary

Historically, disability and parenting have been situated within and between a range of academic and policy literatures. These have tended, more or less explicitly, either to ignore the parenting responsibilities of disabled people, or to construct it in various ways as a social problem. In particular, the absence of disabled parents from mainstream parenting policy and research agendas has served to isolate them further within studies adopting a clinical gaze, or in 'problematising' the parenting of disabled people. Clearly lacking from the debate has been a coherent theoretical and empirical framework for exploring the parenting of disabled people from within a social model perspective, one that is interested in identifying the barriers to equal opportunities in parenting experienced by disabled people. We have seen that researchers from within the disability movement have now begun to establish such a framework.

We turn now to the UK legislative and policy context informing practice with disabled parents and their families.

The legislative and policy context

It is a fact that very few areas of legislation, public policy and practice do not impinge on the way in which families are established and maintained, and the way in which the needs of children and parents are supported or undermined. These include employment law, education policy and practice, tax, income and benefits policies, and macro-economic policies, among other things. In a study of parenting and disability, other areas of legislation and policy also have particular prominence, such as health and community care, transport, housing, and so on.

It is clearly not possible to contextualise our research with reference to all these areas of public policy. What follows, then, is a brief overview of the legislative and policy context most directly relevant to disabled parents – especially, the important twin frameworks of the 1989 Children Act and the 1990 NHS and Community Care Act[7]. The inherent opportunities and problems in these policy frameworks are highlighted with regard to enabling disabled adults to fulfil their parenting responsibilities, and we question the extent to which established ways of conceptualising the needs and welfare of children (as well as parents) can mesh neatly with a social model of disability. The more recent legislative and policy developments in relation to disabled parents are also briefly discussed[8].

Child welfare legislation

The 1989 Children Act offers a potentially enabling way forward in supporting disabled parents. The underlying principle of the Act is that the family home is the best place for children's needs to be met (DoH, 1994), and that:

> when intra-familial supports to the child fail or are absent to the detriment
> of that child, the state has a duty to offer aid to the family, or directly to the
> child to promote his or her welfare. However, the state then has a duty to
> withdraw when parents are once more able to discharge their responsibilities
> to their children. (Aldgate et al, 1994, p 1)

The emphasis, then, is on the state as a backstop, and on intervention that acts
to promote parental autonomy and independence rather than to provide a
replacement for that role. The Act also allows services to be provided to other
members of a child's family, should this be deemed the best way of meeting the
child's needs. This is potentially good news for disabled parents, particularly
given the emphasis of the Children Act on balancing family support and child
protection priorities and activities.

However, we must be cautious about the capacity of the Children Act to
respond adequately to the support needs of disabled parents. First, ample
evidence exists concerning the way in which the principles of the Act have
been undermined by the lack of resources necessary to support fully families in
need. It is particularly important to recognise that the political consensus over
those parts of the Act that were about parental responsibility was not reflected
in political consensus about the material and structural resources necessary to
parent successfully (Parton, 1991). Hill and Aldgate (1996) argue that the
Children Act was introduced at a time of retreat from universal welfare provision,
and towards targeted help to those deemed 'in need'. This has meant that the
discretion of local authorities to set thresholds as to which children in need
(and at what level of need) to provide support for, has left a question mark
hanging over the success of the Act in redistributing the balance between child
protection and family support. Similarly, Tunstill (1997) points out that, while
the Children Act offers a good framework for the provision of family support,
its introduction at a time when the role of the state in supporting families was
ideologically unpopular means that family support aspects of the Act have
subsequently been squeezed.

These issues form the basis of a common concern shared by many disabled
parents: that, while it is extremely difficult to access services that support effective
parenting (on grounds of budgetary constraints, the division of adult and child
social work, and so on), it is very easy to become a target of social work with
regard to the adequacy of parenting and the perceived risk of child neglect and
significant harm. Other researchers have raised similar concerns, for instance
regarding the likelihood that the children of mothers with mental health
difficulties will become targets of child protection proceedings. White points
out that in many cases:

> it appears families receive a child protection package or they receive nothing.
> (1996, p 82)

Green et al (1997) came to a similar conclusion, having interviewed families where a mother was in contact with mental health services, as well as professionals working with them. They reported that the professionals concerned felt an incentive to describe family situations in child protection terms so that they could meet thresholds for service provision. The consequences of this were twofold: first, for the relationship between professionals, and second, for parents with mental health impairments:

> This placed mothers in a situation where they were reluctant to confide fully in the professionals and in a relationship which always had an element of ambivalence ... it was the degree of risk, rather than the degree of need which seemed to determine the threshold to services. It is this issue of professional culture which, together with the lack of resources, is the primary barrier to the provision of an effective preventative service. (Green et al, 1997, p 65)

This echoes work predating the Children Act that found that the reception of children into care – as opposed to the provision of family support – was often the only option offered to vulnerable families (Packman et al, 1986). It is also supported by the experiences of disabled parents who have been offered foster care for their children, but little or no help in parenting their children themselves (Maternity Alliance, 1994).

Most importantly, the fundamental attachment to parental *competence* as an individual attribute or skill permeates the thinking of successive governments on parenting. In particular, the philosophical assumptions behind the 1989 Children Act are in many ways incongruent with a social model of disability. For instance, the test of significant harm is not particularly sensitive to the position that disabled parents might find themselves in when trying to care for, and meet the needs of, their children. Firstly, it is rooted in the assumption that harm is the direct result of actions (or inaction) on the part of parents (Hardiker, 1996), as opposed to broader socioeconomic factors.

Second, decisions about care proceedings involve assessing "the capability of parents or others of meeting the child's needs" (Hardiker, 1996, p 108). Sayce (1999) makes the same point when pointing to the ways in which the legal system can discriminate against disabled people, and deny them opportunities in parenting, by relying too heavily on the assumption that a diagnosis necessarily impairs parenting ability, and therefore sets the interests of the parent and child artificially apart.

Third, the assessment of harm against a criterion of the health and development that could reasonably be expected of a "similar child" (Hardiker, 1996, p 110) emphasises individual capacities above social context:

> Reasonable parents do not suffer disability, any more than they suffer from alcoholism, drug addiction or poverty. All parents come to the judgement seat on an equal footing, however unequal they are in the world outside the court. (Freeman, 1990, p 152, cited in Hardiker, 1996, p 111)

This implicitly assumes that parental ability is a product of the individual, and does not situate parenting within broader parameters of exclusion and social disablement. It will come as no surprise, then, to know that remedies for the perceived shortcomings of parenting focus on a model of individual ability or deficit (a direct parallel to the medical model). Consequently, they focus on ways of changing parents (parenting classes, for instance) far more than on barriers to effective and successful parenting. Similarly, Tunstill argues that efforts to implement family support in the wake of the Children Act have been undermined by the assumption that families should *provide* – rather than *receive* – support. This is a view:

> dependent on a re-invention of the normal family with worrying implications
> for those who cannot or will not conform to the norm. (Tunstill, 1997, p 42)

In addition, the filter of 'children in need' as an administrative category, and the inevitable development of hierarchies of access to services in the context of scarce resources (Tunstill, 1996), have important implications for the ability of disabled parents to access support. In particular, disabled parents have argued that, in order to access support, their requirement to collude with the identification of their children as 'children in need' is a significant barrier.

The most important recent development in child welfare policy and practice is the implementation of the *Framework for the assessment of children in need and their families* (DoH, DfEE and HO, 2000, and hereafter referred to as the Framework). This policy development emerged from a growing consensus that, throughout the 1990s, child protection proceedings had continued to dominate social services activity with families, to the detriment of family support services promoted in section 17 of the 1989 Children Act. This very significant finding was common to a number of studies (especially, Gibbons et al, 1995; Thoburn et al, 1995) carried out under the Child Protection research programme funded by the Department of Health, and published as an overview document known as 'The Blue Book' (Dartington Social Research Unit, 1995).

Importantly, the Framework rests on a particular theoretical approach to examining the constitution of parenting, and to the place of parenting within a number of domains, which permeates current government thinking on family and social policy. The intellectual and theoretical tradition on which policy has increasingly been built is that of an 'ecological' approach to parenting, which traces its development to the work of Bronfenbrenner (1979) and Belsky and colleagues (Belsky et al, 1984; Vondra and Belsky, 1993). An ecological perspective views parenting as a set of activities influenced by three 'domains':

- the developmental needs of the child;
- the capacities and personal resources of parents in meeting those needs;
- the wider social and economic context in which parents operate.

This way of looking at parenting is of potentially great significance for policy and practice in the area of disabled parents, as it draws our focus towards structural factors (poverty, inaccessible housing and transport, and so on) as well as towards the individual strengths of parents themselves. It therefore offers the opportunity for looking at the barriers and difficulties faced by parents rather than automatically assuming that parenting deficits are the responsibility of parents themselves.

However, those implementing the Framework have to find ways of resolving fundamental tensions between these competing conceptions of parental activity. These tensions can be traced back to the theoretical approach to parenting itself embodied in ecological perspectives, and in particular to assumptions made about the relationship between impairment and 'poor parenting'. For example:

> It is unlikely that an individual who is caught up with his or her own psychological concerns will have the ability to decenter and take the perspective of a dependent infant. Without the psychological resources to understand, and consequently tolerate, the daily demands and frustrations of an infant or young child (let alone a teenager), a parent will be hard pressed to demonstrate the patience, sensitivity and responsiveness that effective parenting requires. (Vondra and Belsky, 1993, p 5)

Our argument is that this attachment to the importance of parenting 'capacity' adopts an explicitly medical model approach to disability that is filtered throughout the Framework itself, as well as to commentary on its implementation. For instance, in their paper on the implications of the Framework for learning-disabled parents, Cotson et al (2001) recognise the importance of parental support. However, they also place great stress on the importance of such parents demonstrating their capacity for adapting and learning quickly enough to meet the developmental needs of their children:

> While the learning of new skills may be possible, a crucial issue is whether the rate of learning can be fast enough. Therefore, when assessing whether or not the child's developmental needs are being responded to, or could be responded to, by parents, it is important to identify whether the parents are learning fast enough to be able to adapt to their child's developmental progress. (Cotson et al, 2001, p 300)

Many parents with mild or moderate learning disabilities will, of course, fail to receive support from adult services, as their support needs as *individuals* often fall below ever-tighter eligibility thresholds. They will frequently not have the long-term support necessary for them to demonstrate their effectiveness as a parent, and will often be trying to do so under the cloud of ongoing child protection proceedings. In such circumstances, parents may quite rightly feel as though they have been set up to fail. This is particularly important given current government targets of increasing the number of children adopted as well as the speed at which adoption takes place. It is clear, then, that a lot depends on the *way* in which parenting capacity is assessed as the Framework is put into operation, and on *how* the inherent tension between medical and social model approaches to parenting is played out.

Community care legislation

The key event in the construction of the current adult community care system was the publication of the Griffiths Report, *Community care: Agenda for action* (Griffiths, 1988). This report sought to clarify the roles and responsibilities of various agencies with regard to the 'care' needs of elderly people and disabled adults. Its recommendations – that local authorities should take the lead in assessing need, and in commissioning its provision from a range of (increasingly private-sector) providers – were largely accepted by the government and enshrined in the 1990 NHS and Community Care Act. Disabled people do not enjoy particularly extensive rights under the auspices of this legislation, and are essentially limited to the requirement that local authorities assess need as well as record unmet need (DoH, 1991a, 1991b). The obligation on local authorities to *meet* need is less clear given the resource constraints within which they operate, and the qualified backing subsequently given by the courts in taking resources into account when providing services (Drewett, 1999). In addition, the impetus for change in the way in which community care is organised and provided originated in part from a desire to *minimise* the cost of such 'care' to the state, and to emphasise reliance on the family as the first place to which 'dependent' people should turn (Borsay, 1997).

The development of current community care arrangements runs parallel to the growth of a disability movement increasingly critical of the traditional, top-down, dependence-promoting way their needs have been assessed and (not) met (Priestley, 1998). This critique of welfare production has gone hand in hand with the development of the social model of disability, which emphasises the essentially social nature of disablement (in the design of buildings, workplaces, housing and vehicles, and in prejudicial attitudes) as opposed to the traditional characterisation of disability as resulting from bodily impairment[9]. This theoretical challenge to medicalised definitions of disability necessarily led to a different vision of the role of the state in supporting disabled people. In particular, an alternative discourse developed, emphasising the provision of support to disabled people in ways that promote rather than inhibit independence, and that facilitate control of assistance by disabled people themselves (Morris, 1993a, 1993b).

The importance of the social model of disability for community care policy and practice has steadily grown, and has been encompassed most clearly in the new raft of disability legislation introduced in the 1990s and 2000s. Of particular importance here are the 1995 Disability Discrimination Act and the 1996

Community Care (Direct Payments) Act. The former Act represents an attempt to establish the principles of equal opportunities for disabled people in some areas of public life, including employment. It establishes new obligations for employers and public services with respect to the equal treatment of disabled people. The latter Act allows for the provision of financial support to disabled people in order to enable them to purchase, and therefore assume greater control over, their own personal assistance. Many authorities were slow to take up the opportunity to provide funding directly to disabled people to enable them to control assistance, despite evidence from early studies that this way of meeting need was welcomed by disabled people themselves (Kestenbaum, 1993). Subsequent research has shown that, in addition to the benefits offered to disabled people in terms of personal assistance, direct payments are also more cost effective, given reductions in overheads for local authorities (Zarb and Nadash, 1994).

Furthermore, inherent in the policy guidance accompanying the 1996 Community Care (Direct Payments) Act is an obligation that local authorities develop schemes that "serve all adult client groups equitably" (DoH, 1996, p 4). The origin of this concern for 'equitable treatment' lies in the fear that people with learning disabilities, and people with mental health impairments, might find it more difficult to access direct payments. However, there are clear implications of 'equitable treatment' for the inclusion of parents, and parenting activity, within the scope of the Act (Hasler, personal communication, 2000).

Direct payments will continue to be an important goal for many disabled parents. An important policy development is the amendment to the 1989 Children Act, introduced by the 2001 Health and Social Care Act, which allows for direct payments to be made to disabled parents under a new section 17a of the 1989 Act. This specifically recognises the importance of supporting disabled parents adequately as a way of promoting the best interests of children. However, there remains a concern that this avenue of support is still dependent on the labelling of children as 'children in need' and does not, therefore, address the barrier that this represents for many parents.

Another important recent development has been the introduction of *Fair access to care services* (DoH, 2002, and hereafter referred to as FACS), due to be implemented in April 2003. This policy development is concerned with equitable delivery of services, and with giving local authorities a framework for the consistent application of eligibility criteria for adult services based on clear priorities and understanding of risks involved. Disabled parents see this as an important development, in that it offers an opportunity to make sure that parenting is seen as an activity that disabled people may legitimately need support with. Indeed, the FACS policy guidance states that:

> in the course of assessing an individual's needs, councils should recognise that adults, who have parenting responsibilities for a child under 18 years, may require help with these responsibilities. (DoH, 2002, p 2)

This establishes the principle that parenting is a role for which disabled people can access support from adult community care services. It also offers the possibility that such support does not have to be tied in with child welfare concerns in the way that invocation of the 1989 Children Act or the Framework implies.

In summary, community care legislation, as a route to accessing support for disabled parents, does not require them to accept that their children are 'in need'. It should provide a route whereby disabled adults can seek assistance that underpins and supports their parenting role without having that support provided through the filters of 'risk' and 'need' inherent in children's legislation and policy. However, the climate of scarce resources, as well as means tests and charges written into adult social care legislation, has meant that parenting has seldom featured, until recently, in eligibility criteria in community care assessments. As the SSI inspection of disabled parents' services noted:

> Criteria for getting an assessment and services varied between care groups in adult services but for the majority being a parent was not part of the eligibility criteria nor the priority matrix. In children's services parental disability was one of the indicators of a 'child in need' case. (DoH, 2000b, p 27)

The ability of the FACS guidance to rectify this situation, and the different routes that FACS and the Framework may take in constructing a place for disabled parents within future policy and practice, remain to be seen.

The legislative and policy background to the study of parenting and disability is, therefore, at a crossroads. Existing legislation has often proved inadequate in providing a framework for the delivery of support that includes the parenting responsibilities of disabled people, and that does not alienate disabled parents. The growing acceptance of direct payments as a legitimate vehicle for managing the provision of support, as well as the new policy developments highlighted above, offer a way forward that might enable disabled parents to access support in appropriate ways. (However, the success of such initiatives in reaching disabled parents, and their effectiveness in providing the kind of support required, remain to be seen.)

Finally, it is important to stress that the legislative and policy context has so far been discussed with reference only to England and Wales. Child welfare legislation and policy differs in Scotland and Northern Ireland, and the scope for further divergence in the future is, arguably, heightened by the growing legislative autonomy enjoyed by parts of the UK outside England and Wales. There is insufficient space here to conduct a thorough review of the differences in children's legislation in Scotland and Northern Ireland (for a discussion, see Tisdall, 1997). However, some key differences, of relevance to policy and practice in the area of disabled parents, are worth highlighting, particularly in the context of Scotland. Of greatest significance is the wider definition of 'children in need', which specifically includes children "affected by disability of another family member" (section 93(4A) of the 1995 Children (Scotland) Act). This is a significant deviation: although children with disabled parents may well come under the definition of a 'child in need' in England and Wales, their specific inclusion in Scotland – Tisdall (1997) argues – gives them greater legal protection (for instance, where the support needs of a 'young carer' are inadequately assessed and/or met). Indeed, the term 'child affected by disability of another family member' has been used by some researchers in Scotland (especially those based at the Strathclyde Centre for Disability Research) as an alternative term for 'young carer', an approach which, we would argue, tries to combine a social model approach to disability with a commitment to supporting children as carers.

Scottish authorities are required to deliver less by way of a specific range of services for 'children in need', when compared to the duties imposed by the 1989 Children Act or the 1995 Children (NI) Order, the comparable legislation in Northern Ireland. While this offers greater flexibility in the provision of services, it can also mean that, in an environment of scarce resources, authorities can legitimately provide a more restricted level of support to 'children in need'. Scottish legislation is also more specific about the responsibilities of parents, as well as their rights, with legislation in England having a more vague and general definition of these issues. These, and a range of other legal and procedural issues, make for a somewhat different legislative context for child welfare in Scotland. Indeed, the continuing potential for divergence between policy and practice north and south of the border will be of relevance for disabled parents for years to come.

Conclusions

This chapter has identified the disparate and fragmented literature and policy discourses that encompass disabled parents. We have argued that the theorisation of disability and parenting has been weak, and has been informed by paradigms anchored in medical model thinking and in sets of negative assumptions about the capacity of disabled people to parent, and the likely long-term consequences for their children. This, coupled with the absence of disabled parents from mainstream parenting research agendas, has served to reinforce the isolation of disability and parenting in areas which, by definition, problematise the parenting of disabled people (for example, 'young caring'). We have also discussed the way in which parents – and parenting – have received, until recently, relatively little attention from within the disability movement itself. This book is an attempt to address this empirical and theoretical fragmentation, by presenting detailed data on the experiences of disabled parents from a social model perspective, which sees the parenting of disabled parents primarily as an equal opportunities issue.

However, before proceeding to discuss our approach to the design of our research and the methods employed, one other issue is worth at least brief comment: that is, gender.

It is impossible to study parenting within a gender-neutral framework. Whether in terms of the biological origins of children, or of the socially constructed norms that structure the way in which people take responsibility for – and care for – their children, it is essential to grapple with the differential status and roles laid out for men and women as parents. This concern with the inherently gendered experience of parenting has led several authors to question the usefulness of 'parenting' itself as a term (Brannen, 1992; Allan, 1994; Edwards, 1995; Oakley et al, 1998). For instance, Edwards argues that:

> the gender neutral idioms of 'parenting' act to mask the fact that it is predominantly women who care for children. (Edwards, 1995, p 251)

Our approach has been to retain 'parenting' alongside 'disability' as the central foci of this book (although later chapters do engage with the significance of gender in the parenting activity of disabled people). In so doing, we acknowledge the generally greater role played by women in caring for children, as well as the overrepresentation of mothers, and motherhood, in moral panics, such as those surrounding single parenthood and its relationship with juvenile crime, educational underachievement, and so on (Edwards, 1995). We also acknowledge the importance of other highly gendered discourses in considerations of parenting. For example, an understanding of the experience of both learning-disabled mothers (Cotson et al, 2001) and mothers with depression and other mental health impairments (Sheppard, 1997; Stanley and Penhale, 1999) requires an understanding of the significance of domestic violence in their parenting experiences.

However, we also recognise that the ideological association between parenting and mothering – stretching back to postwar commentators' concern with 'maternal deprivation' (Bowlby, 1965) and to the origins of the concept of 'good enough parenting' in the work of Winnicott on 'good enough mothering' (see Winnicott, 1964; Mortley, 1998) – also acts to exclude and marginalise the role, status and experiences of fathers. Indeed, the remarkable overrepresentation of mothers as research subjects in studies on parenting, and the origins of the disability movement's interest in parenting within explicitly feminist perspectives, caution us to be especially inclusive of mothers *and* fathers in order not to reproduce this exclusion and marginalisation. While it may be right that the term 'parent' masks the disproportionate involvement of women in caring for children, it nevertheless indicates a willingness to include men as parents in a way that much social and family policy research and policy fails to do. The terms 'chairperson', 'firefighter', 'spokesperson', 'police officer', and so on, serve to mask the fact that most of the work carried out in those professions is done by men, yet those terms are used, rightly, because to identify those roles with being male might act as a barrier to equal opportunities for women. Correspondingly, the use of the term 'parenting' in this book, as well as in the design of the study and in methods of recruitment, indicates our commitment not to exclude fathers and fathering from consideration, particularly given the possibility that disabled men may play a greater role than non-disabled men in parenting and childcare given their underrepresentation in the paid labour market (Wates, 1997). We have therefore adopted an approach that is inclusive in terms of disability *and* inclusive in terms of parenting. Appendix One looks more closely at the way in which this commitment to inclusion has structured the design of our study.

Notes

[1] For a full review, see the mapping exercise carried out by the National Family and Parenting Institute (NFPI), and published in Henricson et al (2001).

[2] See, for example, Gibbons et al (1990); Oakley et al (1995); Smith (1997); Mortley (1998); Oakley et al (1998); Roker and Coleman (1998); Barlow (1999); Newman and Roberts (1999).

[3] See, for instance, the publications of Hirsch et al (1985); Radke-Yarrow (1991); Jamison and Walker (1992); White and Barrowclough (1998). Note also the titles adopted for these works.

[4] For attachment theory, see especially Bowlby (1965); Rutter (1966); Rutter and Madge (1976); Rutter et al (1976); Rutter (1981).

[5] See, for the main examples, Keith and Morris (1995); Parker and Olsen (1995a, 1995b); Olsen (1996); Morris (1997); Olsen and Parker (1997); Olsen (2000).

[6] We hope that this book will take its place in this social model tradition, and serve to further our understanding of parenting and disability in terms of barriers, access and equal opportunities.

[7] For an excellent discussion of the different historical and philosophical backgrounds to these sets of legislation, see Hallet (1991).

[8] For further discussion of the current policy and practice context, see Wates and Olsen (forthcoming). Due to a lack of space, we have not expanded the discussion to include other potentially significant developments such as the inclusion of parenting support within the White Paper *Valuing people: A new strategy for learning disability for the 21st century*, or Articles 8 and 12 of the 1998 Human Rights Act, which include the right to respect for private and family life, and the right to marry and to found a family, respectively.

[9] See, among others, UPIAS (1976); Oliver (1990); Morris (1991); Shakespeare and Watson (1997).

TWO

Demographic characteristics of the final sample

This chapter examines the breakdown, by means of a range of basic demographic characteristics, of the families in our study[1].

Stage One

Stage One fieldwork was conducted between October 1998 and June 2000. Interviews were conducted with a parent from 67 families, a child (or children) in 60 of these families, and with 37 partners. The duration of interviews varied widely, with a mean of 133 minutes for parents, 76 minutes for partners and 27 minutes for children. Some of the longer interviews were carried out over two, and occasionally more, visits. Fifty-seven of the parents were mothers – only 10 disabled fathers took part. Twenty-three families were headed by a single parent – only one was a father. Fifty-eight of the disabled parents described their ethnicity as white and five described their ethnicity as Indian (including African-Asian respondents). Only one father was of Indian origin. Two people described their ethnicity as 'other' and there were two refusals to this item. No African or Caribbean respondents were recruited to the study, although different cultural backgrounds were represented in a small number of families where children were born into dual-heritage households.

Where respondents identified more than one set of impairments, they were asked which one, in their opinion, was their 'primary' impairment. In 21

Table 2.1: Sex of parent (by impairment group and family shape)

	Mothers (Dual/Single)	Fathers (Dual/Single)	Total (Dual/Single)
Mental health impairments only	17 (9/8)	3 (3/0)	20 (12/8)
Physical impairments only	25 (15/10)	6 (5/1)	31 (20/11)
Mental health and physical impairments	12 (9/3)	1 (1/0)	13 (10/3)
Physical impairments and sensory impairment	3 (2/1)	0 (na)	3 (2/1)
Total	57 (35/22)	10 (9/1)	67 (44/23)

Table 2.2: Sex of parent (by any mental health impairments and family shape)

	Mothers (Dual/Single)	Fathers (Dual/Single)	Total (Dual/Single)
Current mental health impairments	29 (18/11)	4 (4/0)	33 (22/11)
No mental health impairments	28 (17/11)	6 (5/1)	34 (22/12)
Total	57 (35/22)	10 (9/1)	67 (44/23)

families the primary impairments involved mental health. However, 33 of the parents in total spoke of having some form of current mental health impairments (Table 2.2).

When we approached potential respondents to our survey, we made it clear that we were interested in the experiences of disabled parents. Nineteen respondents, however, did not describe themselves as disabled, and a further eight respondents said that they 'sometimes' described themselves in this way. Less than 60% of the sample, then, responded outright that they were a disabled person (*n*=39), and respondents who described primarily mental health impairments were less likely to describe themselves as disabled (Table 2.3).

Respondents were also asked when their impairment or condition first had an impact on their day-to-day lives. For half of the sample, the impact (though not necessarily its initial onset) began having already become a parent. The impact for the other half had taken place at various points in their lives, from birth to adulthood (Table 2.4).

Table 2.3: Identification as a disabled person (by primary impairment group)

"Would you describe yourself as disabled?"	Primarily physical/ sensory impairments	Primarily mental health impairments	Total
Yes	35	4	39
No	4	15	19
Sometimes	6	2	8
Refused/not answered	1	0	1
Total	46	21	67

Table 2.4: "When did impairments begin to impact on day-to-day life?" (Primarily physical and/or sensory impairments/mental health impairments all considered)

	Mothers (Dual/Single)	Fathers (Dual/Single)	Total (Dual/Single)
Birth or childhood	10 (7/3)	1 (0/1)	11 (7/4)
Adolescence	5 (1/4)	0 (0)	5 (1/4)
Adult, before becoming a parent	17 (11/6)	0 (0)	17 (11/6)
Adult, before becoming a step-parent	1 (1/0)	0 (0)	1 (1/0)
Since becoming a parent	24 (19/5)	9 (7/2)	33 (26/7)
Total	57 (39/18)	10 (7/3)	67 (46/21)

Stage Two

Table 2.5 describes the 12 families recruited to Stage Two of our research. In each family, upper-case letters are used to identify the 'target parent' (for example, MOTHER), although several families had other disabled or ill members. Some details have been changed in order to protect the anonymity of the families.

Note

[1] A full discussion of the methodological issues faced in carrying out this research is given in Appendix One. Further information on the structural context in which these parents were parenting (for example, employment, income levels and housing status in particular) is presented in Chapter Three.

Table 2.5: Basic information for 12 Stage Two families

Family	A	B	C	D	E	F
Shape	MOTHER, father (married), son (12), daughter (7)	MOTHER, father (married), daughter (11), son (8)	MOTHER, father (married), son (19), son (18)	MOTHER, father (married), son (16), son (11), son (8)	MOTHER, father (married), son (9)	Mother, FATHER (married), daughter (14), son (11)
Recruited to project	Word of mouth	Outreach nurse	Outreach nurse	Consultant	Consultant	Consultant
Impairment	Head injury	Epilepsy	Multiple sclerosis (MS)	Mental distress, including depression	Manic depression	Traumatic injury from road accident, leg amputation
Onset/variability	Car crash, approx 15 weeks before first interview	Eighteen months before first interview	Initial onset five years previously	Continuing mental health impairments since birth of first child	Initial depressive episode before becoming a parent – continued difficulties for the past five years	Accident and amputation approx two months before first interview
Employment	Both parents in full-time employment; mother currently on sick leave	Father self-employed (full-time); mother in part-time work	Father employed; mother not working	Father in full-time work	Father in full-time work	Father long-term sick leave; mother part-time voluntary work
Annual income	£65,000+	Not given	£26,000-29,000 (including benefits)	£15,000-18,000 (including benefits)	£20,000-23,000 (including benefits)	Income reduced (sick pay – no overtime). Reduction from £15,000-18,000 to £10,000-12,000

Table 2.5: Basic information for 12 Stage Two families (continued)

Family	G	H	I	J	K	L
Shape	MOTHER, son (10), son (5). Son (14) living with father	MOTHER, father (cohabiting), daughter (16), son (14)	MOTHER, father (married), son (12). Adult daughter (moved away)	FATHER, son (12)	MOTHER, father (married), daughter (11), daughter (9)	MOTHER, father (married), son (14), daughter (6 months)
Recruited to project	Day centre	Local MS society	Local disability organisation	Outreach nurse	National depression organisation	National depression organisation
Impairment	Manic depression	MS	Progressive muscular condition (undiagnosed)	MS	Depression	Myalgic encephalomyelitis (ME) and depression
Onset/variability	Approx six years previously	Approx 15 years previously	Approx 20 years previously	Diagnosis approx two years ago but onset approx 12 years ago	Sudden onset three years ago, diagnosed two years ago	Depression (long-standing) and ME. ME onset approx three years previously, only diagnosed in the past 12 months
Employment	Mother not working	Father full-time carer; mother not working	Mother not working; father not working at first interview	Father not working	Mother not working, receives Disability Living Allowance and Incapacity Benefit; father working full-time	Mother not working; father not working
Annual income	£12,000-15,000 (including benefits)	£4,000-6,000	Previously £35,000+	Approx £6,000	Approx £23,000-26,000	Approx. £10,000-12,000

THREE

Access to support

Introduction

This chapter discusses the findings of our study in relation to the support available to disabled parents. It looks at the way in which both formal and informal sources of support were differentially available to the families in our study, as well as the different ways in which formal and informal sources of support work together to promote or inhibit parenting choices.

It is our argument that the support 'needs' of disabled parents – an adequate income, secure and accessible housing, a network of informal support, access to leisure facilities, among other things – are intrinsically no different to those of non-disabled parents. However, disabled parents often find it harder to access these sources of support, for reasons such as inaccessible environments, negative attitudes and structural disadvantage. Such barriers must be removed so that disabled people can parent with greater control and independence.

We also argue, however, that the exclusion and marginalisation that disabled parents often face cannot be understood without an awareness of other broader forms of disadvantage and social exclusion, such as poverty and racism. In particular, the way in which access to parenting roles for disabled people intersects with the way in which parenting is differentially constructed for mothers and fathers, and with other structural inequalities closely associated with gender, is of great importance. The chapter ends by taking a look at the implications of our arguments for the provision of services to disabled parents.

It is quite artificial to distinguish between the support available to disabled people in general, and that available to them specifically as disabled parents. When parents in our study talked about the lack of service coordination and responsiveness, especially in the period immediately following the onset of impairments, they referred to the effects in terms of the impact both on themselves as individuals *as well as* on the family as a whole. Indeed, while the focus of our interviews was on *parenting*, respondents very often talked about barriers to support applicable to disabled people more generally – issues around access to services and facilities, difficulties in getting information in accessible formats, financial barriers, and so on. Our approach has been to focus, wherever possible, on access to support with *parenting*. However, it has not always been possible, or indeed even desirable, to separate this from the broader context of social exclusion that faces disabled people.

Use of formal support

It is important to emphasise that not all disabled parents are service users. Table 3.1 illustrates the relatively low level of formal service used in the 67 Stage One families.

For some services, a low take-up is to be expected. For instance, our interest in parents with at least one child aged 7-18 meant that only a minority had very young children at the time of interview, which might explain the low use of midwifery services. In addition, differences in the use of services according

Table 3.1: Current use of formal services by Stage One families

	Total number currently using service	Current user:			
		Family shape		Impairment group	
		Dual	Single	PI	MHI
Health visitor	5	5	0	2	3
District nurse	10	8	2	10	0
Midwife	2	2	0	1	1
Psychiatric nurse	6	3	3	0	6
Chiropodist	11	7	4	11	0
Alternative health practitioner	7	4	3	5	2
Psychiatrist	11	8	3	2	9
Speech therapist	0	0	0	0	0
Occupational therapist	20	14	6	17	3
Physiotherapist	13	7	6	13	0
Consultant (outpatient)	31	23	8	30	1
Family planning	1	0	1	0	1
Counsellor	8	4	4	3	5
Psychotherapist	5	1	4	2	3
Home-help worker	12	5	7	12	0
Meals-on-wheels	1	0	1	1	0
One social worker (adult or child)	17	10	7	15	2
Two social workers (adult and child)	3	1	2	3	0
Daycare services	5	3	2	1	4
Advocate	3	1	2	2	1
Befriender	0	0	0	0	0
Voluntary agency	10	3	7	8	2
Self-help group	9	7	2	8	1
Other service	19	11	8	14	5

PI = Physical impairment

MHI = Mental health impairment

Table 3.2: Parental use of any social care services (by family shape and impairment group)

| | Family shape | | Primary impairment group | | |
	Dual	Single	PI/Sensory	MHI	Total
Use	23	17	31	9	40
Non-use	21	6	15	12	27
Total	44	23	46	21	67

PI = Physical impairment

MHI = Mental health impairment

to impairment group can partially be explained by the nature of the service on offer. That is, it comes as no surprise to find that physiotherapy was used exclusively by parents with physical impairments. Similarly, we would expect parents with mental health impairments to use psychiatric nursing services more frequently. However, it is striking (Table 3.1) that parents with physical impairments had greater access to key social care supports such as social workers and home care.

Table 3.2 shows that two thirds of the physically impaired parents in our sample had access to formal, social care support of some kind, compared to around 40% of parents with mental health impairments. Although this is of no statistical significance, it does indicate an important difference in the availability of formal social care support. The table also illustrates that single-parent families were more likely to report using some kind of social care support − 17 out of 23 single parents reporting receiving help, compared with 23 out of 44 parents in dual parent-households.

In total, 17 of our families reported having one or more social workers. The fact that only a quarter of the families in our sample had any social work contact is important in itself, indicating once again that the broader population of disabled parents cannot be characterised as 'service users' in the conventional sense. Where families did have social workers, we asked whether they were from adults' or children's teams − the data are presented in Table 3.3.

Table 3.3: Social work contact with families (by family shape)

| | Family shape | |
	Dual	Single
No social work involvement	34	16
Social worker: child only	1	4
Social worker: parent only	8	1
Two social workers: parent and child	1	2
Total	44	23

Table 3.3 illustrates that seven out of 23 (about 30%) of single-parent families had a social worker, and that in four cases this was a children's social worker. The figure for dual-parent families was only a little over 20% (10 out of 44), with the social worker being based in adults' services in eight of these ten cases. Again, while this may not be of statistical significance, the data suggest that single parents are more likely to have a social worker, and that the social worker is more likely to be based in a children's social work team. This indicates that the nature of social work support for single parents may have a different emphasis, with child welfare concerns being given greater prominence. It also suggests that single parents are less likely to see social work support driven by adult teams, with the likelihood that support with parenting has a lower priority than child welfare and child protection.

Barriers to the use of formal support

What we have seen, then, tells us that many of the families had little or no access to formal services. For some, this was simply a reflection of what they saw as a lack of need, and we must caution against the assumption that disabled parents will necessarily need additional support from formal agencies. For others, the unavailability of support was a major issue, not least because it was often seen as detrimental to health:

> It's the everyday things as well … it's really painful on my bad days getting the kids to school.
> *Mother (PI, MHI), dual-parent family*

This appeared especially so for parents who had struggled to have their impairments recognised at the time of their onset. For instance, several parents with ME reported the negative effect on their health of having to battle to get their condition recognised. Some even reported that medical staff had given entirely inappropriate advice (for instance, to exercise rather than rest), which had subsequently led to a deterioration in impairments and often set them back years in terms of managing, or recovering from, their condition. One parent with ME described a 'medical regime' denying her impairments in the early years, with nursing staff refusing her the use of a wheelchair in order to encourage her to walk. She ascribes two years spent almost wholly in bed to these errors in early treatment, and the absence of appropriate support, during which two of her children were still of school age.

Indeed, the unavailability of quality healthcare, particularly for parents with mental health impairments, was identified as particularly important. Several parents said that the level of support and treatment open to them as *individuals* was so poor that the question of support with *parenting* was simply not on the agenda. One parent was scathing about the treatment available to his wife on the NHS:

It's really incoherent and, I would say, rudderless. Basically, in terms of treatment, they seem to start with the cheap rubbish and then go from there.

Father, dual-parent family (mother, MHI)

The priority for such parents was suitable medical treatment, and only rarely would these families see support in terms specifically of parenting.

Attitudes towards disability and parenting

According to parents in our study, barriers exist to the use of formal support, particularly in the attitudes of those offering such support, or, rather, those acting as gatekeepers to it. Many felt that the inappropriateness of some formal support lay in the invisibility of *disabled parents* in the mindset of professionals. Several parents described how social services had sought to assess their needs as an individual, rather than as a member of a family with dependent children:

My community care assessment didn't really take any notice of the fact that I had two young children.... It was all about me and my needs.

Mother (PI, MHI), dual-parent family

Several parents had requested help with looking after their children; the services, however, were unwilling to recognise that parenting was a valid support need:

The OT [occupational therapist] asked me if I needed any help but I've been told that I can't have it. They've said they would help with personal care.... They would cook for me but not them [the children].... I rang social services to ask them for help – I was in a mess. I said to social services if I didn't cook, wash, etcetera, you would have me for neglect, but I got no answer.

Mother (PI), single-parent family

The conceptual invisibility of disabled parents, discussed in Chapter One, was not, however, limited to statutory authorities. One single mother had been offered low-cost transport to the supermarket once a week by a local voluntary sector group. However, she was unable to use it, initially:

Well, they had agreed to take me shopping and everything was fine, but then they phoned me back and said they could not take children as passengers on insurance grounds. This meant that I simply couldn't use it. I mean, it's as if they assume that disabled people just don't have children. In the end, I argued with them and they got back to me, saying "Yes, you can bring your children, but only because you're a single parent", which I thought was a strange thing to say.

Mother (PI), single-parent family

Many parents also felt judged concerning the suitability of their becoming parents in the first place. As well as the issue of health, several of them reported that social care professionals had told them that "Disabled people shouldn't have children", or had asked "How can you possibly look after a baby when you can't even look after yourself?".

Other parents talked about the availability of support services, yet felt unable to use them given their location or working hours. For example, they were available at times that did not suit the routines of parenting, especially being there for children and having to take them to and from school. One parent, caring for his three children during his partner's periods of severe depression, said:

> I lost my job around the time of her third pregnancy, which involved a lot of travelling to hospital in [nearby town], and problems of what to do with the other kids. I did ask for help from social services but was offered a playschool place at [other side of city] for two hours. After allowing for bus journeys I would have to go straight back to fetch him as soon as I got home, so it wasn't worth it. I was also offered some counselling but it was in town and just impossible to get to given that I had to pick the kids up from school. Once I'm there I can start talking about how it all feels but it's getting there that's the problem.
>
> *Father, dual-parent family (mother, MHI)*

This case illustrates the importance of considering the broader social and economic factors that prevent service use. This is echoed in the Social Services Inspectorate (SSI) inspection of services to disabled parents, which found that buildings-based services were rarely appropriate for disabled parents, given travel time and the need to be home to meet children from school (DoH, 2000b).

Disabled parents also face other barriers to formal support. These barriers are based not so much on negative assumptions about disability, or on the conceptual invisibility of disabled parents in professional thinking, but more on assumptions about 'normal' family life implicit in the way support is offered. In particular, some professionals seemed to make judgements about parenting decisions that resulted in formal support being inaccessible for some parents. One single mother had recently begun to employ personal assistants, but still wanted more assistance getting her children to bed in the evening:

> I was told that I could only receive personal assistance with my baby up until 7.30pm.... I was told by the social worker that 7.30 is an appropriate bedtime and no support will be offered after this. So I am told I can have no more help past 7.30 as that is supposed to be her bed-time, but she goes to bed at nine and that's how I want it.
>
> *Mother (PI, MHI), single-parent family*

Differential access to information

Other difficulties in accessing support concerned the availability and timing of appropriate information. Many parents talked about the paucity of information on services and benefits, particularly around the time of onset and/or diagnosis of impairments. For some, the system actually *limited* the availability of information on offer, with a general unwillingness on the part of professionals to provide comprehensive advice on the whole range of support available:

> I think that an application for DLA [Disability Living Allowance] would be a good starting point in directing disabled people to other benefits and services that they may be entitled to. At the moment the system works to put you off and tell you the minimum.
> *Father, dual-parent family (mother, PI)*

In addition, some parents felt overwhelmed by the sheer rate of change in terms of services and benefits on offer, and in terms of the turnover of professionals with whom they had to deal. This was compounded by the effect that a continual battle for information about support can have on the impairments, energy levels and coping abilities of the disabled parents themselves or of partners taking on 'caring' roles:

> A leaflet should be available to tell you all the support and all the benefits available. Everything is word-of-mouth and accidentally finding out about things. Simply keeping the household together takes so much effort, that there is very little left for chasing benefits or information about things. And we ask for very little as it is.
> *Father, dual-parent family (mother, MHI)*

One effect of the often poor availability of information is the potentially inequitable way in which services are accessed. Several of our study's parents talked about finding out about support only by chance from other, often better informed, parents:

> Everything seemed to lead to a cul-de-sac. For instance, no one ever told us we were entitled to a free wheelchair.... We just overheard someone saying it on holiday and within a week of getting back we'd got one from the Red Cross. After diagnosis there should be a telephone number – a kind of 'start here', because for us it was fragments.
> *Father, dual-parent family (mother, PI)*

Similarly, the degree to which parents felt confident enough to pursue services via the telephone was extremely variable. Some described having to badger professionals for support over the phone (a major obstacle in itself), yet others talked about support being easily accessible "so long as you're prepared to telephone enough of the right people".

There appears, from what we have just seen, to be an information lottery for disabled parents. Related to this is the significance of key individuals or events in triggering effective formal support. We often found hospitalisation of a parent, or indeed their non-disabled partner, to be particularly important. This was due to the fact that a prolonged stay in hospital is likely to bring a patient into contact with a range of professionals (such as occupational therapists), or, in the case of disabled pregnant women, midwives and health visitors. Parents often talked about having a key professional who was able to drive through supports elsewhere in the system, or even in neighbouring authorities:

> All we get now has come via the rehab hospital in [town]. It's down to the fact that the consultant has a very positive philosophy and the desire to see it through, so the other members of his team are progressive as well. They're willing to battle with social services for proper support. When my wife was discharged, she was in a right state ... unable to move. I thought, "I'm not going to get back to work here, am I?". Social services were very helpful at first but after she rallied and help wasn't needed, and then relapsed, I found it impossible to reinstate support. The consultant was brilliant: he really made the social worker squirm at a case conference, forcing them into a corner over giving us more support
> *Father, dual-parent family (mother, PI, MHI)*

Several parents also said that the only factor that ensured that they received information about available support was their membership of a particular voluntary group. This highlights the important role that such groups play, often on an impairment-specific basis, in providing information and support to disabled people. On the other hand, it emphasises the potentially unequal access to information faced by those parents from communities under-represented in the membership base of such voluntary groups. In addition, although ethnicity was not a major variable in our research, it was also clear that language barriers, along with assumptions about the nature of extended families in South Asian communities, could also make accessing formal support more difficult. One parent who spoke little English was trying to get domestic support for himself and his wife. However, he had encountered significant difficulty in finding information about support, and in getting an assessment – telephone calls were not returned, and there was great confusion about whether or not he was entitled to any support.

Further, the importance of family and personal resources is also illustrated by the number of parents who spoke about having accessed support via personal and professional contacts. One professional disabled father had been able to maintain good relationships with his daughter's school, mainly through a personal friendship with a teacher with whom he shared a particular artistic interest. Another parent talked about the support he and his wife received from one of his children's teachers with whom they enjoyed professional connections as part of their jobs.

The availability of appropriate and timely information about the support available is clearly an important issue. However, it is particularly important for those parents who face other forms of exclusion, including additional communication barriers such as the unavailability of information in languages other than English (including British Sign Language) or in formats accessible to disabled parents with other communication impairments. It also includes those who lack personal resources essential in battling for information and support – for example, confidence in using the telephone in dealing with professionals – or do not have personal connections to professionals who are able to circumvent conventional pathways to information, suggest short-cuts, explain jargon, and so on.

Formal support agencies as a source of conflict

For some families, difficulties in accessing support from formal sources went much further. We are aware that many families do not want social services involved in their parenting. For a small number of families in our study, relationships with a range of statutory agencies, and social services in particular, were constructed in *extremely* negative terms. For example, families went to great effort to prevent their children from being placed on the 'at risk' register. The relationship between parents and professionals in this small number of families was characterised by conflict and mistrust, to the point that our questions about how professionals might provide support to them as parents were often met with incredulity. Several parents talked about how conflict with professionals had subsequently made their attempts to receive support more problematic. Others talked about being unable to access necessary support because of a fear that their behaviour would be interpreted negatively, for instance in the case of several parents who were worried about making excessive use of their GP for fear of being labelled as 'neurotic' as well as 'mentally ill'. Other parents talked about what they saw as the unacceptable conditions that were imposed on any offer of formal support, leaving them with no help at all. For instance, one family felt penalised because of one parent's previous criminal conviction, which had led to unfounded rumours concerning the family being circulated among professionals and neighbours alike. In this case, the service professionals made approaches to the mother, implying that more support would be available to her if she 'ditched' her partner. They also made an offer of home care provision by 'teams' of staff – as opposed to individual workers – on what the family saw as spurious safety grounds.

Some parents said that their requests for support had been ignored, only for professionals to take an increased interest in the wellbeing of their children at a later date when the situation had worsened.

> Basically, all the social workers do now is suggest things that are either unwelcome or then don't happen. They have now suggested a psychiatric social worker – I needed one of them 18 months ago when I was on the point of collapse. I asked for a community-care assessment which never happened. At the time I got nothing – even with the emergency team there was so much delay. They weren't there while I needed them, but now they are turning it around and telling me all the things I have to do to keep my kids. I wanted a community-care assessment but gave up banging our heads against a brick wall. Since then, we have been trying to keep social services off our backs. For instance, they insisted on a 3pm meeting on Friday which I refused as I've got to get the kids from school.
> *Mother (PI, MHI), dual-parent family*

This case illustrates that formal services are often unaware of the parenting responsibilities of disabled adults when they offer services or even appointments. More importantly, perhaps, it illustrates that, for some families, the supportive relationship that *might* exist with statutory bodies is subverted by other powerful factors, including the role that social services in particular play in policing families they are concerned about. The mother in this case also talked about struggling with one of her children to the supermarket only to come back home empty-handed after her child refused to enter the shop, having seen a local social worker shopping there. We are not suggesting that social services should jettison their paramount concern with the wellbeing of children. Rather, what we are arguing for is an awareness that extra barriers to support may result if relations with families with disabled parents become so entrenched and negative.

The *Framework for the assessment of children in need and their families*, discussed in Chapter One, emphasises that support by way of direct work with families "may be offered at the same time as family proceedings are in progress" (DoH, DfEE and HO, 2000, p 9). In the light of the experiences of a small number of families in this study, this seems a little optimistic. A small number of our study's families were engaged in deeply negative, conflicting relationships with support agencies, and these families found it difficult to see those agencies as possible sources of support with respect to issues of parenting. The importance, therefore, of keeping channels of support open despite other ongoing concerns about child wellbeing cannot be overestimated. While it is well acknowledged that, at a 'system' level, child protection concerns have often tended to squeeze out family support practice (Dartington Social Research Unit, 1995), it is importance to recognise the potential for this also happening at the level of individual families.

Impairments as barriers?

The parents that took part in our study told us about the hurdles placed in their way when it came to using formal sources of support. As we have seen, some parents also told us about poor relationships with service providers, which made it extremely difficult to see those agencies as sources of support. However, other parents talked about the roots of barriers to the use of services (whether 'special' or mainstream) that are inherent in their impairments. This was particularly so for some parents with mental health impairments, and their partners. For example, one father considered the main reason for not making use of services such as Homestart were his and his wife's forgetfulness and lack of organisation:

> We've been offered Homestart but I'm not so sure about the idea of people coming in to clean ... partly because we would have to tidy up before they came. It's my fault, it's down to me – I don't help myself. Plus, the wife finds it difficult to cope with the idea of regular help, despite the fact that some days she is so depressed she can't lift a finger. Partly, it is about others knowing your business, but also about feeling a pressure to have to put on some kind of public front or face every day.
> *Father, dual-parent family (mother, MHI)*

For others, the standard of their housework – and their control over it – were barriers to receiving outside help. For instance, one mother had periods where she was too depressed to fulfil her usual role of 'housewife'. However, she described a central part of her mental health impairments to be the need to retain control of household matters, and therefore found it extremely difficult and challenging for home-care staff or other family members to take over housework when she was ill.

> It is really difficult to see how any support could be given. When I'm well everything is fine, and when I'm ill I'm not receptive to having any help anyway.
> *Mother (MHI), dual-parent family*

Other parents also talked about difficulties inherent in their impairments that made the receipt of formal support difficult. The husband of a mother with multiple sclerosis (MS) talked about the problems that his wife's poor and erratic memory had caused with regard to formal support. In particular, she would often forget to tell her husband that a particular service had been reviewed or cancelled, or that other changes in her support arrangements had been made. This would lead to gaps in service receipt that her husband would be unaware of for some time and that he would then have to try to reapply for.

Chapter Six examines the implications of these comments, and others, for our understanding of the social model of disability in relation to parenting. They have been introduced here in order to illustrate the importance of recognising that, although services are offered in ways that can present barriers for disabled parents, it is also features of impairments themselves that can frustrate the effective provision of support. Of course, this does not mean that those providing formal services should not seek to adapt their practice in order to remain as accessible as possible.

This section has so far looked at the barriers facing parents when using formal support, according to their own reports. Not least of these barriers is the implicit assumption that disabled people do not have children. The poor availability of information about benefits and services that parents reported, as well as the particular difficulties experienced by disabled parents facing additional forms of exclusion (based on ethnicity, communication impairments, socioeconomic disadvantage, and so on), have been examined also. We have emphasised how conflict between parents and professionals hamstrings attempts to provide support, and have discussed some of the factors internal to the experience of impairments that compromise the suitability and appropriateness of various forms of formal support. These various sets of issues, which structure the ability of formal services to enable the parenting role of disabled people, should inform a process of critical evaluation within those agencies offering support. Access to, and appropriateness of, formal support is contingent on many factors; therefore, those bodies providing formal services should be imaginative and flexible in the way support is offered. We now examine the issue of informal support in our analysis.

Barriers to the use of informal support

Interviews with the parents in our study show that disabled parents' access to the creation, and maintenance, of informal networks of support can be compromised. The reasons for this mirror the barriers identified earlier in this chapter, and include – among many other things – lack of money, inaccessible or unsuitable housing, and the absence of accessible transport:

> I knew most of the parents of my son's friends from the days before I was disabled, but really I've been virtually housebound since and have made no new friends. I don't know any of the other mums at his new school.
> *Mother (PI), single-parent family*

In comparison, several parents talked about having an extensive informal network that was established before the onset of disability and, in so doing, recognised that establishing such a network at this point would be much more difficult.

> I've got a good network here and in the surrounding villages – that's why I moved to the village. I wouldn't be able to build up a network like I have now I'm disabled
> *Mother (PI), dual-parent family*

Not only do disabled parents themselves face barriers to accessing informal support; members of informal networks may also face difficulties in relation to transport, mobility, poverty, and so on. Several parents talked about the increased difficulty in accessing informal support given the impairments and health problems of *other* family members and friends who would normally be called upon:

> My mum and sister are about 10 miles away but my mum is in a wheelchair and my sister is blind … so any contact we have is to help look after them rather than them look after us. On top of that I have to provide a lot of care for my daughter [with learning disabilities].
> *Mother (PI, MHI), dual-parent family*

For another mother, the most critical moment in her recent life as a disabled parent was not the onset and diagnosis of MS three years previously; rather, it was the stroke suffered by her father – on whom she had depended for transport and other help.

Fragmented informal support

Our interviews indicated the extent to which the availability of informal support is by no means straightforward. This is for two particularly important reasons:

1. the *fragmented* way in which informal support is made available to disabled parents;
2. the identification of family members as very much part of the *problem*, rather than as a source of support.

Many parents talked about the restrictions placed upon the availability of informal support. This included friends or family who had strictly limited roles in terms of what they were prepared to get involved in. One parent counted three close friends, one of whom tended to help with lending money or food, whereas the others were much more willing to provide a listening ear when she was feeling down. Several other respondents talked about family members, friends and neighbours, offering help, but only in a limited sense, and on their own terms.

> My dad might cut the hedge or mow the lawn – but there's no way he would go shopping for me…. When my mum was alive she did a lot more housework and shopping.
> *Mother (PI, MHI), single-parent family*

Limits on the accessibility of informal support were not solely the result of boundaries imposed by others. Rather, parents themselves were engaged in limiting their requests for support from family and friends. For example, one mother described her wide informal network, but qualified this by saying:

> I will call on friends for help with shopping, or to go out for lunch.... I
> treasure friendship very much but friends have their own children – however
> nice friends are I don't want to ring and say "I'm desperate", as they know
> that my husband is working at home.
> *Mother (PI), dual-parent family*

Many other parents made a similar point: that friends and neighbours are not
the first people you call on for help, for fear of jeopardising the basis of the
friendship. Recognition of the importance of friends, especially for emotional
support, was balanced with a desire to self-limit any help needed. Many parents
described treading a difficult and often tiring line between calling on family
and friends for much-needed ongoing support, and ensuring that such requests
were minimised in order not to unbalance the reciprocity of friendships and
relationships. For instance, many parents talked about having good neighbours,
but feeling extremely uneasy about having to call on them for help, particularly
if they felt they could not reciprocate. One mother talked about feeling very
isolated, and saw this as a major problem, given the absence of a partner:

> I don't really have any friends living close by and that is a bit of a problem –
> I am rather isolated, although I think my neighbours would help if it was an
> emergency.
> *Mother (PI), single-parent family*

Sometimes, the problem in accessing informal support was one of transport,
mobility and geographical separation. However, some of those quite
geographically close to family and friends often felt isolated from any informal
support. Some described living next door to relatives, but hardly saw them
from one day to the next. For other parents, it was the nature of family
relationships that precluded them from accessing support, with several describing
theirs as 'not that sort of family'. The *presence* of other family members should
not, therefore, be read as implying their *availability* as a source of support (for
instance, in the case of two-parent families, in which one partner has a
demanding job that takes him or her away from the house for extended periods).
Clearly, disabled parents, as well as non-disabled partners, operate with fragmented
informal support networks limited by the quantity and quality of help on offer,
and by a reluctance to over-use it.

Families as part of the problem

It is clear, however, that most disabled parents primarily call on family members
– rather than friends or neighbours – to provide assistance. This is significant,
given the way in which several of the families in our study saw some family
members as part of the *problem*, rather than as a source of *support*. For several
parents, disputes and disagreements within the family were a major source of
stress and isolation, and only served to exacerbate any problems already faced

in terms of disability and/or impairments. One mother, for example, was depressed and was also caring for a daughter with schizophrenia. The mother attributed the severity of her daughter's illness to the bullying and abusive behaviour her daughter received at the hands of her sister-in-law. In addition to stresses felt within the family, she also sought to distance herself from the main South Asian community in the nearby town, and had moved to a town with a largely white population some miles away:

> I like it here. In the Indian community there is a lot of gossip and people talking behind your back, particularly with [child] having schizophrenia. I just wanted to get away as soon as possible.
> *Mother (MHI), dual-parent family*

Clearly, the additional difficulties represented by the prejudicial attitudes of the local community are a key part of the disablement experienced by this mother and her daughter. It also demonstrates how those who might ordinarily be thought of as part of the informal support network can in fact be the source of further difficulty. Of course, this experience is not unique to those from minority ethnic backgrounds[1]. However, we are aware that mental health impairments in particular are often closely related to, and/or exacerbated by, the consequences of racism. This includes the structural disadvantage that black and minority ethnic communities experience, as well as difficulties that non-white mental health service users face when confronted by a psychiatric system that is based on Eurocentric notions of what constitutes mental health and mental illness (Patel and Fatimilehin, 1999).

Other parents talked about doing everything they could to avoid contact with other family members:

> My mum lives in the next village but I have no contact if I can help it. She is a suicidal schizophrenic and manic depressive.
> *Mother (PI), single-parent family*

These views are supported by other studies that have shown that informal networks can be a source of criticism for parents; for instance, single mothers and the parents of disabled children (Jack, 2001). Crucially, others saw members of their family as *directly* implicated in the onset of their impairments; this was especially the case for some parents with mental health impairments. Several of these parents talked about abuse they had experienced as a child, and the impact this had had both on their existing mental health impairments and on subsequent relationships with family members. One father talked about his wife's mother living in the same city, but answered "No" when asked if he considered her to be close by. He continued, saying they were not sure of her address and that lack of contact was partly the result of having no car – but also about 'incidents' in his wife's childhood that had served to prevent her mother from being a possible source of support. Another mother, whose own mother lived in the next village, expressed similar sentiments:

> I would describe my relationship with my mother as very damaging over the years, although it has improved somewhat. Basically, she was really angry with me for having children in the first place, what with my condition. She really crushed me with words.
> *Mother (PI, MHI), single-parent family*

Therefore, we must question the assumption that family members, even when geographically close by, necessarily represent a source of support to disabled parents. This is perhaps most obviously the case in those situations where the availability/desire of ex-partners to stay involved as parents – for instance, as a potential source of support – is compromised by their abusive/violent behaviour in the past. Some mothers talked about their experience of domestic violence in the past, and of the stress involved in trying to manage continued contact with abusive, or formerly abusive, fathers of their children. The stress included balancing the additional support it often represented in terms of parenting, and the perceived benefits to the children of ongoing contact.

Other family members had difficulty in accepting and understanding the nature and implications of mental health impairments, and this served as another problem for disabled families.

> They live up in [other part of country], which leads to all sorts of problems .... They don't fully understand the nature of [wife]'s illness and they have trouble understanding why we don't want to go up and see them when she is only just back from hospital and trying to recover and looking for some peace and recuperation.
> *Father, dual-parent family (mother, MHI)*

Not a one-way street?

So far in this section we have looked at the way in which the participants in our study described and talked about difficulties in accessing sources of informal support. However, our data indicate that disabled parents are sometimes *more* able to create and sustain informal networks of support. This can be for a variety of reasons, including the peer support that often comes from a shared experience of disability, and from the additional time that those disabled parents excluded from full-time employment (or any employment) have to devote to family and community alike. Some parents talked about how the onset of impairments had led to decisions – concerning where to live, for instance – which brought them closer to grandparents and siblings and thereby enabled them not only to use them as support but also to maintain reciprocal relationships and friendships. Indeed, where informal networks were strong, the benefits were not limited to parents: they also enabled disabled parents to make a greater contribution to the community, especially through paid and unpaid work, and involvement in other community initiatives. One single, physically impaired mother said having her mother live in an adjacent part of the building was helpful, not only in terms of ordinary family life but in terms of enabling her to pursue further education, and to work part-time as a volunteer in the community. Another mother pointed to the benefits of having her parents live close by:

> They live in a house whose garden backs onto ours and we moved here to be near them. So if I need help I can ask them or my siblings who also live in the village, especially for practical things like shopping – they are so near and we help each other out.
> *Mother (PI), dual-parent family*

The simplistic view of disabled people as necessarily less able to sustain, and benefit from, informal support, should be resisted. This is especially so given the availability (for some) of support from other disabled parents. Some parents said they knew other people experiencing similar problems, and that this gave them an important informal resource to call upon. Indeed, it was striking how often parents in our study mentioned *other* disabled people when talking about their informal support networks. One father commented that, not only had local disabled people been more helpful generally (than non-disabled people), but that they were simply more available, given their exclusion from paid employment. Similarly, one mother who experienced periods of depression commented on her membership of a support network of other mothers with similar experiences of depression. This reinforces what Campion has to say on the issues of disability and parenting:

> Even in families where disabled parents may need a lot of assistance in managing practical tasks, they may still be the source of emotional strength that binds a family together. Disability alone is not an indicator of the ability of an individual to *care for and support others*. (Campion, 1995, p 139, added emphasis)

As well as the importance of other disabled people in supporting the parents we interviewed, it was also apparent that these parents were themselves often heavily involved in *providing* support to others:

> Well, I'm the counsellor around here. My house is often full of mums from around the village telling me their problems.
> *Mother (PI), dual-parent family*

It was clear that disabled parents were part of support networks that involved *giving* as well as receiving support. Several parents talked about the experience and knowledge they had acquired through the experience of disability and how they had been able to share this knowledge with other disabled parents (for instance, regarding leisure facilities such as theme parks with wheelchair access). Parents often reported that they gave support to other people in their communities, both disabled and non-disabled. For example, one mother had difficulties in attending parents' evenings:

> The last two times I've not been able to go 'cos I've been too busy looking after my friends' kids so that they could go.
> *Mother (PI, MHI), dual-parent family*

It is ironic, given the emphasis in the 'young carer' literature on the likelihood of children missing out educationally, that this mother's difficulties in maintaining contact with her children's school were attributed to the demands of *care giving* as opposed to the requirements for *care receipt*.

In addition to highlighting some of the barriers to informal support that disabled parents can face, this section has also pointed out the informal support they provide to others. We have discussed the importance of fragmentation in terms of the informal support open (or closed) to disabled parents, and have cautioned against any assumption in policy and practice by which the proximity of family and friends represents a supportive and reliable network. This is especially so for those parents who construct their family as part of the origin of their mental health impairments, or who see their family as exacerbating any problems they currently face (for instance, in the case of abusive partners). The issue of how formal and informal networks might *interact* in the support of disabled parents is examined in the next section.

The interaction between formal and informal support

A variety of factors, then, can compromise access to – and the availability of – both formal and informal sources of support for disabled parents. What has also emerged from our research, however, is the importance of the interaction of formal and informal supports, and the importance of conceptualising support in terms of the needs of *people in relationships* rather than, necessarily, as individuals.

Some parents felt that access to formal support had been specifically denied, or restricted in some way, due to the perceived ability of other family members to provide assistance, be that personal 'care', parenting, or other roles. As Chapter Four shows in greater detail, in some cases the age of children had been used as a way of justifying the withdrawal of formal support with implications for the domestic responsibilities of other family members, including children. One self-employed father, using an outhouse for work purposes, felt that social services had been unwilling to recognise his wife's parental role:

> I feel that there has always been an assumption that because I often work at the back of the house, that I would be able to do everything.
> *Father, dual-parent family (mother, PI)*

Many parents complained about the manner in which responsibility for their partner's assistance, or their children, and other household matters, automatically fell to them when formal support was not available. However, the blame was sometimes placed on extended family members for leaving the main 'caring' roles to partners, rather than on social services for withholding support. It was also significant that a number of partners of parents with mental health impairments talked about the strong role they had played in battling for support, and adequate treatment, for their partners. One father described the difficulties he had experienced in accessing support:

> I could have done with support being readily available when the depression started. In the end a lot of help came from [a voluntary mental health organisation] but they were difficult to find; eventually my wife went through a national helpline. If I had been on my own I wouldn't have had the motivation to do it, as the wife has done a lot of pushing for support.
> *Father (MHI), dual-parent family*

In the following case, support became both greater in quantity and more effective once contact had been established, highlighting the possibilities for support when an alliance between informal supporters, the voluntary sector organisation and the GP was forged:

> First it was a real battle, but then, once the wife had put me in contact with [voluntary sector mental health advocacy organisation], who were excellent, and in combination with the GP, who was also excellent, that pressure was put on the consultant who until then had really no appreciation of what we were up against as a family.
> *Father (MHI), dual-parent family*

Other partners talked about a particular role they had in diverting stressful events and situations away from the disabled parent. This role often intersected with gender roles, and often surrounded attempts by fathers to encourage schools to address any difficulties to them rather than their ill partners – often with little success:

> We had a very poor experience with the boys' school. There was a bit of a problem with him ... you know, discipline-wise, and the school kept contacting my wife about it and making her very anxious. I asked them if they could go through me with any problems, in order to prevent this anxiety. I've even made sure that they have my work number, my mobile number ... and I make sure my boss always knows where I am should things happen, but they still don't bother and they continue to phone and agitate my wife.
> *Father, dual-parent family (mother, MHI)*

Parents and partners alike resented the manner in which the system worked – several were quick to point out that, by giving up their work to look after their partners, they had 'saved the state thousands'. Their reward, however, was a small benefit increase, leaving the family worse off and under greater stress as a result.

We also spoke to families who had received advice from professionals that emphasised family self-reliance and served to close the door to any form of professional support. One father, who gave up work to look after his wife and children at home, said:

> Her consultant told me to give up work, as it was not safe for my wife to look
> after a young child while lying down and on medication, simple as that.
> *Father, dual-parent family (mother, PI)*

In this case, the consultant made a judgement not only about the ability of this mother to cope both with a small child and her own impairments, but also about the correct course of action for the family as a whole. This confirms what other studies have said about the importance of professional attitudes in limiting access to support for carers and other family members (see, for example, Twigg and Atkin, 1995). The possibility that support could be provided for this mother that would enable her to look after her child *and* enable her husband to keep working, and therefore maintain a higher standard of living for the family, was simply not considered.

Another parent described the difficulties he had keeping his business afloat as his wife's impairments worsened. Eventually, it became impossible for him to go away on business and leave his wife at home – his business folded and he became a full-time carer. Adequate and earlier support might, this parent argued, have allowed him to keep the business going and prevent the family from becoming dependent on benefit. Another parent talked about a particularly difficult time in her depression five years ago:

> The worst time was when I was acutely depressed. That was a real crisis point.
> My husband gave up work and all we were offered was foster care for the
> children, and to us that was no option.
> *Mother (PI, MHI), dual-parent family*

It is apparent, then, that the interaction of formal and informal sources of support has the scope both to restrict and enable choices for families. Some parents and partners described very positively the balance between statutory, voluntary and family involvement in any assistance they required. Others perceived formal and informal sources of support to be in conflict – formal support was available only when informal support was not.

This section has highlighted the sense of frustration that many parents and other family members feel when an absence of formal support places strains on existing roles and relationships within the family (an issue discussed at greater length in Chapter Five). For disabled parents and their families to be provided with the holistic, flexible and responsive support essential for enabling successful parenting, it is important that formal support is offered in a way that promotes, underpins and enables existing family and friendship relationships. The danger is that other family members are seen solely as *resources*, limiting the availability of formal support. In order to achieve this positive relationship between formal and informal sources of support, a broader understanding of the ways in which support needs can be met, as well as of the underlying origins of those needs, is essential.

Developing a broader understanding of the origins and interplay of support needs

As we have seen, our research points to some of the factors that limit the extent to which disabled parents access, and make use of, sources of formal and informal support. It also points, however, to the importance of recognising the multiple and interacting sources of difficulty that disabled parents face. We cannot overestimate the importance of viewing disability as a single factor among many that structure the daily lives of families with disabled parents. Policy and practice which focuses too narrowly on disability as the definitive issue fails to understand the broader socioeconomic and structural context in which these parents parent their children.

Table 3.4 illustrates the underrepresentation in the paid labour market of those parents in our sample. Only 12 respondents were in regular paid employment of more than 10 hours a week, and a number of parents had never been in paid employment.

Table 3.4 also indicates that paid employment and home-making roles are as gendered for disabled parents as they are for parents generally. Five out of the 10 fathers in our study were in employment of more than 10 hours per week, compared with seven mothers out of 57. Correspondingly, four out of 10 fathers described themselves as 'looking after the home', while 45 out of 57 mothers applied this label to their own activity. Clearly, then, paid employment was the exception rather than the rule for this sample of disabled parents, and this can only partially be explained by the overrepresentation of mothers with school-age children. Thirty-two households were in receipt of income support, and 47 parents were in receipt of DLA at some level. The low level of paid employment and significant levels of dependence on benefits among the families led, unsurprisingly, to many in the sample living near, or below, the poverty line (Table 3.5).

The high level of unemployment in our sample, and the extent of reliance on state benefits, alert us to the role that financial and other resource barriers play in determining the degree to which disablement affects family life and parenting. A parent that has the financial ability to own a fully accessible house and usable car – as the result of a compensation or insurance pay-out, or as a

Table 3.4: Current economic and educational activity of disabled parent (by sex, family shape and impairment group)

	Sex		Family shape		Impairment group		
					PI/		
	M	**F**	**Dual**	**Single**	**Sensory**	**MHI**	**Total**
In the last seven days...							
Looking after the home	4	45	30	19	33	16	49
Provided care for family members	0	7	5	2	5	2	7
Unpaid voluntary work	2	15	11	6	15	2	17
Unemployed/registered, benefit office	1	1	2	0	2	0	2
Unemployed/not registered	0	1	0	1	0	1	1
Permanently sick or disabled	5	35	25	15	34	6	40
Wholly retired from work	1	1	1	1	2	0	2
Waiting to take up work accepted	0	0	0	0	0	0	0
In paid work (more than ten hours a week)	5	7	10	2	5	7	12
On a government training programme	0	0	0	0	0	0	0
In full-time education	0	2	1	1	2	0	2
In part-time education	0	6	3	3	6	0	6
Doing something else	0	3	3	0	3	0	3
Total sample[a]	10	57	44	23	46	21	67

PI = Physical impairment
MHI = Mental health impairment
[a] Respondents may be involved in more than one activity.

Table 3.5: Parental reports of total household income

	Number	**%**
Less than £7,999 pa	16	23.88
£8,000-£11,999 pa	11	16.42
£12,000-£17,999 pa	12	17.91
£18,000-£22,999 pa	5	7.46
£23,000-£28,999 pa	6	8.96
£29,000-£34,999 pa	4	5.97
£35,000+ pa	6	8.96
Do not know	6	8.96
Refused/Not answered	1	1.49
Total	67	100.00

Table 3.6: Housing status (by family shape and impairment group)

	Family shape		Impairment group		
	Dual	**Single**	**PI/Sensory**	**MHI**	**Total of both pairs of columns**
Own outright	5	2	5	2	7
Own with a mortgage	28	5	23	10	33
Owns own home	33	7	28	12	40
Rented: privately	1	1	1	1	2
Rented: local authority	8	11	12	7	19
Rented: housing association	1	3	3	1	4
Other (rented from trust; rented from relative)	1	1	2	0	2
Rents own home	11	16	18	9	27
Total	44	23	46	21	67

PI = Physical impairment

MHI = Mental health impairment

result of remaining in a well-paid job – faces significantly less disability than those parents on income support.

Table 3.6 outlines the housing status of the families in Stage One. Forty families were owner-occupiers, with 27 living in private or public rented accommodation. Not surprisingly, single-parent families were significantly more likely to be living in rented accommodation than dual-parent families – 69% and 25% respectively, numbers that are statistically significant.

Some families were struggling to cope in poorly adapted – or unadapted – homes, which they could not move around in or leave without assistance. One such family, who had been in its current local authority home for 18 months, was struggling in this way with no adaptations having been carried out. The mother had lost her mobility for the previous two weeks, having fallen from a home-made ramp into the back garden. At the time of our interview, she and her husband, like several other parents in the study, were sleeping downstairs in the living room, and the mother was unsure whether she was going to regain some mobility:

> I can't transfer on to the stair lift – it's a nightmare, so my husband has to carry me. The stair lift was here when we moved in. They said they will do an extension with a wheelchair accessible kitchen, bedroom, en-suite bathroom and outdoor ramp, but I'm not sure if and when this will be done.
> *Mother (PI), dual-parent family*

Despite the unsatisfactory housing situation this family experienced, the parents had chosen to stay put rather than move to an alternative, fully adapted property that the council offered to them:

> We are a priority but so are a lot of other people. I don't know when they
> will be done – and the council might sell the houses off. But I like living
> here better than the house before – this is a much nicer house and garden.
> I liked it when I could walk around. The council said yesterday that they
> had a three-bed, adapted house on a rough estate, but we are settled.
> *Mother (PI), dual-parent family*

Of course, housing is an issue of central importance to many disabled people,
whether or not they also happen to be parents. While some in our study lived
in satisfactory homes, for several families this was not the case, with obvious
implications for family life in terms of mobility, access in and out of the house,
sleeping arrangements, and so on.

In addition to the financial and housing disadvantage faced by many families,
parents also talked about problems they had in parenting in terms of the balance
between home life and work life – disability was something of a side issue.
This serves to illustrate that the parenting issues faced by disabled parents are
mainstream and are, in essence, no different to those faced by all parents. The
difference, as we have tried to articulate in this chapter, is the number of
additional barriers that disabled parents face in addressing those issues. It is
also important to remember that, as all parents know, children are often an
independent source of stress. Several parents had children with emotional and
behavioural difficulties and it was primarily this – and not parental disability –
that was identified as a key issue requiring support.

> It has been difficult with my 17-year-old growing up. Brought me and my
> husband down, his mood swings, drinking, banging doors. It would have
> been useful to have someone else around for moral guidance.
> *Mother (PI, MHI), dual-parent family*

One child was asked how he felt about the number of people who came into
the house to assist both his mother and his disabled brother:

> I don't mind really, even though they seem to change all the time. What
> makes it difficult is the fact that my brother sometimes finds it difficult
> when so many people are coming in, and that upsets him, which affects the
> rest of us when the home-care staff leave.
> *Boy (14), dual-parent family (mother, PI)*

Gender and parenting

Of particular importance for understanding the barriers that disabled parents
and their families can face, as well as the nature of any service response, is the
interaction of gender with those factors we have touched on so far. The
experiences that disabled parents shared with us were deeply embedded both

in the importance of gender in structuring the parenting roles that were open to mothers and fathers, as well as in the association between gender and other forms of exclusion.

For instance, we have already touched on the importance of domestic violence for a small number of the mothers in our study:

> I split up through domestic violence, so he's not allowed contact.... The most difficult time as a family was when their dad found us through the electoral roll and came back six years later – and we needed rehousing. I'd had a lot to do with Women's Aid as we'd lived in a lot of refuges. They give you a short-term answer to your problem but not long-term – they'd moved me out of [city] to [another city]; in the end no-one would rehouse us as I had no ties in these other places.
> *Mother (PI), single-parent family*

We have also mentioned the significance that parents attributed to professional assumptions and judgements concerning parenting and/or disability. Even where parents did not report open hostility on the part of professionals to the notion of having children, some felt that other assumptions, often to do with gender, were being made. For example, one mother reported:

> No professional has ever said I shouldn't have any (more) children ... although I feel sure that it was because I am single. I'm sure their approach would have been different if they'd seen me as married.... They just made the assumption that I wouldn't be having any more because I haven't got a bloke.
> *Mother (PI), single-parent family*

Gender, parenting and disability also intersected in the way in which some parents felt able to support and protect their children, especially in what they saw as a difficult local environment. One parent, for instance, talked about the difficulty she had simply being 'a presence' on the streets that her children played on – issues of gender and the absence of a father figure played a prominent role:

> It is difficult to provide support to my boys. By that I mean I wish I was able to back them up a bit more. If I feel they are getting picked on in the street, I find it impossible to get out there and back them up. My son has been bullied before and I know that the fact that I had come from the 'reject shop' was levelled at him. It wouldn't happen if there was a man in the house, I can tell you.
> *Mother (PI), single-parent family*

Family shape also intersects with gender roles within families. Oliver and Sapey (1999) cite a 1979 survey, now somewhat dated, which showed that 16%

of disabled women were divorced or separated compared with a general population figure of 7%. However, for disabled men the figure was 4%, suggesting that marriages were much more likely to end if the woman, rather than the man, was disabled. Similarly, Parker (1993) found in her study of caring within marriage that it was often more disruptive when those more responsible for care giving became disabled than when those more used to being cared for became disabled. Given the importance of gender in the experience of disability, there are likely to be consequences for the experience of parenting, and the differential ability of mothers and fathers to maintain a parenting role. Consequently, we became interested in the extent – if at all – to which families dealt with the disability of mothers and fathers differently.

Our numbers, particularly those of disabled fathers, are too small for statistical analysis; however, our qualitative analysis points to quite a heterogeneous picture of gender roles, with a significant number of male partners engaged in full-time 'caring', often given the lack of alternative, well-paid employment options. Several male full-time 'carers' expressed resentment at the lack of financial support for their 'caring' role. However, we also encountered female partners who were equally resentful at the expectation that they should 'care' for their disabled husbands:

> Basically, single parents get a lot more help than we do. At the end of the day I will become his carer as his MS gets worse. His mum and dad see me here and assume I'll do it all.
> *Mother, dual-parent family (father, PI)*

This is also important because, for this mother, the assumption that she will be a heavily involved carer since she is 'the wife' is attributable as much to the attitudes of other adults in the extended family as it is to any formal response from social and other services.

Gender also intersects with the way in which parents are able to maintain and benefit from informal support. As we have already mentioned earlier in this book, several mothers talked about the importance to them of contact with other mothers. Those without access either to other mothers or their own mother often felt the most isolated:

> When I am depressed it would be nice to have my mum around, especially when I see all the 24-year-old mums shopping with their mums.
> *Mother (MHI), dual-parent family*

Several parents also talked about the problems associated with the involvement of fathers in parenting. A father whose wife had both physical and mental health impairments, and who also experienced health problems himself, was concerned for the wellbeing of his young daughter, and in particular her opportunities for social interaction with other children. He commented on the difficulty he had in using mainstream facilities such as the local *mother* and toddler group:

> Yes, it would have been great for her [child] to go to playgroups, NCT coffee mornings, or something. Most of the kids round here who are her age know probably a dozen or more kids of the same or similar age, you know, and that's because they go to these social things. I mean I started, I took her once down to the mother and toddler group, and I was the only fella there, yeah, and it wasn't a comfortable experience for me, so I just didn't do it again, you know. I didn't feel comfortable with it, it wasn't my place to be. If there'd been like another half dozen dads, it would have been different, but it wasn't so it was just not an option, you know?
> *Father, dual-parent family (mother, PI, MHI)*

In this father's case, the barrier to informal contact was based on assumptions about gender roles that implicitly undervalued fathering – it had nothing to do with his wife's disability. Similarly, a major problem for one mother was the fact that, when her children were younger, baby-changing and other similar facilities would often only be located in women's toilets. The absence of places for her partner to change and toilet the children was identified as the key barrier for the family, rather than the (in)accessibility of toilets for her.

Clearly, the ways in which disabled parents access support is heavily contingent upon other forms of social exclusion and on dominant ideologies about parenting, particularly those based on gendered assumptions about who does and does not – as well as can and cannot – parent.

Support needs are mainstream but barriers are special: the principles of service response

Thus far, this chapter has explored the many complex and interacting ways in which disabled people experience difficulties in fulfilling parental roles. Whereas the essential support needs of disabled parents are no different from those of any parent – adequate income, suitable housing, access to transport and leisure activities, and so on – the additional barriers faced by disabled parents can make these needs more difficult to meet, both as parents as well as for the whole family.

The support needs of families with disabled parents can be generated in a multiplicity of ways, while socioeconomic disadvantage, family shape, gender and other factors can interact subtly to structure the nature of parenting for disabled people. It is vital, therefore, that support services be open, flexible, coordinated and responsive. They must see the support needs of disabled parents as mainstream rather than 'special', and they must be offered in ways that straddle the divides that exist between health, social care, transport, education, housing and other bodies. For example, one mother said she had tried to book an overnight stay with a large national chain of roadside motels and was told:

"There are family rooms, accessible rooms, but not accessible family rooms". Clearly, the response in policy terms to this kind of barrier should be much broader than is possible with a focus only on health and social care provision. An attack on the inaccessible way in which services are offered in the private sector may well be more important in removing barriers for disabled parents than specific measures within health and social care agencies. In addition, the cocktail of factors structuring the way in which barriers are experienced will itself change over time as impairments, children, and relationships grow, change and develop. (This is discussed in greater detail in Chapter Five.)

Most importantly, however, is the need for those offering support to disabled parents to be aware of the family context, and not simply individual need. During our interviews, many parents related tales of how GPs had signed them off work for months at a time for severe mental health impairments, but without considering the impact at home on family relationships. However, we also found examples of support being offered in ways that were much more accessible to disabled parents. For instance, we encountered parents who talked about their GPs making home visits to children with relatively minor illnesses who would ordinarily be expected to go to surgery, in recognition of the parents' mobility and transport problems. Most importantly, there should be an awareness of the different ways – both from within and without – in which different members of families can be supported. Several parents talked about the important benefits to the health of their partner that resulted from the provision of home care and other services to them. Others talked about the important role that formal services (such as family centres) and informal supports (such as grandparents) provided, not only to them, but directly to their children by giving them space to play, and a changed environment, among other things.

Above all, when parents talked about their need for support, it was in terms of their relationships, and their desire to maintain and underpin them. People would sometimes talk of feeling as though they had 'half a wife' or 'half a husband'. The partners of those parents that were inadequately supported often talked about 'feeling like single parents'. Parents talked about feeling 'left out of parenting', and of children growing up 'always going to the other partner for affection'. Partners talked about the importance of commitment to each other, in the face of adversity, and of not wanting to 'farm out' their partners. Partners emphasised that they wanted to remain a husband or wife, rather than become a 'carer'. These are *relational* issues, expressed in relational terms, which serve to underscore the importance at a strategic level of basing formal intervention and support around the desire to protect and enable family relationships.

The following example illustrates the complex and relational nature of support needs. A South Asian family, living in a predominantly white area of a Midlands city, had a mother with both physical and mental health impairments that involved low confidence and self-esteem. Her husband was acting as a full-time 'carer' for his wife and had main responsibility for the day-to-day care of their two daughters, but could speak very little English. They felt isolated from their extended family, which they felt did not even try to understand the nature of the mother's mental health impairments. In addition, the husband had health problems that would flare up periodically, leaving him unable to perform his usual roles of carer and father. The children had had problems at school and the parents had faced a dilemma – whether the English-speaking mother should risk her health by going to the school to sort them out, or whether the father should try and sort them out, despite his minimal English-language skills. In addition, the father expressed problems with parenting that intersected with the transition to adolescence of his daughters and associated gender difficulties "in teaching them about being a woman". The parents also mourned the absence of grandmothers who could take on the role of guiding the daughters through adolescence. In addition, language barriers existed, not only between the family and the outside world, but also within the family, since the children spoke English but very little of their father's mother tongue. At the time of interview, the family had recently returned home from a trip to India that was intended to help the mother's nerves. On their return, they found that they had been burgled, further denting the mother's confidence in leaving the house at all. The husband had asked for support from social services, but his efforts had got lost in the system. Apparently, this was the consequence of a series of misunderstandings between the professionals concerning who should return his calls and/or arrive to do assessments.

This is by no means a unique case in terms of its complexity and the involved way in which different issues around physical and mental health impairments, ethnicity, gender, gender roles, age and gender of children, language barriers, and the local environment all interact. The challenge is to construct policy, practice and service options that are broad enough to encompass this complexity and depth and that are rooted, not in an individualised notion of care needs and support, but in the desire to promote and sustain family relationships. In addition, they must be able to respond to change (this issue is discussed in Chapter Five).

Direct payments and disabled parents: is the future bright?

In Chapter One, we discussed recent changes in the legislative framework that govern the ways in which disabled people can receive support. Of particular significance is the move towards the control of assistance on the part of disabled people themselves and the growth of direct payments provision, whereby disabled people can receive financial support in lieu of services provided directly by welfare agencies. This, the argument goes, enables disabled people to purchase assistance in more flexible ways, and in ways under the control of the disabled person themselves. In the course of our research, we became interested to find out if any parents had made use of direct payments, or independent living fund (ILF) payments, to purchase support with the specific purpose of parenting activity assistance.

Many families were unaware of what direct payments were and who they were for. Given a generally low level of expectation with regard to their entitlement to support, we were not surprised to find that only one family in our study received direct payments. Some of those who were aware of the potential benefits were often denied access to direct payments. One parent described how she had been told that direct payments were restricted to those who needed more than 30 hours of care themselves. This is a clear indication that assistance with rearing children is not considered by her local authority to be a need covered by direct payments provision (the rules governing the ILF specifically exclude support for parenting activities). Another mother, who could not access the upstairs of her home and had been sleeping on the sofa for some years, also said that her application for direct payments had been turned down on the ground that it was not meant to fund assistance with childcare.

Those who employed personal assistants, either through direct payments or through ILF payments, were generally very positive about this mode of support. The sole recipient of direct payments (a single mother with physical impairments) used it to fund one personal assistant; however, she also received an ILF that afforded her a further four assistants. The assistants were viewed as friends, some of whom had been employed by her for a long period. As well as providing her with personal assistance, she also spoke about the ways in which they gave her moral support for her parenting, and provided assistance in a way that allowed her to maintain control. A further three disabled parents received money via ILF arrangements. One father talked about the unreliability that resulted from receiving home care from an ever-changing set of private sector carers and care agencies. He reported that this unreliability only really ended when they were able to employ their own assistants funded through these ILF payments. Other families saw direct payments as an important goal, citing the anticipated benefits in terms of the quality of life for the family as a whole:

> I always have to make sure that someone is with my wife, or that I am contactable and within easy reach at all times. That's why we want direct payments, because if we get it, it will go towards supporting her mobility, someone to travel with her, to be there for panic attacks and so on, and for the baby's safety as well. It also means I am not so tied down as well.
>
> *Father, dual-parent family (mother, PI, MHI)*

Direct payments are still a relatively innovative way of providing support to disabled people. However, as awareness increases of the possibilities they offer for flexible, holistic assistance for families, there will be increasing demands for the inclusion of parenting as a legitimate activity of daily living for many disabled adults.

Conclusions

Support is extremely important to all parents. However, accessing support is difficult for many disabled parents. In this chapter, we have discussed the many ways in which support services and informal networks may be inaccessible. It is important to emphasise once again, however, that the 'needs' of disabled parents are largely the same as those of non-disabled parents, and it is the social and financial exclusion of many parents from a range of mainstream facilities that serves to generate 'special' support needs. This is an important point for those charged with developing policy and practice: the development of a discourse, which takes as its starting point the implicit belief that disabled parents have a particular and distinct set of support needs that therefore require the construction of specialist forms of welfare provision, will ultimately fail to address the essential fact that parenting is differentially accessible for disabled and non-disabled parents. We argue, rather, that the focus must remain on the removal of barriers to participation in parenting and the creation of a more level playing field. We do not support the development of specialist branches of welfare provision aimed at addressing what are spuriously believed to be 'special needs' on the part of disabled parents.

However, we also argue that it is not simply a question of identifying the range of barriers that disabled people face, although these are of central importance. Rather, we argue that an appreciation of the way in which support can be made accessible to disabled parents must be dependent on an understanding of the complex ways in which disability interacts with a wide range of other factors in structuring the parenting experience of disabled people. For disabled parents, an understanding of the place of disability in their parenting and in the life of their family is inherently bound up with, among other things, consideration of the poverty and racism they may experience, as well as the differential ways in which parenting roles are made available to men and women. Indeed, we would go so far as to argue that the process of disablement is itself understandable *only* when viewed from the perspective of these other forms of social exclusion and disadvantage. This means that, while disabled parents as a group share common experiences of barriers (the built environment, the way in which services are offered, the negative assumptions concerning the parenting capacity of disabled people), they also share experiences and forms of exclusion more with non-disabled parents than disabled parents in more socioeconomically advantaged positions, for example.

It is important, therefore, that policy and practice developments involving disabled parents are sensitive to the contingent place of disability in structuring the parenting of disabled people. At a simple level, this involves taking care not to assume that every potentially negative aspect of family life – from divorce between parents to poor exam results and children's behavioural problems – are necessarily related to parental disability. This was a point forcefully made by many of the disabled parents in our sample. At a more sophisticated level, it requires policy and practice that sees disabled parents both as a group defined by common experiences and as divided along much wider lines of social exclusion.

Note

[1] Disability and parenting, however, may be experienced differently within different ethnic groups. Unfortunately, our study did not allow an in-depth examination of this dimension.

FOUR

Children's involvement in domestic and 'caring' work: new insights

Introduction

The origins of this book lie in a critique that we, and others, had made of the conceptual construction of some disabled parents' children as 'young carers'. (The historical background and key arguments of this critique were discussed in Chapter One of this book.) It is natural, then, that we would want to look in detail here at the extent of children's involvement in domestic and 'caring' work, as well as the context in which it takes place.

We keenly avoid labelling family members as 'carers' or assuming that disabled parents do not themselves occupy 'carer' roles within the family. Our aim is to explore the different factors that might influence not only the degree to which children are involved in domestic and caring responsibilities, but also the nature of any involvement. This has necessarily included a concern with the ways in which formal and informal support mechanisms operate to encourage and/or limit the involvement of children in 'caring' roles. (This follows directly from the arguments we made in Chapter Three concerning the difficulties disabled parents can face in accessing support.) It has also included a concern with the influence of a broad set of possible factors on children's involvement, including family shape as well as the age and gender of children. In the second half of this chapter qualitative data is used from our Stage One families to discuss the factors influencing children's involvement in caring and other work, within these four closely related theme clusters:

- parental dilemmas and strategies;
- formal support and 'young caring';
- informal support and 'young caring';
- children as social actors.

In the first half of the chapter, however, we look at what the quantitative data can tell us about the identification of children as 'young carers', their involvement in caring and domestic activities, and their relationship to variables such as gender, age, family shape and impairment group.

Identifying 'young carers'

Our research sample of parents was opportunistic, and cannot be said to be representative of the general population of disabled parents in the UK. In any case, knowledge of the size and characteristics of this broader group is extremely limited. We do not claim, therefore, that the quantitative data presented here paint a picture that is more widely applicable to disabled parents elsewhere. In addition, 'young carer' projects have been specifically excluded as a source of recruitment (although some children were identified by themselves or by their parents as 'carers', and some received specific 'carer' support). Our decision was based on a commitment to maintaining a parent-centred focus, as well as on a concern not to overrepresent families that identified a child as a 'young carer'[1].

'Carers' and 'caring' activity

Disabled parents interviewed at Stage One were told that there has "recently been a lot of talk about 'young carers', children who help to care for a parent", and were then asked: "Would you consider (your child) to be a 'young carer'?" As we discuss in Appendix One, target children were in most instances chosen at random from all children aged 7-18 in the family. Around one third of parents (21 out of 66) said that they considered the target child to be a 'young carer' (see Table 4.1). In addition, however, our pilot work had indicated that we should also enquire as to whether or not children who were not thought of as 'young carers' were nevertheless engaged in 'caring' activities. Approximately

Table 4.1: Parent-identified 'carer' status of target child

	Would you consider him/her to be a 'young carer'?		If no/don't know/refused, is he/she involved in any 'caring' activities?	
	Number	%	Number	%
Yes	21	31.3	23	34.3
No	41	61.2	22	32.8
Don't know	3	4.5		
Refused	1	1.5		
Not applicable	1	1.5	22	32.8
Total	67	100.0	67	100.0
Target child is:				
a 'young carer'	21	31.3		
involved in caring activity	23	34.3		
not involved in caring activity	22	32.8		
not applicable (no child in house)	1	1.5		
Total	67	100.0		

half of those parents (23 out of the remaining 45 parents) who thought that the child in question was not a 'young carer' *did* think that he or she was involved in caring activities. This left us with a roughly equal three-way split between target children regarded as 'young carers', children involved in caring activities (but not labelled 'young carers'), and those reported to have no involvement in caring (Table 4.1).

Child characteristics and 'caring' status

Table 4.2 shows that older children (ages 12-19) are no more likely to be labelled 'young carers' than younger children (ages 4-11). On the face of it, this is a surprising result, as we might expect children's involvement in domestic work to increase with age. The result is especially interesting, given that parents have also reported much less involvement in task-by-task caring and domestic work by younger children than by older children (see Table 4.6). The apparent contradiction is important since it indicates that parents' use of the label 'young carer' is, at best, only partially related to what children *actually do*, and is perhaps more related to broader social relations within the family. (Qualitative analysis sheds more light on the different ways in which the domestic work of *younger*

Table 4.2: Proportion of target children identified as 'young carers' or involved in 'caring' activity (by age, sex and parental impairment group)

	Child details							
		Age					Sex	
	Number	4-11	12-19	Mean	Median	Range	M	F
'Young carer'	21	8	13	12.86	14	7-17	12	9
Involved in 'caring'	23	11	12	10.91	12	4-18	11	12
No 'caring' activities	22	7	15	12.32	13	5-19	8	14
Total	66	26	40	66	66	66	31	35

	Parental details			
		Primary impairment group		Mental health impairments present?
	Number	PI/Sensory	MHI	No	Yes
'Young carer'	21	17	4	8	13
Involved in 'caring'	23	16	7	13	10
No 'caring' activities	22	12	10	12	10
Total	66	45	21	33	33

PI = Physical impairment
MHI = Mental health impairment

children is constructed. This is discussed in greater detail later in this chapter.) Table 4.2 also shows that the sex of the target child bears no relationship to the likelihood of that child being labelled a 'young carer' or as a child involved in 'caring' activities. This finding is consistent with Dearden and Becker's (1998) survey of children attending 'young carer' projects.

Impairments and 'young caring'

Although there was no *statistically* significant difference between impairment groups in the extent to which parents identified their target child as a 'young carer', parents with physical impairments were more likely to identify their children in this way. Under one fifth of parents with primarily mental health impairments labelled the target child as a 'young carer' – yet this rose to 40% for physically impaired parents. Beyond this, no significant differences were found between parents with mental health impairments and those without (Table 4.2).

Family shape

An important issue in the 'young caring' debate is the extent to which single parents are less able to protect children from involvement in 'caring' (see Appendix One). In other words, does the presence of a partner (disabled or non-disabled) make it easier for families to meet the support needs of the disabled parent without recourse to including children? Table 4.3 breaks down the 'young carer' status of the target child according to family shape. For the

Table 4.3: 'Young carer' status of target child (by parental impairment group and family shape)

	'Young carer'	Involved in 'caring' activities	Not involved in 'caring' activities	Total
Impairment group				
Physical/sensory impairments				
Dual parent	10	12	9	31
Single parent	7	4	3	14
Total	17	16	12	45
Mental health impairments				
Dual parent	2	4	7	13
Single parent	2	3	3	8
Total	4	7	10	21
All				
Dual parent	12	16	16	44
Single parent	9	7	6	22
Total	21	23	22	66

sample as a whole, and for each primary impairment group, single parents were more likely to describe the target child as a 'young carer'. That is, nine out of 22 single parents described their child as a 'young carer', whereas this was the case in only 12 out of 44 parents in dual-parent families. Similarly, differences occurred between the level of involvement in various 'caring' activities of children in single-parent, as opposed to dual-parent, families (discussed in greater detail later in this chapter).

Rhetoric and reality: what do children actually do?

Our research has shown that about a third of the disabled parents in our study considered at least one of their children to be a 'young carer'. Here we briefly consider the relationship between this finding and children's actual involvement in 'caring' and domestic work, as well as the contact families had with 'young carer' organisations and services.

Children's involvement in domestic work

To what extent does parental identification of children as 'young carers' – or their involvement in 'caring' activity – correspond to reported levels of involvement in both housework and care tasks? Our parent questionnaire asked about target child involvement in a broad range of household tasks: cooking, cleaning, washing up, changing bed clothes, shopping, laundry washing, ironing, vacuuming, and picking up any other siblings from school (Table 4.4). (Information on caring tasks of a more personal nature was collected in a slightly different way and we discuss these data later in this chapter.) Very few

Table 4.4: Parental reports of target child's involvement in domestic work

	Never	Sometimes	Regular	Regular and main responsibility	Total
1. Cooking for family	35	26	3	2	66
2. Cleaning bathroom	54	11	0	1	66
3. Washing up	35	20	8	3	66
4. Changing bed clothes	40	22	2	2	66
5. Shopping	24	32	10	0	66
6. Washing clothes	46	17	3	0	66
7. Ironing	52	14	0	0	66
8. Vacuuming	40	22	3	1	66
9. Fetch siblings from school	65[a]	1	0	0	66

[a] Including those with no school-age younger siblings

Table 4.5: Level of involvement of target child in domestic work

Points	Target children (total number)	Level of involvement
9	13	Low
10-12	23	Low to medium
13-16	22	Medium to high
17-24	8	High
Total	66	

children were reported to have regular involvement in activities other than shopping or washing up; fewer still assumed the main responsibility for any of these activities.

We wanted to carry out further analysis that differentiated between high and low involvement in domestic work. Therefore, an overall 'level of involvement' score was generated for each target child, by attributing four points for each activity in which he or she had main responsibility, three for regular involvement, two for occasional involvement and one where he or she had no involvement. The score for each child could range, then, from nine (no involvement in any task) to 36 (regular involvement and main responsibility for all nine tasks). As Table 4.5 shows, this allowed us to sub-divide the target children into four groups with regard to total levels of involvement.

- low;
- low to medium;
- medium to high;
- high.

We can see in Table 4.6 that those children identified by parents as 'young carers' were unlikely to have a low involvement in household activity. However, a similar proportion of those identified as 'young carers', as well as those reported to be involved in 'caring activity', had a medium-to-high or high level of involvement. It is also interesting to note that *all* of the children reported to have a high level of involvement had a parent (or parents) with primarily physical impairments. Furthermore, living in a dual-parent household increased the chances of a child having a low level of involvement – only one out of 22 children lived in single-parent households, compared with 12 children in 44 dual-parent households, were reported as having low involvement. Again, these differences were not found to be statistically significant.

It appears, then, that the increased (though not statistically significant) likelihood of single parents labelling a target child as a 'young carer' is borne out when one examines the child's actual levels of involvement in domestic work. However, in other areas the label appears less related to what children

Table 4.6: Involvement in household tasks (by reported 'young carer' status, age, parental impairment group and family shape)

| | | Level of involvement | | | | |
	Low	Low to medium	Medium to high	High	%	Total
'Young carer' status						
'Young carer'	1	6	9	5	31.8	21
Caring activities	4	8	8	3	34.8	23
No caring activities	8	9	5	0	33.3	22
Target child age						
4-11	9	10	6	1	39.4	26
12-19	4	13	16	7	60.6	40
Impairment group						
Physical/sensory impairments	7	16	14	8	68.2	45
Mental health impairments	6	7	8	0	31.8	21
Family shape						
Dual parent	12	15	13	4	66.7	44
Single parent	1	8	9	4	33.3	22
Total	13	23	22	8	100.0	66

actually do. For instance, Table 4.6 shows that older children are more likely to have medium-to-high and high levels of involvement (23 out of 40) compared with younger children (seven out of 26). However, Table 4.2, as we saw earlier, demonstrated no difference in the extent to which the label 'young carer' was applied by parents to older and younger children. Similarly, Table 4.6 illustrates that high levels of involvement were limited to children of parents with primarily physical impairments, although Table 4.2 showed that impairment group had little bearing on whether parents considered their target child to be a 'young carer'. Again, these data indicate that the construction of a child as a 'young carer' is often minimally related to what children actually do by way of housework.

Children's involvement in 'caring' work

It was relatively straightforward to inquire about the range of household tasks that a target child may be involved in, since these are tasks typical to most households. However, we could not assume that parents would have any additional care needs. Therefore, a more sensitive way had to be devised to ask about the need for – and provision of – personal care. To do this, we adapted the Meltzer's (1995) Psychiatric Morbidity survey, such that, for a range of areas, parents were asked whether or not they had any personal assistance needs, as well as who, if anyone, provided that assistance. It was possible, therefore, to assess the number of parents who described one or more of their children as assisting with these caring activities. We created these summary variables to describe the support received in each of the nine 'caring' tasks:

- no help required;
- help required but none received;
- help received from formal/informal support only;
- help received from children with other formal/informal support;
- help received from children only.

Our nine 'caring' tasks:

1. personal care;
2. transport;
3. medication;
4. household chores;
5. practical tasks;
6. paperwork;
7. financial matters;
8. checking you are OK;
9. dealing with outside agencies.

Table 4.7 gives a breakdown of our sample for each of the nine 'caring' tasks, and for the five summary variables listed above. The first thing to note is the high number of parents who described themselves as 'requiring no assistance' with most of the tasks identified, and especially with personal care tasks. Hence, while children were involved in household chores in 23 families (usually alongside other sources of support), only eight families reported children as helping with personal care, and only 10 families reported children assisting with medication. It is also interesting to note that parents identified as an important area of unmet need having someone who could check that they were alright.

These data also point to very low levels of child involvement in providing assistance to parents with mental health impairments. Whereas we might have expected, in the previous section on domestic work, lower levels of involvement from these children, we here expected to pick up greater involvement when looking at 'caring' tasks such as helping with medication and checking that parents were OK. Our result was a sample of parents with mental health impairments reporting little requirement by way of assistance. This possibly reflects the characteristics of the sample, in particular that they had relatively moderate mental health impairments and/or were recruited and interviewed during a period of relative good mental health.

In addition, Table 4.7 suggests that family shape is important in determining levels of child involvement. Where children were involved in household and caring tasks, this involvement was typically alongside other sources of formal and/or informal support for children in dual-parent families, but tended to involve sole involvement on the part of the child in single-parent families. This finding is supported when one examines some of the areas of possible support need in more detail.

Table 4.7: Child involvement in our nine 'caring' tasks (by family shape and impairment group)

					'Caring' tasks				
Do you need help with:	1	2	3	4	5	6	7	8	9
ALL									
No help required	37	25	44	13	17	35	54	26	39
Help required, none received	3	2	2	6	7	4	7	12	4
Help received from:									
Formal/informal support only	19	32	11	25	39	23	6	19	24
Child[ren] with other formal/ informal support	4	4	6	19	3	3	0	7	0
Child[ren] only	4	4	4	4	1	2	0	2	0
Not answered	0	0	0	0	0	0	0	1	0
Total	67	67	67	67	67	67	67	67	67
Family shape (dual/single)									
No help required	23/14	15/10	29/15	10/3	12/5	24/11	35/19	23/3	30/9
Help required, none received	1/2	2/0	1/1	3/3	5/2	3/1	4/3	6/6	2/2
Help received from:									
Formal/informal support only	16/3	23/9	8/3	22/3	27/12	15/8	5/1	10/9	12/12
Child[ren] with other formal/ informal support	2/2	4/0	5/1	9/10	0/3	2/1	0/0	4/3	0/0
Child[ren] only	2/2	0/4	1/3	0/4	0/1	2/0	0/0	1/1	0/0
Not answered	0/0	0/0	0/0	0/0	0/0	0/0	0/0	0/1	0/0
Dual/single	44/23	44/23	44/23	44/23	44/23	44/23	44/23	44/23	44/23
Impairment group (physical and/or sensory/mental health)									
No help required	16/21	9/16	25/19	3/10	5/12	20/15	40/14	18/8	27/12
Help required, none received	3/0	1/1	2/0	4/2	6/1	3/1	2/5	8/4	3/1
Help received from:									
Formal/informal support only	19/0	28/4	11/0	17/8	31/8	19/4	4/2	11/8	16/8
Child[ren] with other formal/ informal support	4/0	4/0	5/1	18/1	3/0	2/1	0/0	7/0	0/0
Child[ren] only	4/0	4/0	3/1	4/0	1/0	2/0	0/0	2/0	0/0
Not answered	0/0	0/0	0/0	0/0	0/0	0/0	0/0	0/1	0/0
Physical and/ or sensory/ mental health	46/21	46/21	46/21	46/21	46/21	46/21	46/21	46/21	46/21

Table 4.8: Child involvement in helping with household chores (by family shape)

	Dual parent	Single parent	Number
No child helps with chores	35	9	44
At least one child helps with chores	9	14	23
Total	44	23	67

Table 4.8 illustrates a statistically significant association between family shape and the involvement of children in household chores.

Children in single-parent families were approximately three times more likely to be assisting with chores than children in dual-parent families (61% as opposed to 20%). This association is also found in other areas. For instance, the data suggest that children in single-parent families were much more likely to be assisting with practical tasks than those in dual-parent families (Table 4.9), although the generally low level of involvement means that we must be cautious when interpreting the statistical result.

Table 4.7, as we have seen, also shows lower levels of involvement in caring tasks on the part of the children whose parents have mental health impairments, including checking that their parent was OK. These data suggest that children are only likely to be involved in assisting *physically* disabled parents – involvement in assisting parents with mental health impairments, therefore, is extremely rare. (This is especially interesting, given that we used the Psychiatric Morbidity survey in order to capture and measure the need for assistance of parents with mental health impairments.)

Table 4.9: Child involvement in helping with practical tasks (by family shape)

	Dual parent	Single parent	Number
No child helps with practical tasks	44	19	63
At least one child helps with practical tasks	0	4	4
Total	44	23	67

Table 4.10: Child involvement in assisting with personal 'care' (by impairment group)

	PI/Sensory	MHI	Number
No child helps with personal 'care'	38	21	59
At least one child helps with personal 'care'	8	0	8
Total	46	21	67

PI = Physical impairment
MHI = Mental health impairment

The greater likelihood of the children of physically disabled parents being involved in particular types of 'caring' (albeit in the context of generally low levels of involvement) is reproduced when areas of potential support need are analysed in more detail. Table 4.10 illustrates a significant – but unsurprising – association between impairment group and the involvement of children in personal 'care'.

This statistically significant association between parental impairment and children's involvement in providing assistance extends to help with getting out and about and using transport, and assistance with household chores (Table 4.11).

The finding is very clear: almost half of parents with primarily physical impairments described some child involvement in providing assistance with chores; yet only one out of the 21 parents with primarily mental health impairments did so.

Our data, then, suggest a strong association between physical impairment and child involvement[2]. It can reasonably be speculated that this was because parents currently experiencing severe mental health impairments were less likely to take part in the research than those who felt their illness was in the past, or at least not greatly affecting the present. It may also be because parents with mental health impairments were less likely to identify support needs in the first place.

Table 4.11: Child involvement in assisting with household chores (by impairment group)

	PI/Sensory	MHI	Number
No child helps with chores	24	20	44
At least one child helps with chores	22	1	23
Total	46	21	67

PI = Physical impairment
MHI = Mental health impairment

It is to be expected, then, that they then went on to report lower levels of involvement on the part of their children. Their reluctance to identify support needs is an important issue, and reinforces Chapter Three's discussion concerning the (reduced) likelihood of parents with mental health impairments seeing 'support' as something they thought they needed, or at least as something that they would be entitled to. Or, finally, it may be that as researchers we were less skilled in enabling parents with mental health impairments to make a connection with their experience of illness on the one hand, and the possible need for assistance on the other. It is inherently easier to engage parents who identify physical support needs than it is to engage parents for whom the relationship between impairments and assistance is more complex.

Something that really caught our attention was the fact that, despite these strong differences in what parents report children as actually doing (see Table 4.7), there was no significant difference between the likelihood of physically impaired parents and those with mental health impairments labelling the target child as a 'young carer'. Again, this suggests that the relational context of the giving and receiving of assistance is more important than the actual 'doing' of household and other 'caring' work.

Children's perspective on domestic and 'caring' work

It was important to us that what children thought about their involvement in domestic and 'caring' activity was reported in our study. The views of children have value in their own right, of course; we were also interested, however, to see when (if at all) the perceptions of parents and children tallied.

The responses of the 60 children interviewed are presented in Table 4.12. Comparing the reports of children with those of their parents (presented in Table 4.5), children report greater involvement for each of the areas identified, the sole exception being cooking a hot meal for the family. In addition, from the child's perspective, their involvement is 'regular', rather than 'sometimes'. It is important to understand that both the children and parents in our study were giving *subjective* reports of child involvement in domestic and caring work. Our data were not gathered prospectively (for instance, using diaries or timesheets). It is likely, then, that both within and between these groups the notion of 'regular' and 'occasional' involvement differs. In particular, what children consider 'regular' involvement may instead be reported by their parents as 'occasional' involvement. It is also possible that the reports of children and parents are mediated by a concern to conform to particular norms. For example, parents may be sensitive to the public perception that they rely too heavily on their children (and may therefore tend to underestimate child involvement). Children, on the other hand, may want to emphasise their helpfulness within the home (and may therefore tend to overestimate their involvement).

In terms of personal care, some comparisons can be drawn between children's reports and parental responses to our questions adapted from the Psychiatric Morbidity survey. For example, 12 of the children reported helping with

Table 4.12: Children's reported level of involvement in household and 'caring' tasks

	Regular involvement	Sometimes	Never[a]	Total
Make your own bed	23	28	9	60
Make other people's bed	2	20	38	60
Cook a hot meal for the family	6	21	33	60
Do the shopping (including going to the corner shop)	19	26	15	60
Do the vacuuming	10	38	12	60
Clean the bathroom	3	20	37	60
Wash up (including dishwasher)	10	38	12	60
Help parent with stairs	5	12	43	60
Help parent with medication	6	15	39	60
Help parent with dressing	3	9	48	60
Stay in to keep (disabled parent) company	3	35	22	60
Help parent to wash or bathe	0	13	47	60
Cook for parent	6	28	26	60
Help parent go to the doctors	3	17	40	60
Do the ironing	2	17	41	60
Look after siblings	9	18	33	60
Fetch younger siblings from school/nursery	0	7	53	60
Wash clothes (including loading washing machine)	8	28	24	60

[a] Including 'not applicable'.

dressing, either on a 'regular' or 'sometimes' basis (Table 4.12). Similarly, 13 children reported 'sometimes' helping their parent to wash or bathe. However, only eight parents reported any involvement by any child in personal care (Table 4.7). Similarly, only 10 parents reported any child involvement in assisting with medication (Table 4.7), while 15 children reported 'sometimes' helping, and six reported 'regular' involvement (Table 4.12). There is an even greater disparity when one compares the number of children who say they stay in to keep their parent company and parental reports of a child either 'checking' that they are OK, or staying in to be with them. Three children said that they 'regularly' stayed in with their parent to keep them company, and 35 said that they 'sometimes' did so (Table 4.12); only nine parents reported child involvement in this area (Table 4.7)[3].

Our interest in whether or not the reports of parents and children tallied was to emphasise children's and parents' *understanding* of their involvement in 'caring' and other work. Perhaps it is not surprising, then, that each group interprets 'care' differently. (However, the data we have presented suggest that disparities do exist in the extent to which parents and children report patterns of involvement. These disparities merit a study all of their own, but one that will have to wait for another day.)

Table 4.13 presents children's reported involvement in greater detail. From it, we see that 14 out of 21 target children in single-parent families reported cooking hot meals for the family, as compared with 13 out of 39 target children in dual-parent households. Similarly, 17 out of 21 target children in single-parent families reported specifically cooking for their disabled parent, compared with 17 out of 39 target children in dual-parent households. Children in single-parent families also report greater involvement in helping with shopping. More accurate data could be gathered if more specific questions on the number of *times per day*, or per week, that children perform certain tasks were asked. However, it is clear that when children are asked about involvement in specific sets of tasks, they – like their parents – report higher levels in single-parent families than dual-parent families.

Table 4.13 also highlights some differences between children of parents with primarily mental health impairments and children of parents with primarily

Table 4.13: Children's reported involvement in tasks (by family shape and impairment group)

	Family shape		Impairment group	
	Dual (39)	**Single (21)**	**PI/sensory (42)**	**MHI (18)**
	Does task	**Does task**	**Does task**	**Does task**
Make your own bed	35	16	38	13
Make other people's bed	16	6	18	4
Cook a hot meal for the family	13	14	21	6
Do the shopping (including going to the corner shop)	26	19	31	14
Do the vacuuming	31	17	35	13
Clean the bathroom	18	5	17	6
Wash up (including dishwasher)	31	17	34	14
Help parent with stairs	12	5	17	0
Help parent with medication	13	8	19	2
Help parent with dressing	6	6	12	0
Stay in to keep (disabled parent) company	27	11	30	8
Help parent to wash or bathe	7	6	13	0
Cook for parent	17	17	26	8
Help parent go to the doctors	13	7	16	4
Do the ironing	15	4	13	6
Look after siblings	21	6	17	10
Fetch younger siblings from school/nursery	4	3	5	2
Wash clothes (including loading washing machine)	24	12	26	10

PI = Physical impairment

MHI = Mental health impairment

physical and/or sensory impairments. For example, children of parents with physical impairments reported a greater level of involvement in terms of helping their parent with medication. It is also interesting to note that they were also more likely to stay in to keep their parent company, given that violence and observation on the part of children whose parents have mental health impairments are frequently cited in the literature on 'young caring'.

'Young carer' service provision

Disabled parents were told that "in some areas there are 'young carers' groups that organise activities and provide support for children who have a disabled or ill parent". They were then asked whether or not there was such a group in their area. Nineteen parents knew of a 'young carer' group (and half of these parents had identified their child as a 'young carer'). As Table 4.14 shows, a majority of parents (36) were not aware of such a service in their area (one third of these identified their target child as a 'young carer')[4]. This suggests that those parents who knew about a 'young carers' group in their area were more likely to define their child as a 'young carer'. This could reflect one of two things. Firstly, parents who identified their target child as a 'young carer' were more likely to have come into contact with professionals who might refer children to the local project, or at least provide information about it to the family. Or, secondly, it could be that awareness of a local 'young carer' group might encourage parents to think of their children as 'young carers', irrespective of their involvement in household and caring activity. For instance, parents may see 'young carer' as a label that increases the chance of their children gaining access to the facilities on offer at such projects.

There were no significant differences between parents with physical impairments and parents with mental health impairments with respect to

Table 4.14: Knowledge of a 'young carer' group in the area (by 'young carer' status, primary impairment group and family shape)

	Is there a 'young carer' group in your area?				
	Yes	No	Don't know	%	Total
'Young carer' status					
'Young carer'	10	1	10	32.3	21
Involved in caring activities	2	6	14	33.85	22
Not involved in caring activities	7	3	12	33.85	22
Impairment group					
Physical/sensory	14	7	24	69.2	45
Mental health	5	3	12	30.5	20
Family shape					
Dual parent	10	7	26	66.2	43
Single parent	9	3	10	33.8	22
Total	19	10	36	100	65

Table 4.15: Attendance at 'young carer' groups (by 'young carer' status, primary impairment group and family shape)

| | Does (target child) attend a 'young carers' group? | | | |
	Yes	No	%	Total
'Young carer' status				
'Young carer'	7	14	32.3	21
Involved in caring activities	0	22	33.85	22
Not involved in caring activities	0	22	33.85	22
Primary impairment group				
Physical/sensory	5	40	69.2	45
Mental health	2	18	30.8	20
Family shape				
Dual parent	3	40	66.2	43
Single parent	4	18	33.8	22
Total	7	58	100.0	65

awareness of the existence of 'young carer' projects locally. Our data, however, suggest that single parents were more likely to be aware of the existence of a local 'young carer' project than parents in dual-parent households (although, again, the finding is not statistically significant).

Table 4.15 gives a breakdown of the attendance at 'young carer' groups of the target children in our sample. It shows that one third of those labelled as 'young carers' were in fact attending a 'young carers' group. No difference was found between the likelihood of the children of physically impaired parents attending a 'young carer' group compared with the children of parents with mental health impairments. However, our data suggest that the children of single parents were more likely to attend a 'young carers' group than children in dual-parent households.

In sum, then, the quantitative data suggest that children's involvement in 'caring' and domestic work is generally low. Furthermore, the use of the label 'young carer' is often unrelated to what children actually do. This is reflected, for instance, in the fact that no difference was found in the extent to which older and younger children were labelled 'young carers', despite the fact that, according to parents' reports, the actual involvement of older children in a range both of domestic and 'caring' activities was higher. It also appears that the children of single parents are consistently reported both by themselves and their parents to be involved in greater amounts of domestic and caring work than the children of dual-parent families. (However, the small numbers involved mean that statistical significance is rarely reached.) We also found gaps in the extent to which parents and children reported children's levels of involvement – that is, children consistently reported higher levels than their parents did.

Finally, the data on developmental and self-care skills collected through use of questions from the Looking After Children (LAC) schedules (see Appendix

Two) suggest that the children of the disabled parents in our sample are comparable with those in the broader, general population. In particular, there is no evidence that children of disabled parents are unusually advanced, or 'falsely mature', in their acquisition of developmental and self-care skills.

'Young caring' in context

The first half of this chapter discussed quantitative data on children's contribution to domestic and 'caring' work. Our interviews, however, also generated a wealth of qualitative material on the context of children's involvement (or non-involvement) in this work, and the meaning and significance given to it by family members. The starting point is the fact that parents were, on the whole, very well aware of the public debate surrounding 'young caring', and consistently expressed the desire to minimise involvement of children in assistance:

> I am very conscious to keep them out of my care. I very occasionally would ask them to do things, but only if nobody else could. I can care for myself and there are usually other adults able to help out.
> *Mother (PI), single-parent family*

In another family, the father had sole responsibility for all household work and was concerned about the impact of any caring responsibilities on his children's schoolwork and exam preparation:

> Housework is not shared out in this family, I basically do it all and sometimes I'm unhappy about that. But deep down it's what I want, to leave the kids free to get on with their lives, they work hard in their own right with their GCSEs coming up.
> *Father, dual-parent family (mother, PI)*

Other parents described their anxiety about the level of responsibility that would be involved if their children took on caring roles. One mother, who described her son as a 'young carer', said:

> When I feel grotty he'll get milk from the shop – that's important to me as I live on cereals and if I asked him he'd do it. He's here all the time.... It might make him more 'caring' or more understanding when he's older but I don't know if he feels responsible for me. I don't want him to feel that way.
> *Mother (MHI), single-parent family*

As we have already said, most parents were aware of the term 'young carer', and were keen to point out ways in which they had prevented overinvolving their children in care. They expressed anxiety about the amount of help required of their children, and pointed to the factors that helped or hindered them in preventing children from taking on what might be seen as 'caring' roles.

Our analysis of the data from Stage One interviews led us to cluster the perspectives of disabled parents around four closely related themes. These involved:

- the dilemmas faced, and strategies adopted, by disabled parents in preventing child involvement in caring;
- the role that formal sources of support play in protecting children from taking on, or alternatively encouraging children to adopt, caring roles;
- the influence of features of informal support networks that help to prevent children from inappropriate caring roles;
- seeing children's contribution to domestic and caring work as something that is negotiated and contested, and which therefore depends also on the active role of children in taking on and/or resisting involvement in caring and other work, and not solely on the presence or absence of other forms of support.

It is to each of these themes that we now turn, to examine them in more detail.

Disabled parents and 'young caring': dilemmas and strategies

Many parents in our sample expressed the desire to see their children grow up with the skills needed for independence. This was expressed in terms of the 'normal' expectations that parents have for their children. For some, however, particular decisions had to be taken and strategies followed regarding child involvement in 'caring' and other work. This was most often expressed in terms of a dilemma between what *needed* to be done in the house and what the *right* level of involvement for children should be. Responses to these dilemmas were varied. One partner said:

> I think it's unfair to expect too much of them. I'd rather have things not done than put more pressure on people who already feel put upon.
> *Father, dual-parent family (mother, PI)*

Other parents talked about the detriments to their own health that resulted from making sure their children were not overinvolved.

> I don't want to turn my children into carers, so I probably do more than I should.
> *Mother (PI), single-parent family*

Why aren't my children young carers? Well, when I'm ill, I've always tried and managed to do as much as I can so they don't have to, things like cooking and cleaning.
Father (MHI), dual-parent family

Disabled parents often talked about the impact on their health of these kinds of trade-offs – between the need for assistance on the one hand, and the need to limit requests from family members (including children) for support on the other. This was particularly so for those families who described hostile and contested relationships with formal support agencies. One mother had resisted the decision by social services to put her children on the 'at risk' register, and for one of them to be placed in voluntary care. For her, a public perception that she depended on her children for support would only fuel the social services' desire to instigate child protection action. Instead, her strategy included reliance on microwaveable food, since she had difficulty in chopping vegetables and opening tins, even though she was concerned about the effect of such a diet on the health of all family members. Similarly, she was also upset at the poor state of her garden:

But I would rather have grass six foot in the air, than have people think I am getting my kids to do too much.
Mother (PI, MHI), dual-parent family

Other parents talked about the 'rules' that they had developed in order to limit and manage the degree to which children could (or did) take on 'caring' roles. For example, when a hot meal was being cooked, a single mother and her daughter had made an arrangement whereby the mother would position herself at the cooker and take control of stirring and managing the heat, while the daughter did all the chopping, laying the table, and so on. Another family had rules concerning the children being in the house when the only adult present was the disabled mother. The mother said that the decision not to involve children in 'caring' was deliberate and part of an 'agreement' with her husband. However, this decision also involved limitations on *her* freedom, as her husband illustrated:

Basically, on Saturdays, when I take the lad to play football, we have a rule that if she [mother] is out of bed and downstairs before I go, then she must stay downstairs, and if she isn't yet up, she mustn't get up until I come back. Otherwise the youngest two are going to be at home and dealing with her falling down the stairs.
Father, dual-parent family (mother, PI, MHI)

We can see how parents have adopted strategies that allow them to retain a sense of control over their family life, but which also involved trade-offs. One single mother in our sample had decided to put her bed in her living room, since she had difficulty using the stairs and was already locked in a battle with the local authority regarding the provision of a downstairs bedroom extension. She acknowledged that this restricted her children's ability to bring their friends home, and also involved leaving them unsupervised upstairs, with associated implications for their safety. However, it was more important for her to locate herself centrally and not to feel shut away in an upstairs bedroom on days when she could not get out of bed. This mother did identify her son as a 'young carer' and talked about the number of schooldays he and the other children had missed. However, she attributed this more to the inaccessibility of the upstairs of the house than to any 'caring' responsibilities they took on: she often found it very difficult to make sure they got up and ready for school in good time.

Another example highlights the difficult dilemmas that some families face in using available informal support to minimise children's involvement in caring. One partner was the family's full-time 'carer', despite some formal input for his disabled wife and disabled daughter. His poor health was a major concern, and there was a constant fear of what would happen if his own health problems worsened:

> If I am having a bad day, then I just have to crash out, leaving the others with no one to look after them. If my health really fails, then what will happen? I'm worried that all I will be offered is residential care for both of them. This is where my son steps in. Ordinarily his life isn't really affected at all, although I would like to be able to get to his football matches more, but often I'll need him to step in and just be in the house while I have to go out shopping, for instance.
> *Father, dual-parent family (mother, PI)*

Gender roles compounded the difficulties faced by this family. The husband was in the position of providing personal care to his wife and his 16-year-old daughter. Both he and his wife were extremely uneasy about him having personal care responsibilities for a teenage daughter:

> What do you do when she doesn't want you to change her [sanitary towel]? If you ignore her saying 'no', it could easily be seen as abuse. If you leave it alone, it could be seen as neglect.
> *Father, dual-parent family (mother, PI)*

Faced with such dilemmas, the family was trying to minimise the impact on their other, non-disabled child, in terms of his involvement in caring, demonstrating the complex factors that underlie attempts by families to minimise child involvement in caring work:

> I have to be constantly aware of not leaving my wife and daughter alone. This means that spontaneity goes out of the window, as I always have to

make sure that someone is there with them. It also means I miss out on seeing my lad play football on the weekends.
Father, dual-parent family (mother, PI)

Parents are acutely aware, then, of the need to prevent overinvolvement of their children in domestic and caring work. This supports Parker's work (1993), which points to the great efforts made by disabled people to prevent and minimise the impact of disability on family members, and children in particular. Various strategies are deployed in their attempts to do this, including increased responsibility for the other parent (in dual-parent families), the overexertion of disabled parents (often in ways detrimental to their own health), and the management of household tasks in practical ways that minimise children's involvement.

Formal support and 'young caring'

Many dilemmas faced by disabled parents are underscored by an absence of appropriate services, adaptations and support from formal agencies. For example, in the case of the mother who needed to relocate her bed to the living room (discussed earlier in this chapter), her dilemma is structured by the failure of her local authority to deal with the inaccessibility of her house. In this section, we examine our data concerning the relationship between the availability of formal support and the nature of children's involvement in caring and other work.

It is important to recognise at the outset that a small number of parents lived in houses that were fully accessible and adapted to their needs, enabling them to carry on parenting and take responsibility for housework and self-care without the need for formal support at all. One physically impaired mother had a completely adapted house paid for by an insurance settlement. She hesitated to describe herself as a disabled person and was fully enabled as a parent, despite being a single parent and living on benefits, which are characteristics more likely to be associated with stressful parenting.

However, there were several cases where parents made a direct association between reporting their child as a 'young carer' and the lack of formal support available to them.

> I see both my children as 'young carers' out of necessity.... They really do more housework than they should, so help with cleaning and cooking in particular would be very helpful. It's different if they want to help me rather than having to help me.
> *Mother (PI), single-parent family*

A physically impaired mother and single parent, who received little formal or informal support, saw both of her children as young carers "because I'm disabled, I have no choice". It is striking that many comments about the *necessity* of child involvement in caring were made by single parents, supporting data presented earlier on the higher levels of child involvement reported by single parents.

However, many partners in dual-parent families referred to *their* involvement in caring as a by-product of the lack of formal support. There were many cases where a partner felt that their presence was 'taken for granted' by services, and that services to support the disabled parent were not being made available. Some partners did see caring as part of the relationship, but for many this was also seen as the only option, either because of the lack of an alternative, and/or because of a sense of responsibility towards their partner. One father, who had become a full-time carer for his wife, said:

> I will do everything I can for her because she is my wife, but at the end of the day who else is there to do it?
> *Father, dual-parent family (mother, PI, MHI)*

Another father felt that 'caring' for his wife was his job:

> I've never been one for asking for help. I married her so it is my responsibility – I don't want to farm her out.
> *Father, dual-parent family (mother, MHI)*

What these testimonies teach us is that inadequate formal support has implications for *all* family members, and not simply children at risk of taking on caring responsibilities. Interestingly, our interviews with children also highlighted cases where they themselves saw formal services as important in limiting what they would otherwise have to do. For example, one boy described how a 'nurse' (more likely a home-care worker) would come in every day when his mother was in hospital, and tidy up. We asked him about how it felt to have people coming in to help his mum, and he said:

> It's OK.... At least when she comes in to help my mum it means I don't have to help her.... It means I can play out more and stuff.
> *Son (11), dual-parent family (Mother, PI)*

Clearly, then, there was awareness among parents and children that the receipt of formal support services played a part, or could potentially play a part, in limiting the extent to which children (particularly in the case of single-parent families) were drawn into 'caring' roles[5]. A small number of parents reported that formal support had been withdrawn, or withheld, on the grounds that children in the family had reached an age at which they could be expected to help out. If this is the case, then, it is clear that in *some* circumstances the provision of formal support to disabled parents acts to *encourage* – rather than restrict – child involvement in 'caring'. One 12-year-old girl mentioned that she had known important emergency numbers from the age of seven, and took responsibility for calling the doctor on the rare occasions that her mother fell in the house. Until recently her mother had received home-care assistance with ironing and vacuuming. Her father said that home care had been withdrawn at the same time as assistance in getting their daughter to school had stopped (in the week of her 12th birthday). He felt that part of the justification for this was the fact that his self-employed status often meant he worked in buildings close to the house. He deduced that the withdrawal of home care implied that both he and his daughter should take greater responsibility for domestic and caring work. For this family, the burden of reduced formal support was placed on each of the family's three members. When asked what extra support she might like, the daughter said:

> It's hard work and tiring. Home help stops when you are 12. That's wrong, because you get more homework and tests, not less. Now I have to go to the shop more. Mum has to do the ironing now, which makes her leg worse, and dad is always having to stop work to go to the shops and things.
> *Daughter (12), dual-parent family (mother, PI)*

Other families said that formal support was offered in a way that either ignored the impact on family members, or that made assumptions about the willingness of family members to meet any additional needs:

> When my husband was too ill to work the GP just signed him off for two months. I went mad because I knew I couldn't cope with him at home ill all the time. I argued and argued and eventually he was offered three days a week at a day centre and a CPN [Community Psychiatric Nurse] as well.... He's only ever seen two CPNs and only when I have demanded it.
> *Mother, dual-parent family (father, MHI)*

Another parent described how home care had ceased to be provided about five years previously, when social services "stopped paying for it". This mother told us how the kitchen had become almost completely inaccessible as her impairments had worsened. She was now completely reliant on her husband and children for cooking, washing up, and so on. Indeed, when we asked her what adaptations were required for the house, she specifically linked the need for kitchen alterations with the future departure of her children, now well into their teenage years. In this case, the indirect effect of increasing home-care charges had been to increase the extent to which both the father (himself with health problems and physical impairments) and the children took responsibility for housework, with consequences for the son's life beyond – and not only within – the family:

> A 17-year-old boy should not be folding clothes in a launderette all day – he should be out dating.
> *Father, dual-parent family (mother, PI)*

Another way in which parents felt as though formal services did not reduce reliance on family members was in the limits placed on the kind of work that home-care workers could do. For instance, one single mother received home care in the form of general domestic help and a cook two days each week. She said that the problem with home care was that they could only do the lighter tasks that she could generally manage herself through the day:

> What I would really like is help with the more energetic things such as hoovering which I can't manage myself and which I have to ask my son to do.
> *Mother (PI), single-parent family*

We also came across a small number of families in which disabled parents were receiving substantial formal support in the shape of home care, personal assistance funded from the Independent Living Fund or direct payments, and so on. For these families, the receipt of this support was instrumental in reducing the extent to which children were involved in caring and housework. However, it also became clear that even comprehensive care packages had not led entirely to the withdrawal of children from caring roles. Again, it was often single parents who were most affected by this issue. One single mother had recently employed two personal assistants following years of having relied heavy on her son (now aged 17) for often quite intimate care. The arrival of more comprehensive personal assistance had significantly reduced – but not eliminated – his caring role, and she still described him as a 'young carer'. She said that they had both found it difficult to adjust their relationship to take into account the arrival of personal assistance. Her son elaborated:

> Even though my mum has a lot of help now, and I don't have to do as much caring, it is still difficult and a lot of pressure to live with someone with ME and depression.
> *Son (17), single-parent family (mother, PI, MHI)*

Another single mother had substantial formal and informal support during the week, but relied on her 10-year-old son at other times:

> Mostly I would say he is not a 'young carer', although occasionally, at nights, he just has to take over. Mostly, I'm just his mum, so if he stubs his toe he comes over for a cuddle, but there are times he takes over mentally and physically.
> *Mother (PI), single-parent family*

The 'office hours' kept by many forms of formal support were also mentioned by partners as the reason they still felt themselves to be carers. For some parents with physical impairments, professional staff carried out personal care, such as assistance with going to the toilet, for much of the week, but left it all to partners (and occasionally children) at other times. Similarly, partners of parents with mental health impairments often felt that, even though their partner might be receiving support through a GP or a CPN, they still took much of the responsibility for fighting for services and for recognition of their partner's support needs. Additionally, parents with mental health impairments were often less likely to see domestic support as something to which they were likely to be entitled, despite sometimes expressing the need for it to prevent overreliance on other family members[6]:

> When I am in a depressed phase, I just don't have the motivation to do the domestic things that normally I love, like cooking.... They become a real burden. It would be nice to have something like meals-on-wheels but that's a bit unrealistic.... Something like that wouldn't be available to me.
> *Mother (MHI), dual-parent family*

It is clear that the availability of formal support to disabled parents is a centrally important mechanism whereby children are protected from being overinvolved in 'caring'. For the most part, children's caring involvement was at a low level (running errands, fetching drinks, and so on), although some parents expressed concern about the responsibility it involved on the part of their child, rather than the sheer level of involvement. Again, those most concerned about this were single parents:

> He does more than his mates – but only because he says that his friends' mums say things like "My word, you hoover!" But for me its not what he does exactly, but the responsibility he has for things. For instance, he will remember to lock the house up at night and put the milk away, and put the cat's stuff away. He also takes responsibility for me on bad nights, he just takes over and gets on with things.
> *Mother (PI), single-parent family*

Caring at nights and weekends, and in response to the more unpredictable things that happen in family life, as in the above case, resists replacement by formal services. This means that, in the absence of direct payments which would give disabled parents greater flexibility and control in the receipt of assistance, and in the context of the role that formal services can play in cementing and extending the caring responsibilities of other family members, as we have seen in this chapter, it is impossible to consider the role of formal services in preventing 'young caring' without considering also the role of informal support.

However, let us take a look at what parents said about the support offered by 'young carer' projects. We mentioned earlier that seven target children in our sample were attending 'young carer' groups. And we found that parents approached the support on offer at 'young carer' projects in a variety of ways. One mother was enthusiastic about the 'young carers' group that her son was attending, and felt that there were no problems with her son's involvement in caring:

> I suppose he sees both sides – he sees the way we are, being disabled, and his friends' parents are able-bodied. He goes out with the ['young carer' support group] and they meet up at weekends with other teenagers in the same situation. Sunday week they are all going to London for a day – before Christmas they had two shopping trips. He's been going for one and a half to two years. It's made a big difference – yes, it has.
> *Mother (PI), dual-parent family*

One mother said that, given the lack of support available, her children had no choice but to be 'young carers'. And for her, the lack of available places at the local 'young carer' group was a major problem:

> The welfare worker told me Barnardos have a club for 'young carers', but they've closed the books – they are full. My children are 'young carers' out of necessity – they shouldn't have to do it, it's different if he *wants* to help me rather than *having* to help me.
> *Mother (PI), single-parent family*

For one white mother with mental health impairments, it was important that her daughter – whose father was Asian – attended a 'young carers' group attached to a local Asian mental health organisation. For some parents, the needs of their children could be met by a 'young carers' group, although they did not actually see their children as 'young carers'.

A mother with complex mental health impairments was disappointed when her children refused to go to the 'young carers' group, as they did not want to be picked up by a special bus. She saw neither of her children as 'young carers', but said:

> I'd have loved them to have gone – it would have given them a chance to speak to other kids and to be a kid.
> *Mother (MHI), single-parent family*

Her eldest son said that he did not currently talk to any of his friends about his mother's mental health impairments and that it was hard to talk to people as he thought that they would 'take the mick'. This points to the fact that, while children may not need support in relation to caring, they often require a supportive environment within which to talk to others about their experience of parental disability and their parents' experience of disability.

What we can see, then, is a complex and sophisticated relationship between a willingness to define children as 'young carers', the perceived support needs arising out of being a 'young carer' and/or having disabled parents, and the availability of 'young carer' support provision. Parents, it seems, approach the labelling of their children as 'young carers', and the question of their children receiving support through 'young carer' provision, in a number of ways. These are informed not only by what children actually do, but also about their perceived support needs in relation to a range of factors. These factors include ethnicity, the need for youth club provision irrespective of 'carer' status, the interchangeable use of 'caring about' and 'caring for' to describe their relationship with their children, and so on.

In addition, children themselves negotiate and contest the 'young carer' label and the suitability of 'young carer' provision. These complexities perhaps help to explain why, in the context of a generally very low level of involvement in 'caring' and household work by children, such a high proportion of parents were willing to label their children as 'young carers'.

Informal support, family structure and 'young caring'

It appears from our research that dual-parent families are in a better position to share out assistance and household tasks in a way specifically designed to prevent child involvement. For example, one mother did not perceive her target child as a 'young carer', despite the fact that he helped looking after his younger siblings. This mother referred to an 'agreement' with her husband:

> It's what we wanted – we talked about it. If they wanted to be involved, they could have, but really there's been an agreement with my husband.
> *Mother (PI, MHI), dual-parent family*

Similarly, another mother said:

> Between me and my husband we get things done.... We have a commitment that she will not become a 'young carer'.
> *Mother (MHI), dual-parent family*

For many single parents, the desire to keep their children out of caring roles is less easily realised. This supports other evidence concerning the choices that parents make about their children's gender roles in assisting with household work (Morrow, 1996). This evidence suggests that, even for households where gender divisions are strong, difficult circumstances will often lead to the dissolution of these divisions. Rather, the necessity for help from whoever is available takes precedence. In short, boys and girls are equally likely to be labelled 'young carers' by their parents.

Dual parenthood, however, provides no guarantee that children will be insulated from taking on 'caring' roles. One father, whose wife was also disabled, said that his son had missed about 10 schooling days in the previous year, in order to help out whenever his father's leg problems flared up. Indeed, parents in several other dual-parent families talked about the enhanced roles for children when the 'other' partner was ill, heavily involved in paid work, or during a 'bad' spell when they themselves had impairments. This indicates that families in which *both* parents are disabled, and therefore face barriers to accessing support, may be particularly susceptible to relying on their children for assistance.

Even when parents felt that they currently had the resources to minimise children's involvement, there was often a fear that this might not always be the case:

> I won't let them get involved in caring for their mum. I've seen how it screws them up when she has to go into hospital, how they worry. They've got their own lives and I don't want to force it on them. However, I am worried about what will happen if something happens to me.
> *Father, dual-parent family (mother, MHI)*

The shape of any particular family also intersects with other key factors in determining levels of support available to parents, and therefore the likelihood that children will be involved in assistance. One important factor is parental employment and its role in structuring the availability of support to disabled parents and their children. The low level of paid employment in our sample of disabled parents meant that most children in the sample had at least one parent who was at home throughout the day, and several children gave this as the reason why they did *fewer* household tasks than their peers.

In dual-parent families, where the partner was in employment, there were often low levels of support available within the family, given the absence of the non-disabled partner for work reasons. In one family, an eight-year-old girl told us that, when her father was at work, one of her roles was to telephone the doctor or neighbours whenever her mother fell over. Another family faced serious dilemmas over the employment of the non-disabled partner. The father's work took him away from home on weekdays; however, he was well paid, and this enabled the family to have a quality of life that would not be possible were he to give up work and become a full-time carer. However, his absence meant that his disabled wife and his increasingly disabled son were left short of support, especially between the end of home-care support, the arrival of his son home from school and bedtime:

> This last year has been desperately difficult, what with me working away and being needed so much at home. It has meant that my son couldn't go out at all in the week. He would simply come home and wait for the home-care person to come and put him to bed.
> *Father, dual-parent family (mother, PI)*

This example, and others where one partner had well-paid – though often very demanding – employment, illustrates the difficulty in assuming that single disabled parents are inevitably more likely to depend on their children for assistance. In other words, dual-parent families may decide that the partner's earnings are so important to them that they live with a level of informal help that is similar to that experienced by single parents. It also shows that being concerned about who is available to care for a disabled family member or members is, in fact, only one of many other, broader concerns. (In the example above, these concerns included the lack of stimulation and variety in the son's life and issues of safety when no assistance was available.)

Children's caring involvement is not simply related to whether the family had one or two parents. Several parents, for instance, expressed views on their children's involvement that were clearly influenced by conceptions of gender and age. One partner, who was also disabled, talked about the significance of age when deciding appropriate levels of help from his 10-year-old daughter:

> It's important that my daughter doesn't do too much for her mother, but as she gets a bit older then I think she will do a lot more.
> *Father, dual-parent family (mother PI, MHI)*

However, age was not the only factor: gender, too, informed this father's attitude, since he was keen to compare her involvement in household tasks with that of the daughters of other members of his extended family. Although he had said that his daughter did more housework than the other children of her family, he also said:

> She is really a little bit lazy. When we go as a family to my cousins, their daughters are much more helpful, taking your cup and washing it up as soon as you have finished your tea.
> *Father, dual-parent family (mother PI, MHI)*

This means that the housework and caring expected of children in families with disabled parents is often as much a matter of gender and age expectations as it is of disability and the need for care. Expectations based on age and gender, however, are not straightforward. Some parents, for example, stressed how important it was that children were asked to do *less* around the house as their GCSEs approached. One partner talked about a period four or five years previously when his wife had been very depressed. He said that the family was lucky in a way, since their eldest children were old enough (they were then aged about 14 and 15) to be fairly independent in terms of activities, and did not need much supervision or input. Their youngest child, on the other hand, was too young to be involved in social activities outside the house (she was then aged eight), requiring the partner's time and commitment. In other words, the age gap between his children made it easier for him to care for his wife on a full-time basis.

In addition, our respondents tended to describe the entire agenda of domestic work and assistance in very different terms for children under the age of 10, roughly, compared to adolescents. This is an important point in childhood: it is the age, for instance, when children generally move from primary to secondary school, with important implications for parental access, mobility, and so on.

(These issues are discussed later in this book.) When parents were asked about the involvement of younger children in housework, they frequently talked about the difficulties in 'fending off' requests from children to assist, with cooking for instance. For several parents, the overenthusiasm of younger children concerning involvement in domestic tasks was an important issue to deal with. If not managed properly, this issue was potentially detrimental to their health. One mother with mental health impairments described the impact on her health of the constant demands of her five-year-old to help in the kitchen:

> I discourage her from being involved. Well, she is a bit young but also it is very tiring and I have to try and conserve energy for the sake of my mental health.
> *Mother (MHI), dual-parent family*

Another partner talked of how he tried to keep his four young children – all below the age of 10 – out of the kitchen. He was concerned about the danger they might put themselves in, as well as the fact that he simply could not afford to have them getting in his way.

With older children, the most typical response regarding housework was one that many parents will recognise: the difficulty of getting teenagers to tidy up, or do anything to keep the house clean and functioning! The apparent fact that children's involvement in housework is conceptualised differently for older and younger children is important in the 'young caring' debate. It challenges the dominant assumption that children's involvement in housework is primarily a product of parental impairment. Instead, the management of children's involvement, or overinvolvement, is about the age and gender expectations that parents have of their children, and the desire to be involved, or not involved, on the part of children themselves.

Children as social actors

It is clear that children are actively engaged in constructing and/or resisting caring roles and household responsibilities. For instance, children often told us about their contribution to household work and caring in terms of the other things important to them in their life. One boy had a job in a local restaurant and was also studying for his GCSEs:

> I do what I can, but often I'm not here to help. I've got my job, my exams and my girlfriend, so really I don't have time to help.
> *Son (15), single-parent family (mother, PI)*

Another boy, whose mother, sister and father were all either disabled or had complex health problems, was not involved in significant caring. His father, however, described his role as 'keeping an eye on' his sister and mother when he (the father) had to go shopping. When interviewed, the boy situated his involvement in terms of schoolwork and his educational priorities:

> Well, I suppose I do play out less than my school friends. Sometimes, it's 'cos my dad needs to go out, but the other kids at school don't seem to care about their schoolwork or their exams, but I do.
> *Son (14), dual-parent family (mother, PI)*

In several interviews, children felt capable of expressing resentment about the extent of assistance they were required to give to their parents. Sometimes, as we have seen, this was expressed as a desire for greater formal help for their parents in order that they might be afforded more free time. However, children also expressed resentment towards what they saw as unreasonable demands made by parents themselves. One boy eloquently described his pride in being the eldest child and the only one able to open the stiff hall door. However, he also felt very put upon:

> Mum makes me do things around the house that I'm too small for. Sometimes I have to help mum put her socks and shoes on and sometimes she has no pants on, and I don't like it. She's angry with the world, so has a grudge against me.... She makes me do so much, I'm only a kid.
> *Son (10), dual-parent family (mother PI)*

One older child said that, while he was growing up, he felt that his father had used his mother's impairments to try to get him to do much more than his friends and other children of his age were expected to do. Now that he had left school and was in work, he said that he was better able to 'stick to my guns' and so help less when he was called upon. The fact that he also had primary-school-age siblings who were now more able to help out his mother also enabled him to say 'no' to his father more often. In contrast, when some children in our sample were asked whether they needed any support, several said they wanted to be taught how to do even *more* things to help their parent(s). One nine-year-old said that she wanted cookery lessons so that she could cook meals for her mother. Again, this typifies the different approach to 'helping' expressed by or about younger children.

Another example illustrates the fact that children approach involvement in caring and domestic work with their own sense of what is right and wrong, and their own reasons for taking on – or resisting – 'caring' activities. One 15-year-old boy took significant responsibility for helping his father, who in turn was the main carer for the child's mother. He was asked whether he thought his level of involvement was fair:

> Yes, I think so. Things just need doing so I help. I want to help because if
> I take some of the work off my dad, then my mum and dad will be more
> relaxed and happy.
> *Son (15), dual-parent family (mother, PI)*

Here, the child clearly felt he had things to gain from being a 'carer' in terms of contributing to family harmony, even if this meant restrictions on his free time and social opportunities. This indicates that children are actively engaged in decisions, trade-offs and dilemmas of their own when negotiating a caring role for themselves. We discuss the age difference here and earlier when reflecting on how things are different for children aged 10 and under. That is not to say that all teenagers have the same degree of freedom in negotiating caring roles, but that children in general will be, in many cases, active in carving out or resisting a role for themselves and that this makes 'young caring' more complicated than existing theory caters for.

Finally, as we have also seen, children can actively demand a greater level of involvement in housework as a 'play' activity. The following two examples – each involving 10-year-old boys – illustrate the difficulty in striking a balance between wanting children to do more to help, and dealing with the stress that their involvement causes, especially, as in the second example, when this balance needs to take account of employment obligations.

> Sometimes I need to rely on him, and sometimes he relishes this and wants
> to help, sometimes too much .... For example, when I'm tired it's too much
> effort to battle over the things he wants to do, like using the kettle, which I
> don't like him doing. At other times, he gets fed up with helping and I can't
> get him to do anything.
> *Mother (PI), single-parent family*

> I think that my son does do more than his friends – sometimes voluntarily,
> sometimes not – but you have to balance it with wanting them to have their
> childhood. The thing is, with my working hours it's important that when I
> get back I can get on with what needs doing. Sometimes he wants to help
> so much he tries to do things he isn't capable of, so sometimes you're faced
> with trying to rein him back a little bit.
> *Father, dual-parent family (mother, PI)*

Conclusions

Despite a generally low level of involvement in 'caring' and domestic work, our quantitative data show that a third of parents labelled their target child as a 'young carer'. Another third said the target child was involved in 'caring activities'. No significant differences in the application of the label were found between boys and girls, or between younger and older children. Single parents and dual parents each talked about children being involved in caring activities; however, single parents were more likely to describe the target child as a 'young carer' in the fuller sense of the word. This pattern is repeated in what single parents say their children do, and in what the children of single parents perceived themselves as doing. It is further supported by evidence that child involvement in caring work in dual-parent families is likely to be alongside other sources of help, as opposed to in single-parent families where children are more likely to have sole involvement in providing assistance.

What we have been stressing throughout this chapter is the importance of placing 'young caring' in the context of the *meaning* attached to children's involvement in providing assistance. In particular, the presence or absence of formal alternatives is key in understanding children's involvement. However, this can only be understood in combination with the (un)availability of informal support and the role of family shape, age and gender in structuring expectations of children. Each child's age is particularly important with regard to caring involvement. That is, qualitative analysis suggests that the whole issue of younger children assisting with domestic work is played out within an entirely different framework based on play and enthusiasm (on the part of the children), and the need to manage and occasionally fend off this enthusiasm (on the part of their parents). We have highlighted the dilemmas faced – and strategies adopted – by disabled parents in order to prevent their children adopting 'caring' roles, as well as the potentially negative impact this has on the parents in terms of energy levels, the management of impairments, and so on. Similarly, attention was drawn to the role that children play as active negotiators and resistors of caring roles.

As far as we can see, then, the existing theoretical approaches to defining 'young caring', as well as policy and practice responses to it, are underdeveloped. Our argument is that, politically and practically, the response to 'young caring' should take the form of interventions aiming to underpin the parenting role of disabled adults and to provide them with the option of not having to ask children for assistance. However, fulfilling this depends upon a more sophisticated understanding of the context in which 'young caring' takes place. In all, this includes an awareness of:

- the meaning attributed to children's involvement within family relationships;
- the role of factors (such as family shape) in structuring both the quantity and nature of any 'caring' carried out by children;
- the different framework used to explain and respond to the involvement of younger as opposed to older children in caring work;
- the active role taken by children in negotiating and resisting 'caring' roles for themselves.

Notes

[1] Dearden and Becker (1998) have examined the characteristics of this group in some detail.

[2] However, as we have mentioned earlier, this may reflect a bias in our sample. That is, parents with mental health impairments in our sample may have been relatively well at the time of our interviews, compared with earlier periods in their lives, as well as compared with the broader population of parents with mental health impairments as a whole.

[3] Since different wording was used in the parents' and children's questionnaires, there is a danger of overestimating these results.

[4] Of course, there may not have been one in some areas, although most parents did live within an area covered by a 'young carer' project.

[5] We are prevented from testing statistically whether or not those parents in receipt of specific services were less likely to consider their children as 'young carers' as a result of the small numbers that took part in our survey. Furthermore, absence of formal input, as we mentioned earlier in the text, may indicate a fully accessible home environment rather than an enhanced need for informal care.

[6] In Chapter Three we highlighted the fact that this perceived ineligibility for formal support was compounded for some parents, since they found it difficult to deal with people coming into the house to provide support.

FIVE

The life course: dimensions of change in parenting and disability

Introduction

This chapter examines the importance of change in the experiences of disabled parents and their families. This involves focusing on hopes and experiences of becoming and being parents, within a life-course perspective. By this we mean exploring choices and expectations around parenting, from childhood through adolescence and into adulthood. Parenting is often perceived as a 'normal' feature of independent adult life. And yet attitudes towards disabled people do not always reflect this. We argue, therefore, that a life-course perspective is vital to the debate of parenting and disability, and the policy shaped to deal with it[1].

The relative invisibility of disabled parents, particularly when compared to the exposure of children who have been defined as 'young carers', is related to the concentration of social policy on the beginning and the end of the life course. This is also reflected in approaches to the support of family life; that is, research on family transitions is largely concerned with the transition to parenthood (and the early parenting years), and transitions into adulthood. The concept of the life course is more flexible than the previous conception of the lifecycle, which presented a normative description of key stages through which each individual passed. However, the experiences of disabled people can be defined and restricted by a policy framework that continues to individualise the life course.

> For those disabled people who do seek to operate as independent 'adults' two issues seem central – work and parenting. Idealised constructions of adulthood emphasise parenting and partnering as a signifier of adult status. (Priestley, 2000, p 430)

Our findings are intended to comment on the significance of change, both in terms of the experiences of disabled parents and their families, and in terms of the ability of formal and informal supports to respond. We have been concerned to present our examination of change in the broadest possible terms. Therefore, we have looked not only at the implications for parents of the changing needs of children as they grow up, but also at the changes that take place in family composition, and in the nature of disability impairments. Our analysis, then, highlights the importance of understanding that the experience of disability is closely linked to the changing experience of parenting, and the changing demands of the parenting role. This broader context of change also requires inclusive definitions of parenting to be as important as inclusive definitions of disability.

Impairment, disability and the life course

In Stages One and Two, we included parents whose impairments predated parenthood as well as those who were already parents at their onset. For half of the Stage One sample, the impact (though not necessarily the initial onset) of their impairments began after having become a parent. Therefore, the parents in our sample, irrespective of impairment group, reported various 'starting points' in their life as a disabled person. This allowed us to examine the experiences of those who were disabled people before becoming parents, and those who had already had children beforehand.

We can state in broad terms that, in most families where disability long predated having children, we found parents were less likely to see their impairment as central to their experience of parenting. However, we are unwilling to make overgeneralisations on the basis of such a classification of different experiences. Not only did some respondents find that a pre-existing impairment was significantly altered having become a parent (for women, this was often as a result of pregnancy), families also experienced other significant changes that altered family life (such as changes in the employment status of parents).

Clearly, it can be difficult for some people to pinpoint a particular period in their lives when they felt that they had become a disabled person (indeed if they felt that way at all). The point of diagnosis often bore no relation to the parent's experience of onset, especially for those parents who felt that their mental health and/or physical impairments should have been identified and recognised at a much earlier stage by medical professionals.

Reference to the diagnosis of a condition or pinpointing the 'onset' very much represents a medical approach to what may have been a gradual process. Furthermore, this process may have been a reflection of increasingly inaccessible environments (in the broadest sense) rather than deteriorating impairments. Although receipt of a medical diagnosis can provide a key to support (such as disability benefit), the diagnoses themselves were not always considered to encapsulate either the personal experience or the history of impairment. Some parents reeled off numerous diagnoses that they had received over the years, variously accepting and rejecting the labels applied to them. This was most often the case in relation to mental health impairments.

It became quite natural, then, for some parents to link adulthood experience of impairment to childhood experiences. For example, we interviewed a number of women who discussed their mental health impairments and their experience of parenting specifically alongside experiences of abuse or difficult family relationships in childhood. We also spoke to parents with physical impairments who stressed that while no 'diagnosis' occurred prior to their becoming a parent, they felt that the deterioration of their physical functioning had begun during childhood. For example, one man described how he began to find walking difficult as a young teenager, yet was in his 30s before he was eventually diagnosed with multiple sclerosis (MS). Some of those with gradually developing impairments felt that not much could have been done to speed up a diagnosis. Others spoke, however, of how there had been reluctance on the part of professionals to take their symptoms seriously. In short, then, our research sample included a group of people who felt that they had become parents after the onset of impairment but before they received a diagnosis, medical intervention and/or support.

Let us now turn our attention to some specific difficulties faced by those parents who, having had their impairment identified, had felt unsupported – and effectively disabled – in their desire to become parents in the first place.

Disabled people's experience of the transition to parenthood[2]

Some of those who had experience of disability before becoming a parent spoke about their own and other people's (including professionals') attitudes. Consequently, it was possible to gain detailed insights into key barriers faced by some disabled people as potential parents, such as professionals who had been either supportive or unsupportive when they expressed their wish to have children. (Of course, our sample's parents had successfully gone on to become parents, despite the barriers they had faced[3].)

One single parent with four children provided us with a stark reminder of the lack of encouragement in employment and parenting she had experienced as a result of her segregated education as a disabled child. Not only had she received little or no support in terms of taking qualifications, low expectations were also expressed about her potential for having a partner and for having children.

> A teacher told me I would never have kids – I was 14. She said "You'll never have children, no one will have you".
> *Mother, (PI), single-parent family*

When we interviewed this parent, we found that she had a stable and adequate income (largely through compensation payments), a well-adapted home, her own transport and a strong sense of her own ability as a mother. Indeed, her feeling of 'if they could see me now' was expressed by other parents who felt that others had not expected them to make a success of parenting. Expressing one's enjoyment of parenting also proves to oneself, as well as to others, that you can have and bring up children. For these parents, the problems – rather than the possibilities – associated with parenting had been stressed.

> I suppose it's nice to know I could carry a child.... I've proved to people,
> I've done it, as I didn't know I'd be able to have children.
> *Mother (PI), dual-parent family*

Respondents indicated how professionals in their adult life had sometimes reinforced this disapproval. Some mothers described how they had been dissuaded on health grounds rather than any (overt) prejudice. In these situations, it was often stressed how access to supportive healthcare workers had been very important in deciding to get pregnant, and in managing any difficulties experienced during pregnancy and labour. One woman, now a single parent, had been warned by doctors of the potential physical stress of pregnancy. She stated specifically that, since her husband was a health professional, she "knew what was available and what my chances were". Another mother with physical impairments said that her GP had expressed the view that she could not look after herself, let alone a child. The difficult relationship that developed from his attitude meant that her support in pregnancy came instead from her hospital consultant and a gynaecologist.

Social care and other professionals were also reported as having occasionally expressed disapproving attitudes. One mother said that a social worker had told her that "disabled people shouldn't have children if they cannot look after them". Another single mother, who had experienced long-term mental health impairments, said "I've had social workers tell me not to have them [children]". This message – that to be a parent with 'mental illness' or 'disability' is irresponsible – is bound up with beliefs that disabled parents are unable to provide security for children, as well as concerns about the child's own 'mental health', be that the result of a genetic, social or behavioural risk. Beresford and Wilson argue that this dissuasion from parenthood continues to be experienced by mental health service users. The current message is that they:

> have a moral responsibility not to have children in the interests of preventing
> further unnecessary suffering. (Beresford and Wilson, 2002, p 547)

This was the message given to many of the parents in our sample. Even among those who had not received such explicit 'advice', often the feeling was that it was broadly considered inappropriate for disabled people, who themselves required support, to have children. This attitude could be read into experiences of conflict with services. For example, one mother said that she and other disabled people could feel guilt about having disabled children in the first place. Although she did not overtly link this to her difficult relationship with social services, these feelings of guilt are likely, at least in part, to reflect the way in which she had felt defined by services as a *problem* to her family, rather than more positively as a *parent*.

It is clear, then, that negative attitudes towards disabled women in particular led to anxiety in childhood and early adulthood about their future prospects for relationships and children[4].

The immediate advantage of an increased visibility of disabled mothers and fathers is that it challenges the attitudes of non-disabled adults. It may also broaden the parental aspirations for (and of) younger disabled people in relation to the transition to adulthood. The experiences of women can be particularly pertinent, since some may require specific medical care during pregnancy to protect themselves and/or the child.

Pregnancy and postnatal care

For some women in our sample, pregnancy had implications for their physical and/or emotional health. In many cases, a successful pregnancy was emotionally satisfying for those who had not previously been encouraged to become a parent. Other positive personal experiences reported were relief from physical pain, to a more positive attitude among disabled parents than might be experienced by non-disabled parents to the potential of impairment in a child. In addition, some women received increased support from formal services with regular access to a general practitioner, consultant or nurse, which was often immensely reassuring.

For some women, pregnancy posed a threat to their own wellbeing, such as those who had to change, or temporarily stop taking, medication that could potentially harm the foetus. For them, medical advice and other support had been very important and reassuring. However, these women often reported that professionals were unsympathetic to their specific needs during this time. Most often, it was parents with mental health impairments who spoke about these issues, although they are clearly relevant to parents with other health concerns (such as epilepsy). For example, one mother who had manic depression said that she did not take her medication during pregnancy, because of the risk to her child. She did not return to medication after her son was born, and had no outpatient care until she was admitted to hospital with her baby a few months later. She believed that her consultant was "obviously one of those people that didn't think I should have children". Indeed, during her pregnancy her husband, who also had a mental health diagnosis, had spent some time in hospital on a psychiatric ward. During a visit to her husband, and therefore outside of a formal consultation, a professional thought it appropriate to comment negatively on her pregnancy. What, then, of the importance attached to the individual consultation and confidentiality, at least within psychiatrists' public accounts of their relationships with patients?

> I got pregnant and he [husband] got ill [laughs] but I was fine throughout.... Even visiting you in the ward when the consultant said to me, "I believe you suffer with manic depression?". I said, "Yes". He said, "You do realise you will be ill soon?". Because, there was me with my bump. I said, "Thank you very much". [Laughs]. You know, that's *really* helpful.
> *Mother (MHI), dual-parent family (Family E, Interview One)*

This mother's experience illustrates how, in addition to the day-to-day difficulties inherent in parenting (such as a lack of appropriate support), parents could be faced with such negative and demeaning responses from professionals to news of a pregnancy. Needless to say, such pressures and attitudes could lead to pregnancy itself being a traumatic experience. In a small number of families, we heard how termination of the pregnancy had been chosen or considered, sometimes at the suggestion of a medical practitioner. We did not specifically ask about this, but parents would describe their own decision processes. For example, one couple told us how they had only decided against a termination because the trauma of an abortion was more likely to be detrimental to the mother's mental health than having another child to look after. On the other hand, however, continuing with unplanned pregnancies could also be traumatic. One woman told us that she had previously had a termination after contraception had failed, at a time when she was already planning a sterilisation. The subsequent sterilisation failed, owing to medical negligence, and she became pregnant again. She then had a second termination as she felt she could not continue with that pregnancy having previously terminated one. In addition to the stress felt given these experiences this mother suffered physical ill health resulting from poor medical care, and she felt the combined stresses were linked to her later development of a neurological impairment.

Women who had experienced problematic, or previously unsuccessful, pregnancies reported how this could make the transition to parenthood and ongoing parenting more difficult. For some, increased levels of distress were experienced, and pregnancy or the postnatal period marked the first time in which a diagnosis (sometimes of postnatal depression) and/or psychiatric care had been received. For example, one woman told us that she first started taking antidepressants after miscarrying. Although she had experienced some mental health impairments before this, they were not recognised by a professional until after the miscarriage.

As we have already seen, mothers with physical impairments were sometimes advised not to have children because of the physical demands of (and risks to) pregnancy and childbirth. Before successfully giving birth to her daughter, one woman in our sample had experienced miscarriages. These had the effect of planting seeds of doubt about whether or not she would be able to carry a child for long enough for it to survive. Consequently, when she did have her baby, she felt that her previous lack of confidence in the pregnancy prevented her from bonding well with the child.

We had a number of mothers in our Stage One sample who reported that MS, depression or back problems developed or worsened just before or after the birth of their child. For parents with a physical impairment, the emotional consequences of an increased severity in impairment following pregnancy were often stressed more so than the impairment itself. We look at this further later in this chapter when considering the experience of parenting young children.

Changes in family composition

In Chapter Six, we focus specifically on parents' experiences of their ongoing relationships with partners and children. Here, we want to deal with the important way in which the experience of parenting can change over time through alterations in family shape. We do this by looking specifically at parents' reports of their decisions to have (or not have) more children, the ending of relationships with partners, and the experience of losing a child.

Decisions to have further children

In Stage One, we asked the disabled parent to say whether or not they had considered having more children in the future (Table 5.1). The vast majority of parents felt that their families were complete, with only five parents seeing future children as certain or likely.

While one child was a positive choice for some parents, others spoke of how they had hoped for further children. Although this is an experience shared by other families, parents did sometimes talk about the consequences of this in the context of parental impairments:

> Some days I thought it would be nice for my daughter. For instance, if I was
> ill, she would have a playmate.
> *Mother (PI), dual-parent family*

Several parents gave a similar reason for wanting another child. Therefore, decisions to add to the family were made *despite* any concerns about impairments and health problems. One father, for example, described how his wife's MS worsened considerably after the birth of their third child; yet they were

Table 5.1: "Do you think you will have more children in the future?"

	Number
Currently expecting	2
Yes	1
Probably yes	2
Probably not	5
No	53
Don't know	2
Not answered	2
Total	67

determined that this daughter should have another sibling due to the large age gap between her and her elder sisters.

Earlier in this chapter, we saw that professionals could have an important part to play in enabling disabled people to become parents in the first place. Often decisions to have further children were made in negotiation with health professionals – 20 parents had been advised at some time by professionals not to have any – or any more – children. None of these parents felt that they would be likely to have any more children, with 17 certain that they would not. However, professional responses to potential or actual pregnancies ranged from specific advice in the context of a consultation, to casual remarks. Sometimes it was simply the manner in which the professional responded to a parent that conveyed their (sometimes influential) disapproval. One single mother diagnosed with manic depression, who had two children living with her as well as an older child living with her ex-husband, said that she would not have any more children. In fact, her psychologist made a 'funny face' at her when she said she wanted another baby. Similarly, people received input from others in inappropriate circumstances. For example, a paediatrician whom a mother visited with her son made a comment aside from her son's health problems:

> He wanted to give me counselling so I wouldn't have more kids – he kept saying, "Are you pregnant?".
> *Mother (PI), dual-parent family*

Parents whose family life was already operating under considerable pressure often internalised the feeling that it was something wrong with their parenting that had lead to difficulties. Earlier in this chapter we referred to a mother who said that social workers had told her not to have children. She was a single mother, whose sons' had emotional and behavioural difficulties, and she felt that both she and her sons had been unsupported over a number of years. While she did not talk specifically about her own childhood, she did volunteer information about her difficult years before becoming a mother, including having had a custodial sentence as a young woman. She thought that she would probably not have another child, despite having also said that she would quite like another one. While recognising that her sons had difficulties with which they required more support than they received, she also expressed her own feelings of failure. She stated that if she were to have another child:

> I might get it right this time.
> *Mother (MHI), single-parent family*

A father's impairment could also influence a couple's decision about whether or not to consider having another child. Not one of the disabled fathers in the Stage One sample thought that they would have any more children. It may be less likely for professionals to offer 'advice' to families in the case of a disabled father, and perhaps this is in part due to assumptions concerning men's role in parenting. A father with MS told us that no professional had ever talked to him about whether or not he wanted more children, but that it had been an important issue to himself and his wife:

> MS is very important. We do talk about it – my wife would like to [have another child]. I know it would be a struggle and now I'm not working.
> *Father (PI), dual-parent family*

It would be wrong to suggest that many of the parents in our sample were unhappy about their decision to have no more children, or that their impairment was always a central factor in this. Rather, just as some parents had mainstream considerations at the fore when deciding to go ahead with more children (such as wanting a sibling for a previous child), many felt that their families were complete, and/or had concerns about money and employment issues – sometimes linked to disability – which led them to decide against further pregnancies.

Others were pragmatic about their decision not to have more children on health grounds. However, mental distress (linked to either a mental ill health diagnosis or painful experiences during pregnancy) also featured. Two such parents were among a small group who stated that soon after their last pregnancy they or their partner had been sterilised:

> I sent him [partner] to the doctors after our son was born as I didn't want more. If I'd had any more, I'd be gone – I wouldn't be living.
> *Mother (MHI), dual-parent family*

> I said I didn't want no more. They [professionals] said don't get sterilised until Sally is one – how horrible that pregnancy was. When Sally was one I was sterilised. I don't think my spine would take another pregnancy anyway.
> *Mother (PI, MHI), dual-parent family*

The responses of the parents in our sample therefore suggest that very few had in-depth advice from professionals concerning their decisions to have more children. Anyhow, many felt that this was a decision they could make on their own. Fathers particularly seemed to be least likely to receive information from medical professionals (for instance, on potential support available). While some mothers felt they had received good care and information, others felt that there was often limited information and *directive* – rather than *supportive* – input. Some felt that professionals were trying to police decisions that they felt capable of making on their own in the light of information provided. This highlights a need for parents to have access to good-quality information and advice, and in appropriate settings. Our data also show that decisions about whether or not to have children are closely interwoven with concerns about disability (public and professional attitudes, the anticipated extra difficulties, and so on) and impairments (for example, the effect of pregnancy on existing impairments, and the effect of taking or not taking medication during and after pregnancy, among other things).

Relationships: endings and their consequences

Single parenthood, rather than impairment itself, was often put forward by some parents in our sample as the main source of strain in parenting. Significantly, the earlier chapters of this book indicated the additional barriers faced by single parents in accessing support, as well as the additional socioeconomic disadvantage faced by disabled parents, and the likelihood that the children of single parents would take greater responsibility for domestic and 'caring' work.

As part of our research, we did not pursue details about separations, or the death of a child's other parent. However, parents were often open about their past relationships, and why they had ended, and the extent to which children maintained contact with a non-resident parent. As one would expect, where impairment had been present before a relationship began and had remained relatively stable, the impairment was not usually seen to be a factor in a separation. A small number of parents, however, and particularly those with mental health impairments, identified destructive or abusive relationships that had exacerbated and/or focused upon their distress. One woman told us that, although her last partner found her manic depression 'hard' to cope with, she differentiated this relationship (from which she continued to derive support) from her previous marriage:

> My ex-husband used to say "You're a psycho" – he was verbally abusive.
> *Mother, (MHI), single-parent family*

While a high level of input from the child's other parent could be a great support, for others it impacted on their own relationship with their child, and particularly the extent to which they felt a child should provide them with support. The only single father in our sample, who was also interviewed at Stage Two, continued to care for his son in close negotiation with his son's mother. So much so, in fact, that the mother called in during the first interview and the father felt it improper to consent to his son's taking part in the research without asking her permission. Their separation had occurred at the same time that his health difficulties began and he was unsure about whether or not these were related. He was concerned not only about protecting his son from involvement in care tasks, but also about criticisms from his ex-partner:

> I mean there are occasions, you see, when I fall down at home…. I can't pick myself up. I know that he wants to help me then, but I can't ask him to do that…. He's not quite old [enough?]…. And apart from that, his mother would give me a hard time if she thought I was using him as a carer.
> *Father (PI), single-parent family (Family J, Interview Two)*

Parents also raised concerns about how much to inform an ex-partner about their impairments. Another father in our sample, who had shared caring tasks with his daughter's mother (and who had re-partnered), felt unable to explain his impairment to his daughter. He was held back by the worry that his ex-partner would rush the child to the doctors to 'have her checked out'[5].

The extent to which non-resident parents continued to have contact both with the disabled parent and their children was clearly an important factor for most single parents and 'reconstituted' families. Single parents identified perceived threats to their children's wellbeing, which reduced the capacity of the child's other parent to sustain their involvement in parenting. These factors ranged from the other parent living abroad, to their coping abilities, and to alcoholism. For such single-parent families, accessing the support of a child's other parent was not always an option. Families who had experienced domestic violence faced particular difficulties. Where an ex-partner was perceived to be a continued (physical or emotional) threat, and where the parent felt undersupported, the consequences were often isolation and fear. One mother told us how she and her children had to change their family name and sever all ties that could link them to her children's father. After some time at a women's refuge, they had a protracted period when they were moved to various 'safe houses' before finally settling in a village. Here, however, the family (and the mother in particular) felt extremely isolated. Another single mother, the victim of her ex-partner's violence from when their child was just six months old, expressed fear. She had been unable to isolate herself from him completely, and her ex-partner had at times tried to abduct the child, despite an out-of-court access agreement. At the time of our interview, the father had recently been seen waiting close to her son's school, causing her to be concerned that he might again try to take the child.

These experiences can be contrasted with a small number of families where an ex-partner maintained very strong links with the day-to-day lives of the family. For example, a mother talked about the important part played by her son's father, who not only maintained regular contact with their child, but was also heavily involved in supporting her domestically (with household chores that she found very difficult to carry out during periods of mental distress). As with other single parents, therefore, the long-term impact of a separation on parenting responsibilities was very varied.

Loss of a child

Within our interviews, there were three ways in which parents had experienced loss in a parenting relationship:

- the death of their child;
- their child(ren) being taken into local authority care;
- their child(ren) moving to live with another parent.

One family highlighted how the loss of a child prior to the mother's disability had in fact strengthened family coping resources. A Stage Two family (Family C) had lost their youngest son when he was five years old, before the onset of his mother's MS. The parents felt that this loss had significantly affected how they and their two other children had subsequently coped with both the mother's diagnosis, and the progression of the condition. The father viewed his two remaining sons as having always been there to provide support, and felt that the family's earlier loss had equipped them to deal with their upset at their mother's diagnosis.

Unfortunately, we found one clear example of how formal services exacerbated the difficulties of a family who experienced the death of their disabled child. This was one of our families interviewed at Stage One and Stage Two (Family H), who, between interviews, had been bereaved when their teenage daughter died suddenly. Preceding this, there had been a long battle with local services for support for both their daughter and the mother, in which they had eventually succeeded in obtaining home adaptations and direct payments. The grief experienced by this family was exacerbated by a social work report prior to their daughter's death that had expressed the view that the mother was not an appropriate model for the daughter to 'emulate' as a disabled person, since this did not aid her development. This was in contrast to the feelings of the mother, who felt that their different impairments had actually provided them with a special relationship of camaraderie. Since the child's death, the swift approach of the benefit agency for information, and subsequently slow processing of the family's benefits, at a time when they were looking to meet funeral costs, had created further hurt. Their grief was further impinged on by a plan by local services to have the family convert the daughter's bedroom into a bathroom in their plans for adapting the family home. The primary sources of support for the family had been their local church and their daughter's school. Both groups had expressed sadness at the girl's death, and showed concern for the family's loss. These basic human responses were sadly lacking in the actions of the formal agencies.

We also heard of social services expressing disapproval towards a young man's decision to return to live with his mother, after having been in local authority care. For a long time, his mother had been living on her own as her children were living in various local authority placements. Her husband had died after a long illness when their children were very young. She described each of her sons as having had 'behavioural special needs', and she had often been unhappy about the inadequate support they had received. She saw the estate where she lived as a threatening place for her children to live, and felt she could do little to protect them. She and two of her children had experienced violence from neighbours – she saw this as the cause of her children being looked after by the local authority. At the time of our interview, her eldest son had returned to live with her, after living with his girlfriend's family for a short time, and he had regular contact with his grandparents (although his younger siblings did not). His mother told us that his plan to return home was not treated positively by a social services team leader. In fact, he had been warned that, if he did live with his mother, he would feel guilty "because your mum's disabled".

Both of these cases highlight long-term difficulties that can be faced by parents who struggle to receive supports that are relevant to their family's needs as a whole. Of particular concern is the way in which disabled parents in both families appear to have been considered as 'problems' in themselves.

Three disabled parents did inform us that a child of theirs had been adopted into another family. One woman, who spoke briefly about a baby she had given up for adoption, said that, in retrospect, she felt that she should have accepted the emotional support that had been offered to her to help her come to terms with this loss, which in any event was considered to have been her only possible course of action. Another family, however, who had lost custody of one of their children some years ago when she was only a baby, talked about the effect that inadequate support had had on their confidence in their abilities as new parents. In particular, the requirement that the mother prove her ability to look after an infant – while on an adult psychiatric ward and barred from using the staff kitchen to sterilise bottles or make feeds – was seen as overwhelming and unfair. Her hand impairments also made using old-fashioned nappy pins difficult; yet her difficulty in using them was interpreted as a deficit on her part, rather than the environment in which she was expected to parent. Subsequently, her lack of confidence came to be used against her and her husband as evidence of inadequate skills, which was used to justify placing their child for adoption.

For single parents, there was sometimes the option of a child living primarily at the other parent's home. One mother, interviewed in Stage One and Stage Two (Family G), had three sons, one of whom had moved to live with his father, over 100 miles away. This was a result of his emotional and behavioural problems, which had been present in the years following his parents' separation: he had 'dissolved' his mum to tears, and failed to keep to work plans with the child psychologist and the social worker. In the Stage One interview, the mother said that her son had decided that he wanted to go to his father, although she was not sure whether her son now felt that he had made the right decision. However, just over a year later at the Stage Two interview, it became clear that there had indeed been significant difficulties. Her son (now aged 16) had left his father and his stepmother (who were apparently treating him poorly) and was living at a friend's house:

> In the end it got really bad and he ran away to his friend's house and they've kept him there ever since and that was about 18 months ago.
> *Mother, (MHI), single-parent family (Family G, Interview Two)*

Her son, then, remained resident *near* to his father, but still a long way from his mother and younger brothers. While this seemed to be a difficult situation for his mother, because of her concern for her son, it was a situation she could at least accept, especially since having seen for herself the situation her son was now in. She felt that his friend's family had "turned him around" and that he was now looking forward to living with a group of other boys while taking his A levels. It was also important to her that they were now very close emotionally, and that he visited her and his brothers regularly, for holidays and weekends[6]. However, at the second interview, she also talked about how it was difficult for him to slot back in on these visits, and referred specifically to her mental health impairments:

> It is hard because ... he knows I'm not so well, I don't do things. I don't do the washing up and I've got a thing, what people laugh at: ... even though I don't do the washing up I don't like germs, and if I don't do it for four days all I do is just go squirt, squirt with the germ spray and walk away and leave it. But, they're all so efficient and they want to do the washing up, "Come on [middle child], let's do the washing up". He doesn't wanna do it, you know, and I say "Oh leave it, don't worry about it", you know. It's just because he lives in a different household.
> *Mother, (MHI), single-parent family (Family G, Interview Two)*

Parenting over time

As we specifically sought families with older children (who might be willing to be interviewed) in our recruitment strategy, our research includes more information about parenting those children of school age. However, a small number of families included young babies or toddlers, and many more parents we interviewed also discussed issues relating to parenting younger children in depth. Here, then, our focus is on parenting children of pre-school age and on parents' changing experience of their children's education.

Parenting young children

Of course, when parents discussed difficulties in parenting younger children, what featured prominently were the issues of time limitations and tiredness faced by all families. Some parents, though, felt that they faced specific physical, emotional and social problems. One mother we spoke to in Stage Two compared her experience of having a baby prior to her ill health with her current experience of having a young daughter while suffering from ME. She herself had concerns that she was unable to provide her daughter with the range of experiences that her son had encountered. When she was first interviewed, her daughter was six months old. Her ME had made it physically very difficult for her to get out of the house, and she was unable to drive. On the rare occasions when she met other mothers with small children, she could still feel isolated as a disabled parent:

I mean, I think one of the things that I've learnt over the last year ... as a disabled parent, disabled parents are not part of mainstream society at all. I mean, even when I go to an NCT [National Childbirth Trust] coffee morning, even though that's quite rare, you are the only person, I mean, you're there with your walking stick, and you know, you're sort of, sometimes you have to ask other people to change a nappy, or lift the baby into the car.
Mother (PI, MHI), dual-parent family (Family L, Interview Two)

Although she felt there had been an improvement in some aspects of her wellbeing, at the Stage Two interview the mother explained how, now her daughter was older and heavier, childcare tasks could threaten her health, particularly by intensifying her fatigue. Since her son was now older, she had the option of involving him in caring for his sister, and she and her son would both be involved in bathing her, and would split other tasks between them. She felt that, although they were adapting to circumstances, this was far from satisfactory. This family had been unable to gain access to any formal support, and their informal support consisted of a friend of the parents taking their young daughter out for fresh air every day. The husband explained how he saw the situation:

There is no provision for the children of disabled parents, especially young children. You know, the children's team won't fund it 'cos the child isn't disabled, the disabled team won't fund it because the child the parent wants support with helping isn't disabled, you know?.... But to improve the quality of life for both, somebody should say, "Right, well, this needs doing", you know, it's a need that's not identified. But hopefully with more and more people who are disabled having children, pressure will come to bear, but at the moment people write rules and they like to put people in boxes and if you don't fit the box there's nothing there.
Father, dual-parent family (mother, PI/MHI) (Family L, Interview Two)

The potential long-term impact of those particular stresses faced when caring for young children and lack of support for parents provide a good example of the importance of looking at disabled parents' experiences over time. For example, in one of our Stage Two families, the mother's depression did seem to be specifically postnatal, and later linked to demands associated to parenting a child with autism. The father described his wife's mental health history as follows.

Well we were married about two years when [our first son] was born and after he was born [my wife] had ... what they said was postnatal depression and was ill for about four years. And sort of got over it a bit and had [our second son] and then she had it again for a couple of years and then we had [our third son] and we had it again for a couple of years. And then she got better after that and then we found out about [our second son's] disability and we had a lot of problems with the school he was at. So [my wife] was ill again after that and has been ill for about three years now. So she's been ill on and off for ... about 16 years now.

Father, dual-parent family (mother MHI) (Family D, Interview One)

For others, postnatal depression was linked to physical impairment rather than to a response to childbearing. For example, one mother found her impairments had deteriorated following her final pregnancy and subsequently experienced severe depression. It was only after this last pregnancy that her spina bifida-related impairments began to impact on her day-to-day life. She felt that, had she and her family been better supported during the early days, when she was coping with small twins and her own impairments, her emotional problems would not have been so debilitating. There were broader social and economic consequences for the family. It was this profound depression, rather than her physical support needs, that had led her husband to give up work to become a full-time carer.

Parenting school-age children: maintaining contact with schools

In Chapter Four of this book, we discussed the balance that parents tried to strike between allowing young children to be involved in household activities (due to their desire to lend a helping hand) and ensuring that they would not become overinvolved. In particular, parents expressed the view that, as children grew older, the importance of them being able to concentrate on schoolwork and exams increased. However, while parents often felt that they were able to organise their parenting within the home in a way that was satisfactory to them, greater difficulties often emerged when they discussed the extent to which they could gain positive working relationships with schools.

While many parents in our sample had no contact with social services, health services (other than general practitioners), the benefits system, or local authority housing departments (and so on), each one had direct experience of sending children to school and of trying to maintain what they saw as satisfactory levels of involvement with the education system.

Two thirds (44) of the disabled parents that we interviewed had been able to attend a parents' evening in the past 12 months. The majority of parents were fairly satisfied with the level of contact they had with schools: 23 felt contact was 'good', 25 felt that it was 'adequate', and 15 that it was 'less than adequate'. However, interesting findings emerged from our data regarding the importance of change in influencing the way in which parents were involved in school life. In particular, several factors often conspired to make it increasingly difficult for parents to maintain the level of involvement desired as their children progressed through the education system.

The number of parents who commented on the difference in terms of accessibility between primary and secondary schools was striking. The relative inaccessibility of secondary schools was partially a straightforward issue of the physical environment of the school. For example, several parents talked about difficulties they had encountered when attending open days at their children's new secondary school, given the older architecture, the separation of schools into various sites on a single campus, and the reliance on stairs both inside and outside the school. One parent commented:

> His secondary school has been much more difficult to access, although they
> are trying to address it. Basically, it is a school built for non-disabled students
> and that affects us as parents.
> *Father, dual-parent family (mother, PI, MHI)*

Other parents talked about the assumptions that lay behind access problems they had encountered at secondary schools. One non-disabled father commented on the fact that in recent years only he, and not his wife, had been attending parents' evenings:

> In the last few years it has only been me really that's been going to parents'
> evenings. The primary schools were much better, I think, because they have a
> kind of pushchair mentality which obviously people using wheelchairs can
> benefit from.
> *Father, dual-parent family (mother, PI)*

That primary schools are likely to take access issues relatively more seriously because of the likelihood of parents also having pushchairs lends weight to broader arguments concerning the willingness of schools to respond to the access needs of children much more positively than to the access needs of their parents, despite the apparent overlap of interests between the two groups. It could be argued that more recent initiatives that have looked at disability, access and education have been rigorous in their examination of the needs of disabled pupils, but less so with regard to the educational needs of the children of disabled parents (DfEE, 1999). Indeed, this reinforces our argument concerning the invisibility of disability as a parenting issue (since research into disability and family life is dominated by a focus on childhood disability). Here, then, is a clear example of how disabled adults can be excluded from a key element of their parenting role.

However, the factors inhibiting involvement in secondary school education were not limited to issues of access; rather, they were compounded by other interrelated factors. For instance, one mother talked about a particularly difficult period when social services had contemplated placing her son on the 'at risk' register. The strong relationship the family had established with their son's form teacher at primary school was seen as extremely supportive, and the input of the teacher, being a person who appreciated the problems faced by the family, was seen as very important. The mother contrasted this strong relationship with a single form teacher at primary school with the absence of relationships with teachers at secondary school.

Distance is another factor exacerbating the difficulties of disabled parents' involvement in secondary schools. Primary schools are typically much closer to where children live than large secondary schools, since secondary schools' intake comes from a much wider catchment area (particularly in rural or semi-rural areas). This can often compound any transport and mobility barriers that disabled parents already face.

Closely related to this is the central role of parental choice in their children's schooling, especially in the secondary sector, where children are increasingly likely to attend schools other than the one closest to their home. One father described the different ways in which the practicalities of family life had changed as his two children went from attending a local village school, which was within walking distance of their home, to attending a secondary school in the nearest large town, 20 miles away. This led to the loss of informal networks for parents and children alike, as other children from that year group went to a wide variety of schools. While this happens in many families, the difficulties were compounded by the fact that his wife was recovering from a period of severe depression, which had precipitated hospitalisation. Taking medication meant that she was unable to drive, forcing the family to confront the problems that the daily use of public transport often entails, especially as she did not have the confidence to accompany her children to school. The family did receive support from the father's employer, who allowed him to leave the office earlier and catch up on work later in the evening, and by the willingness of a family friend to 'baby-sit' the children at his office until their father was able to drive them home from school.

This case illustrates how the changes that ordinarily occur as part of family life, such as the progression of children through different parts of the education system, can be experienced very differently by disabled parents. Our interviews strongly suggest that, when children move from primary to secondary school, it can be much more difficult, for a variety of reasons, for disabled parents to maintain the kind of ongoing contact that they would like. This is particularly significant given the importance of the shift from primary to secondary school at a moment when parents might be successfully engaged and support offered (Henricson et al, 2001). Difficulties in maintaining contact with schools may be particularly acute for parents experiencing dramatic change in other areas of their lives, and especially for those with progressive and deteriorating conditions. One single mother talked about the very rapid 'death' of her informal network. Not only had her son moved from primary to secondary school, but her impairments had worsened and she had lost her only form of assistance with transport when her own father had suffered a stroke.

Recent changes in parental impairment: onset and variability

We now consider the extent to which parents felt as though their parenting responsibilities were adequately understood by professionals. Often, with retrospect, parents felt that there had been a lack of awareness of the potential consequences of impairment and disability for people's family lives. For instance, one father described his wife's consultant delivering her diagnosis thus:

> He said "You've got MS – some people change from butter to margarine. You've just got to get on with it".
> *Father, dual-parent family (mother, PI)*

While for some parents impairments developed gradually over time, others experienced either a sudden (and often physical) development of impairment, or great variability (often mental health impairments). This group was our prime concern throughout Stage Two of our research.

Sudden onset

Many of the respondents we spoke to in Stage Two had recently experienced either the onset of a condition or a traumatic injury. Parents often highlighted the impact that this had had on their children, which could in turn lead to greater demands on them as parents. In two families, a parent had experienced a traumatic injury, as a result of a road traffic accident. In each case, the injuries sustained were reported as having had a particularly strong impact on the family's daughter, who wanted to be close to the disabled parent. One father described the situation as follows:

> Our daughter has found it quite difficult to cope with mummy not being quite as she was and ... possibly she's been traumatised by it because she wakes up at night at the moment, not every night but some nights, and she wants to come in and sleep with us. So we've sort of erected a sort of makeshift bed, which we put up every night, next to our bed. But, and she's fine, you know, she'll sleep there, but then mum can't sleep, so she ends up going off to our daughter's bed.
> *Father, dual-parent family (mother PI), (Family A, Interview One)*

Similar responses were reported from a mother who had recently started having epileptic seizures. Her daughter had witnessed her first seizure and had seen her mother taken to hospital in an ambulance.

> To be honest with you, when it first happened our daughter used to be a bit, she used to sometimes get a bit upset, because she used to think, you know, say she'd had a bit of a bad day at school, she'd sort of, like, come home, she'd think, she'd be worried about me, a lot, at first, when she'd go to school. She'd, like, rush home from school to make sure that I was all right. And that I had come home from work.
> *Mother, dual-parent family (PI), (Family B, Interview One)*

Professional advice and support in relation to parenting seemed to be most likely to be forthcoming when impairments were seen as more stable and predictable. A rare example of a father feeling that his doctor was more than aware of his need to be involved in family life was given during our Stage Two interviews. He had recently had his leg amputated, and there was concern on the part of his consultant to organise operations in a way that would ensure that he and his wife had a holiday with their children. His wife told us his story:

> So right from day one when, when he was first in hospital and I said, "We've got a holiday booked in July, do you think I ought to cancel it?". And he said, "No." He said, "You want to try and go on that holiday, whatever happens, you're going to need it by then". So I mean, all along we've been asking every time we've sort of, every month we've gone, "Are we still all right for the holiday?". "Yes, yes, you're still going on that holiday." Then when the problems started with the knee, we said, "Does this mean that the holiday's going to be ... [cancelled]?". He said, "No way, we'll work, we will work round that, you give me your holiday dates and I will make sure we work round it".
>
> Mother, dual-parent family (father, PI), (Family F, Interview Two)

While the mother was positive about the consultant's family awareness, the father did feel surprised at the extent to which the early input focused on his medical needs when emotionally the family as a whole had other needs, such as counselling support. He also felt his own emotional needs were overlooked, since while he was on the ward the hospital staff had seen him as a 'coper' and even suggested that he try to cheer up another man who was not considered to be dealing with his injuries so well. Therefore, even when health professionals were family-aware, there could be a lack of psychological support for both disabled parents and their families.

Variability

When parents spoke about whether or not their impairments had an impact on their parenting, or talked about the support they required, a key feature was the extent to which their condition was viewed as stable. Related to this was the extent to which people felt future changes could be foreseen, and whether parents felt that they could hope to maintain or achieve their desired level of independence (or interdependence). Concerns about ongoing deterioration, relapse, or more rapid variability could make thinking about the future difficult, especially when the family did not feel positive about the extent of support experienced, be that currently or in the past.

Many of the parents we talked to spoke about the importance of achieving a period of stability. For those parents who felt that they were currently more stable in their condition, it was clearly hoped that this would be something that could be maintained in the long term. For one family taking part in Stage

One of our research, the father's variable mental health impairments highlighted the way in which families have to keep on adjusting, and how concerns and difficulties can remain even where a previously 'ill' parent is currently perceived as 'well'. The father had needed extensive periods of sick leave from his job, since his severe anxiety and depression made it difficult for him to leave the house. At the time of our interview, he was pleased with his progress and with the medication he was taking, and was back at work. His wife and daughter were both keen to state that his problems were behind him, although his wife maintained that she continued to be concerned about his future health.

Parents also talked about how they had learned more about their condition over time, so that variability could eventually become more manageable. However, apparent improvements could also come at a cost for parents. For instance, a mother with ME (Family L) told us on our first visit that her level of fatigue meant that she was unable to drive. On our second visit, she reported that she was able to drive now, but that it would have significant costs for her after a trip out:

> The fact that I'm driving now means that the fatigue is worse afterwards. So, I mean, I'm wiped out today because we took the cat to the vet yesterday …. Although it is a good thing that I can actually drive a little bit, it, it tends to backfire on me because I'll do something and then I'm, you know, sort of completely wrecked for two or three days afterwards.
> *Mother (PI, MHI), dual-parent family (Family L, Interview Two)*

This need for self-care might be particularly difficult to express to services or through benefits assessments. This mother spoke of how it could be very difficult for people with ME to access benefits, partly because of its variability and also because of the lack of recognition of it as a condition. Her concern was widely expressed by those with variable conditions, and particularly those who had mental health impairments:

> But certainly it's something that is a cause of concern for anybody with disabilities, the fact that they can just take your benefits off you like that, and it's very worrying.
> *Mother (PI, MHI), dual-parent family (Family L, Interview Two)*

Likewise, variability in condition could also mean insecurity about access to support, and about future income.

Looking to the future

Planning for the future, then, is greatly affected by variability in impairments, and uncertainty about future services and benefits. Parents themselves spoke of concern (and sometimes fear) about their future, and that of their family, including financial wellbeing and the potential physical and emotional costs of 'caring' on family members. We referred earlier in this book to Family C who felt their personal resources to respond to the mother's MS had been strengthened by their shared experience of the terminal illness of one of their children. However, the father did indicate that it was the 'not knowing what might be round the corner', both in terms of the MS and of support, which made planning for the future difficult. Concerns about impairment and personal, family and social resources were often discussed alongside economic concerns.

Finances

For some parents, the opportunity to stay in – or return to – work was a key issue. Work could be seen as important for both financial security and social contact. For each of the Stage Two parents who had experienced traumatic injuries, the question of whether or not they would be able to return to work was of central importance. One parent received support, both from her employers and a psychologist, enabling her to return to her professional job. The other was a father who had worked in a factory – he, on the other hand, experienced greater insecurity about a possible return to work. His employer had said that they would keep his job open for two years, but he had already received letters that offered him voluntary redundancy.

> Never been on the dole in me life, I've always found something to do. I've never been out of work and I don't want to, I don't want to sit and go to an office and sign on.... If I have to I will do but I, I'll strive to get a job somewhere.... I'll feel like I'm just dragging everything out of the system and I don't want to do that I want to – I still want to put into it if I can, but if I can't in the end, well, I'll have to accept that, but then that's going to be a bit more of my self-respect gone.
> *Father, dual-parent family (PI), (Family F, Interview Two)*

Concern about future employment among parents who had a longer experience of impairment, and who had remained in work, was greater when variability was a feature of the condition. There were cases of extremely supportive employers, but it was often unclear whether this support would be maintained in the long term. Only 12 of our parents had any regular paid employment; therefore, in dual-parent families where a partner had continued to work, the ability of the partner to stay in employment was often a key concern:

> As I say, you know, the pressure's on me, well, to carry on working. I mean, ... there's two ... pensions or, you know, I've got to provide a retirement for two of us. There's not many people know that, once you finish work, you cannot have a private pension. That's one of the first things that happened, when my wife finished work. Before we got any benefit, or anything, there was a letter through from the ... pension company to say, "The pension's on hold".
> *Father, dual-parent family (mother PI), (Family C, Interview Two)*

Similar pressures were felt in families where neither parent was employed. A father discussed how he and his partner might use a future inheritance, given the lack of access they had to financial services, particularly mortgages and pensions:

> So then we've got to think right, well, we've got to put all that money into a house, we won't get a mortgage 'cos we're not working. I mean, it's the same, same thing as, like, you can't get a pension if you're not working. I mean a lot, a lot of these things you find out over the course of time.
>
> *Father, dual-parent family (mother, PI), (Family L, Interview Two)*

Parents therefore did discuss the impact of disability on current and future plans, and often felt that information to support this was gradually accrued rather than readily available.

Conclusions

Our study has focused primarily on current support needs, but we have also been able to sketch out some of the key issues involved in parents' experiences of family life over time. It is important to include what might be viewed as 'mainstream' experiences (such as contact with schools and financial security) alongside other factors specific to the experience of disability and impairment. Our research highlights that experience of disability and parenting over the life course must be grounded in the changing social and economic framework within which parenting and family life takes place.

Our focus has been disability, time of onset and variability in impairment with reference to the life course. Some of the parents we interviewed discussed the impact of negative attitudes towards disabled people becoming parents: we argue that this reflects their relative invisibility (in contrast to 'young carers') in public and policy discourses. It is clear that, for some of our respondents, having a family was achieved despite a lack of support or approval from others, including both family or professionals. Indeed, within our sample we found clear evidence of how disabled people were actively discouraged from expecting access to Priestley's (2000) two cultural signifiers of independent adult life – employment and parenting. Negative attitudes could continue to be expressed by professionals from the beginning of pregnancy through to parenthood. While parents would often welcome information concerning parenting with an impairment, some clearly felt that they were being given little room to make, and little respect for, their own decisions (for instance, about having more than one child), given the explicit disapproval of others.

What our research has also highlighted is the potential long-term impact of the demands of parenting young children alongside little or no support. For example, physical or mental health impairments – even where they predated having children – could be exacerbated by (and experienced as) creating day-to-day difficulties for the first time having become a parent. Our brief review of changes in family shape and the later onset or impact of impairment (a family life course) highlights the importance of understanding the experiences of impairment and of disability in the context of relationships. This is the focus of Chapter Six.

Notes

[1] Normative concepts of the life course are extremely influential in shaping social policy, and the invisibility of disabled parents reflects the way in which disabled people are often excluded from such expectations of adulthood.

[2] Each of the parents in our sample had children aged at least four years. Consequently, our research did not focus on the experience of becoming a first-time parent.

[3] Since our sample does not include disabled people who did not become parents, we have been unable to consider what factors are important for those who decide not to have children, or feel that they were dissuaded from becoming parents.

[4] Unfortunately our sample did not include a sufficient number of fathers to measure whether or not disabled men had felt similarly limited in their expectations, and how these expectations had impacted on their experience of becoming parents.

[5] Despite having only two fathers in single-parent or reconstituted families on which to draw, their experiences suggest to us that fathers feel more limited than mothers do in their ability to make decisions about how to involve their children in disability-related family issues. This is likely to be due to the higher level of involvement of mothers in these cases than we found of fathers in the other single parent or reconstructed families.

[6] Research has not yet paid sufficient attention to the difficulties faced by children when returning to live for brief periods with their disabled parent. Instead, it has concentrated on the experiences of resident children. This situation is perhaps more often relevant to disabled fathers, and merits further attention.

SIX

Individuals, families and relationships

Introduction

This chapter restates our commitment to a *social* model of disability, enabling us to identify the social and environmental barriers that disable parents. Throughout this book, we have used our data to argue that a commitment to enable, support and underpin family roles and relationships must be central to any appropriate intervention. We further stress here that, for many disabled parents, the extent to which they are able to access roles and relationships both inside and outside of the family can have an impact on how they experience the parenting role.

In reporting individual experiences of parenting we must also explicitly recognise that tensions exist between individual and collective approaches to the experience of impairment and disability. We clearly reject any solely individual approach to disability that locates the experience of disability within individuals rather than within families or wider relationships. The dominant outcome of our research has been that adequate theoretical understanding of disability and parenting is only possible within a framework that encompasses both the social and the personal factors that shape people's experiences of impairment, illness and mental distress.

This chapter is our contribution to a critique that some disabled writers (for instance, French, 1993; Crow, 1996) have made of the capacity of the social model of disability to encapsulate fully their experience of *impairment*, while recognising that this is not its raison d'être. In doing so, we begin to reconsider how impairment is conceptualised. Within this research we wished to compare the experiences of parents with physical impairments and parents with mental health impairments. While conducting the study, it became clear that while a mental health 'diagnosis' (or 'impairment') was one way in which distress might be defined, in any final analysis both mental health impairment (usually defined by doctors) and mental distress (that is, a personal experience) ought to be considered. This involves building on the development of social model approaches to mental health and therefore moving away from relying on a concept of 'mental health impairment' to a consideration of 'mental distress'. So, as we highlighted earlier in our discussion of terminology (see page vii) we now refer primarily to mental distress.

Our theme throughout this chapter, then, is that parenting stands at the intersection of public and private worlds. In other words, while our social model enables us to identify the social barriers that shape disabled parents lives, it is also important to understand the personal ways in which this is experienced.

We believe that this approach can help to contribute to the social model's 'renewal and continued relevance' (Shakespeare and Watson, 1997).

Disability, relationships and parenting

Much research thus far into the experiences of disabled parents has taken an individual, medical model approach (see Chapter One of this book). By maintaining a focus in our research on the barriers that parents face in their parenting role, we have also sought to distinguish between impairment and disability in a way that is consistent with a social model of disability.

> *Impairment* is the functional limitation within the individual caused by physical, mental or sensory impairment. *Disability* is the loss or limitation of opportunities to take part in the normal life of the community on an equal level with others due to physical and social barriers. (Barnes, 1991, p 2)

This distinction is the basis of academic research, disability campaigns and theoretical development that has located the discrimination and exclusion of disabled people in social organisation. It enables us to maintain a focus on the barriers facing disabled people when they attempt to access and maintain socially and personally valued social roles. For us, then, taking part in 'normal life' is not to be understood simply in terms of the individual operating in the social world as an atomised body. Rather, a personal experience of the 'normal life of the community' inherently involves relationships with others (friends, neighbours, colleagues, family, and so on). This fact is obscured by reducing such relationships to distinguishing the 'carer' from the 'cared for'. Indeed, approaches that polarise the interests of disabled people and 'carers' fail to acknowledge shared concerns in relation to community care policy and practice (Parker and Clarke, 2002).

We have been eager to explore barriers in the parenting experience of the parents in our survey within the context of family roles and relationships. In Chapter Three, for example, we detailed the experiences of parents of not having their family role as a parent taken into account by others (such as social services, health services, and the private sector). For example, we saw how a 'strong' partnership between disabled parent and partner could aid access to services and information. Yet such a partnership could also be considered by those same services as a sign of sufficient personal resources, leading, ironically, to inadequate formal support being offered. Elsewhere, we examined the way in which a focus on parental 'care needs' has led to the identification of 'young carers' as a welfare category. Our assertion – that supporting relationships means supporting people to enjoy a relationship with their children or partner beyond the limited categories of social services – is within the context of social disablement. However, as Beckett and Wrighton have argued, opening up aspects of personal relationships to services can make disabled people feel vulnerable:

Expressing needs related to social interfacing becomes particularly difficult
if it also means making visible feelings and relationships more commonly
experienced in the private sphere. (Beckett and Wrighton, 2000, pp 997-8)

Yet the relationships that disabled people have with friends and family members
requires considerations beyond limited welfare categories.

Partners' relationships

While some single parents did talk about previous relationships, separations
were often discussed in terms of other difficulties faced beyond impairment or
disability (see Chapter Five). However, in their review of the psychology of
disability, Finkelstein and French (1993) report that those who acquire substantial
impairments frequently experience serious problems with their relationships,
particularly if those relationships were already under strain. Furthermore, Morris
(1989) reports that the onset of impairment and disability can exacerbate pre-
existing tensions within relationships. Our research suggests that this is often
as a result of the demands imposed by a community care system that often
equates the existence of a partner with a primary source of 'care'. Through our
review of the way in which assistance was provided informally within family
relationships, it is clear that for many married or cohabiting disabled parents
support at home was mainly provided by their spouse.

Disabled people and their partners often emphasised that support within the
relationship was a feature of their personal commitment to one another, rather
than of an adoption of 'carer' and 'cared for' roles. However, the management
of impairment, the experience of disability, and the difficulties raised by illness
could lead to frustration (and in some cases resentment) within the relationship.
Many couples were placed under extreme pressure by an expectation on the
part of formal services that partners would provide extensive support, even
when this was felt to be barely possible. That is, becoming a 'full-time carer'
was often by default rather than choice: concerns about a disabled parent's
quality of life (and even safety) led to partners leaving their jobs or being laid
off when their home commitments became incompatible with employment.
Partners could feel there was considerable pressure on them to stay well, whether
in terms of maintaining employment or providing assistance at home. For
example, one husband and wife had both experienced mental distress, and they
shared the same mental health diagnosis. The husband considered himself to
have recovered and wished to stop taking medication. However, he could not,
because of his concern with what would happen if both he and his wife
experienced severe mental distress at the same time.

Disabled parents also voiced their concern about the impact a lack of alternative
support was having on their partners' health. While parents or partners only
rarely stated that the pressure was threatening their commitment to their
relationship, parents often expressed anxiety about what would happen 'should

anything happen to him/her'. This source of this anxiety was perceived as a threat to both the partner's health and to the health of the relationship itself.

There was often great awareness of the importance of both the disabled parent and the partner maintaining other roles. For example, maintaining employment, education or voluntary activity was viewed as highly important for both financial and personal reasons. In some cases, parents indicated how a recent onset of impairment had altered the balance of their relationship. This may have been due to that fact that the opportunities for pursuing external roles had changed, or the allocation of tasks within the household had changed. Or, perhaps, the (satisfactory or unsatisfactory) degree of a partner's understanding had become an issue.

Even when partnerships were experienced as mutually supportive, there could still be discomfort experienced throughout changes in the relationship. A mother interviewed at Stage Two of our research told us how she and her partner had previously been relatively 'independent', with both having nights out with other friends as well as with each other. Now that she was medically unable to drive and consequently less spontaneous in her social life, she was more dependent on her partner's availability:

> I wouldn't say that … he likes me being tied to the kitchen sink. Sometimes
> I say to him, "Hey, you like this, don't you. 'Cos I can't get out and about".
> You know, that sort of thing.
> *Mother (PI), dual-parent family (Family B, Interview One)*

Other parents, on the other hand, reported how their relationship had been strengthened *alongside* concerns about feeling too dependent on their partner. Reduced mobility for one parent (whether related to physical impairment or mental distress) could mean that they were less likely to be able to access other friendships and that the presence of their partner became more important to them. These parents articulated how they wanted to ensure that their relationship did not develop into an overly dependent or 'care' relationship, but this was difficult, given a lack of alternative support. This was very often the case in terms of emotional support: some parents stated that they did not want to rely exclusively on a partner (or friends), but that a partner was usually the main available listener. In Chapter Five, we touched on the experience of a father who had recently experienced a traumatic injury, and was concerned that neither he nor his family had received any form of counselling. Of his relationship with his partner, he said that:

> It's really, well, we were close anyway. I don't think we could be any closer.…
> [But] when she goes out on Tuesdays and Fridays, them two hours, I hate it.
> … She needs to have a break from me, and I hate it.… Sometimes I say to
> her, "I wish you didn't have to go today", just to make a joke of it, and she'll
> say, "Well, I don't have to", and I say, "Yes, you do". And she'd stay at home

and we'd just sit here all day, just sit like you and I are sitting, doing nothing, and just sit talking. And we've never been so close as we are now.
Father (PI), dual-parent family (Family F, Interview One)

In a small number of two-parent families, partners who had extensive involvement in supporting their disabled partner indicated that this had had a negative impact on their relationship[1]. At its most extreme, one husband, who had stopped working to support his wife through a physical impairment that caused her extreme pain, stated that it was like having "lost my wife". Another man, whose wife experienced mental distress and would retreat upstairs leaving him with the children, felt he had "half a wife". Others referred to feeling like a lone parent. Often these statements were made specifically in terms of household tasks, for instance that the disabled partner rarely (if ever) cooked and cleaned, or would withdraw from activities with the children. In such cases, then, people were referring to the fact that a previously predictable role had altered beyond recognition. However, negative feelings about the current state of a relationship could also be overtly linked (for both partners) to the impact of tiredness, frustration, and emotional distress, which were often the consequences of a lack of other sources of support as well as the demands of the parenting role.

Parents and partners sometimes expressed the view that, of the people within their community or friendship network, those with experience of disability had been of most support to the family. This *support through understanding* was also experienced within the parents' relationship. For instance, some parents benefited from their partner having also experienced mental distress. For example, one mother told us about previous poor relationships that she had experienced, and about her current relationship with a man who had also had periods of depression:

Its helping my depression – he's very understanding and can reassure me. But some of them have just been using me and I didn't really understand what I was doing.
Mother (MHI), single-parent family

In relation to mental health, partners' understanding of the distress could impact on how the relationship was experienced. For example, anticipated improvement that was not realised sometimes lead to despondency. One father described how his marriage was going through "a rocky spell" – he linked this to his hope that, after nearly 20 years of his wife's depression, some level of improvement could be reasonably expected. For him, this frustration was exacerbated by her reluctance to accept support (such as membership of a depression support group). In another family, a wife whose depression was not improving felt that this made it more and more difficult for her husband to cope, which had an increasingly detrimental effect on their relationship.

Experience of the parenting role

Parents were often keen to state explicitly their feelings about parenting with reference to their own sense of identity. This research provides greater detail about mothers because there were more women than men in our sample. However, women did seem to be more likely to talk about how mothering was, or might be assumed to be, central to their sense of self. Therefore, some mothers reported strong maternal feelings, while others reported that mothering was not instinctive or central to their self-identity. However, feeling that mothering was not a central role did not mean it was not a valued one. For instance, one mother told us that, while she was not strongly maternal and could have 'gone without' having children, she was deriving great pleasure from her son.

The extent to which people had access to other roles clearly had an impact on how they felt about parenting. We have already mentioned how few of the parents in our sample were in employment, although this was not always seen to be the result of parental impairment. Some full-time parents stressed that their children benefited from them not working. They presented this as meaning that more love and warmth was provided to their children. However, having *chosen* to be a full-time parent was perceived more positively than having full-time parenting presented as a *fait accompli* given as a result of being excluded from the workforce. For example, in the case of a disabled mother who already valued the role of homemaker and did not see impairment or disability as barriers to other possibilities and opportunities, gender rather than disability was the main structuring factor. However, other parents spoke of loneliness and other distressing circumstances. One woman whose employment and marriage had ended after the onset of her mental distress felt bereft of any role. Not only did she feel that she was being stopped from having more children, but she also found it difficult to say what exactly it was that she enjoyed about parenting. When expressing sadness that she would not have more children, she focused on the importance of the infant care-giving role.

> I would like to – nobody would let me – all my kids are in four- to five-year gaps. I feel I have no role at the moment. I just sit at home and do nothing until I pick up the children. Nobody will let me have more children.
> *Mother (MHI), single-parent family*

The parenting role could also be interrupted, for example, by a period of hospitalisation or 'respite care'. Even when this respite was generally perceived by the parent as positive, it might still disrupt parent–child relationships. One woman explained that her children sometimes said that she did not care about them, and that this was partly a reflection of their lack of understanding about her mental distress. Her regular respite – when her children stayed with their (reluctant) father, or a mother's friend – was particularly difficult for them. On returning home, there could be strains in their relationships:

I get a hard time when I come home.
Mother (MHI), single-parent family

Children's responses to parental absence could heighten parents' wish to have a strong presence in their children's lives, as well as their concern about how events were affecting the child. For some parents there was continued or sometimes increased involvement in their children's day-to-day lives, and an awareness of children's relationships with other significant adults. One mother was struck by her daughter's attachment to her teacher, which was highlighted to her when, on a school trip, the daughter moved from the group she was meant to be in (that is, with her mother) to go to sit with her teacher:

I thought "Oh gosh, here's another role. I'm not doing very well for roles this week". Lose the mothering role in a minute. My daughter would rather be with her teacher.
Mother (PI), dual-parent family (Family A, Interview Two)

The daughter's teacher had showed particular interest in her daughter's art work, and, in a later interview the mother referred to the teacher as 'quite a mother figure' who had indeed had a positive relationship with her daughter. The mother was currently on sick leave from work, and hence the reference to role loss was related to some dissatisfaction at not currently being involved in previous professional responsibilities, rather than implying less involvement with her children.

Other parents were deeply concerned that others were taking on part of their parenting role in their day-to-day lives. This was sometimes expressed in terms of *disability*. For example, one mother expressed how her husband was becoming more responsible than she was for her baby daughter and this was because of a lack of home-based support that could have helped her to manage her myalgic encephalomyelitis (ME). However, others did locate this in terms of their *impairment*. For example, one woman felt that her children had learned her 'limitations' from an early age, and so were more likely to go to their father for support or advice.

Children's understanding of impairment

Some parents had difficulties explaining their impairments to their children. For others, however, it was considered either straightforward or unnecessary. For instance, one mother told us that she had not really talked to her child about her multiple sclerosis (MS) beyond reassuring her that she was not going to develop it just because her mum had. Others just said it might come up in general conversation, but that there was no real need to sit and discuss the impairment in detail.

On the whole, parents felt it was important that what information was provided to children came primarily from them. This did not mean that parents did not appreciate support in explaining the nature of their impairments to their children (although such support was rarely available). Only in relation to MS did we find parents who had found information suitable for young children – a book about a mother with MS available from a voluntary sector organisation.

Clearly, some impairments were more difficult for children to understand than others. However, parental experience of a particular impairment could vary significantly between families. In one family, for example, where a father had MS, his wife felt that the children had simply developed an understanding of it, and so there was no need actively to explain or discuss it:

> No – we just live with it really. Because it's fairly stable, we know it quite well, so we live with it. It doesn't keep catching us by surprise – it's familiar to us. We know the problems and get around things.
> *Mother (Father, PI), dual-parent family*

However, when there was greater uncertainty, parents could try to strike a balance between telling children too much (and provoking possible anxiety), or too little (through being overprotective, cautious or uncertain themselves). For example, one woman said that she speaks to her children about her own MS:

> as much as I can. It's not like you can say this is how it is – no set pattern.
> *Mother (PI), single-parent family*

This mother raised another issue expressed among some of those who had variable conditions: that it could be useful to be able to ask someone else to explain an impairment or distress to children. When she had a relapse, she said she was unable to talk to her children about what was happening, and said that not only would she have liked more information herself, but also she would have liked someone to have been available specifically to talk to her children. Another single parent, this time experiencing depression, explained how a professional key worker's input had helped her child to understand what was happening.

> I wanted her to [explain to my daughter] as I was really quite low one day and acting not quite right. A few weeks ago – it was the first time anyone talked to her about it. It was helpful – made her feel that it was not all her fault.
> *Mother (MHI), single-parent family*

It is a delicate balance to strike: arming a child with enough information to protect them (from taking personal responsibility for the parent's impairment or distress, and from unnecessary fears, for example), but also protecting them from taking on greater responsibility for the parent's continued wellbeing as a result of having greater information. Some parents wanted their children to understand medication, for example, but not for them to feel overly responsible for it. Furthermore, in relation to parental mental distress, some parents wanted their children to have an understanding that it was 'not their fault', but at the same time wanted to protect them from the traumatic personal experiences sometimes associated with it, which might involve wider family relationships. The extent to which children were involved in regulating of the amount of information they received about impairment was also interesting. One single parent stated that she answered her children's questions about her mental distress but did not want to keep reminding them about her own problems. Another single parent, whose impairment arose from post-polio syndrome, told us that she tried to give her daughter information but that "she doesn't like to think about it".

Parents sometimes reported that, as children grew older, they could become more self-conscious about parental impairments. This could be overtly linked to bullying experienced by children as they started secondary school and were meeting new children. And some parents anticipated future difficulties despite the fact that parental impairment had not yet been an 'issue' in their children's relationships:

> [The children] know no other so its not had an effect. I do have potential
> fears – especially at [son's] school – they don't know and he might get teased.
> *Father, dual-parent family (Mother, PI)*

This is an example of how the barriers faced by people with impairments are reproduced in the lives of those close to them. Some children said that, when they needed someone to talk about difficulties faced by their disabled parent, they had a number of friends and friends' families that were available. However, other children said that they had kept these difficulties entirely to themselves, or had been very definite about which friends they were able to talk to. Some children did talk about a lack of understanding from others, and/or their embarrassment in discussing their parent's impairment. Therefore, their own personal experience of their parent's impairment and disability was not something that was made public. And when it was made public, it could be experienced as embarrassing or upsetting. One daughter said:

> Just keep it to myself – it is embarrassing to talk about it because nobody else
> has a mum like that.
> *Daughter (12) (Mother, PI), dual-parent family*

She indicated that she had been 'called names' in her village, and her father commented that her those of her own age "have highlighted things before" about her mother's impairment.

Parental mental distress could be particularly difficult for children to talk about to other children. This can be understood in the contexts of difficulties individuals themselves face in developing an understanding of mental distress, the dominance of the medical model in public understanding (including genetic explanations), and media and policy focus on risk, danger and mental health. For example, one daughter found it difficult to invite friends back to her home. She had told none of them about her father's mental distress, and having tested the water she felt uncomfortable and unsafe about disclosing this information. She herself found her father's erratic behaviour and his distress uncomfortable and difficult to understand. The story line of a young man experiencing schizophrenia in a TV soap opera, however, had helped her gain some more insight into her father's behaviour and feelings, in part through understanding her father's diagnosis (manic depression) as illness[2].

What is clear, then, is that the private experience of disability and impairment – on the part of parents and children alike – is influenced by external relationships and perceptions. Tanner highlights very clearly the personal consequences of pressure to conceal her mothers' mental distress, both within and outside the family:

> Reflecting on my childhood and later experiences, I feel that much of my distress and discomfort has been caused, not so much by inherent features of the 'aberrant' behaviour of my mother, but by the shame and stigma associated with that behaviour; in other words, by socially constructed phenomena rather than ones appertaining to either my mother as an individual or the family unit. (Tanner, 2000, p 290)

Wider attitudes towards impairment and distress, and a lack of contact with others who had direct experience of disability, could clearly lead some children to be unable to draw on the support of others their own age.

The social model, impairment and illness

Our discussion raises questions about the extent to which (and ways in which) parents distinguish between their experiences of impairment and of disability. Some parents clearly did so, and this was most often the case when impairment was stable, predictable or highly manageable. Indeed, we have already stated that within our research there was a small number of parents for whom accessible and adapted housing, good transport arrangements and financial security have meant that their impairment is largely insignificant to their involvement in parenting activity. Other parents, however, placed illness and impairment at the very centre of their parenting, such as when a parent feels sad at not being able to pick their child up to comfort them when they have hurt themselves, or carry a child upstairs to put them in bed when they are asleep:

> It's the small things, like when the kids were small and they would fall asleep downstairs, I would have loved just to scoop them up and take them upstairs, but I couldn't. It's not a big thing but sometimes I do regret not being able to do that kind of thing.
> *Father (PI), dual-parent family*

For some parents, then, an inability to do something with or for one's child can not be replaced by the hands and arms of a personal assistant. Parents also expressed concerns about the extent to which their ability to be fully involved in childcare and other family activities was limited by exhaustion resulting from impairment. One woman, who had rheumatoid arthritis (RA), said:

> For me tiredness is a major factor affecting family life. It is a symptom of
> RA and is a major problem. I can walk but I know my limitations and have
> to watch what I do. It's in the legs so it is about knowing limitations.
> *Mother (PI), dual-parent family*

This woman highlighted how she had to develop her own strategies in order to be able to avoid severe bouts of tiredness. Support enabling individuals to manage such difficulties was often expressed in terms of self-support and family input. Parents experiencing mental distress often found it particularly difficult to highlight ways in which their family life and personal relationships could have been improved by input from formal services or in terms of the removal of barriers. They often referred to insufficient or inadequate health service care, rather than a lack of social support. This was expressed in terms of unsatisfactory aspects of the medical management of distress, waiting lists for psychotherapy, and the difficulty in achieving referral to a community psychiatric nurse. When support was received, it was often outside the home (in hospital or a day service); consequently, professionals rarely had contact with partners or the wider family.

Renewing the social model?

Pain, fatigue and emotional distress are important aspects of many impairments which parents in this study discussed in relation to their parenting. A number of writers who have worked within the social model approach have argued that integration of the lived experience of impairment into the social model of disability will enable a richer understanding of the way in which social barriers operate. For instance, Crow has put forward an argument for a renewed social model of disability that focuses both on disability as a social concept, and the individual's bodily experience of their impairment over time. She concludes that:

> Disability is still socially created, still unacceptable and still there to be changed;
> but by bringing impairment into our total understanding, by fully recognising
> our subjective experiences, we will achieve the best route to that change, the
> only route to a future which includes us all. (Crow, 1996, pp 72-3)

Her argument is that, by downplaying the bodily experience of impairment (such as pain, fatigue, emotional distress), some disabled people are at risk of being alienated by those focusing exclusively on the *social* origins of disablement.

Indeed, this distinction between impairment and disability has led to uncertainty about who exactly the social model of disability includes. The issue is particularly vague in relation to those people impaired through chronic illness, learning disability, or mental distress.

Others have argued that the division between impairment and disability is too simplistic. This arises from a tension which we highlighted at the beginning of this chapter, between the need for a model that focuses on the *collective* experiences shared by all disabled people on the one hand, and, on the other hand, one that takes account of the different ways in which impairments are experienced in a disabling society. French (1993), for example, discusses her own experience of visual impairment with reference to the social model, and has described her own inability to read non-verbal cues as a barrier to interpersonal communication. She suggests that such a barrier could be understood as 'something in between' impairment and disability. She recognises the importance of challenging the ways in which a link is routinely made between impairment and illness (or other 'symptoms' of impairment, such as pain), but feels, too, that these should not be wholly ignored.

Many authors recognise both the political power of a clear-cut separation between impairment and disability, and the difficulty this raises in terms of what constitutes an impairment. A failure to integrate this issue into the theory relegates an understanding of impairment to physical/medical explanation.

> Indeed, there is a powerful convergence between biomedicine and the social model of disability with respect to the body. Both treat it as a pre-social, inert, physical object, as discrete, palpable and separate from the self. The definitional separation of impairment and disability which is now a semantic convention for the social model follows the traditional, Cartesian, western meta-narrative of human constitution. The definition of impairment proposed by the social model of disability recapitulates the biomedical 'faulty machine' model of the body. (Hughes and Paterson, 1997, p 329)

Such mind–body dualism can be oppressive to those experiencing mental distress, as well as those with physical or sensory impairments. One mother informed us that, although she felt that her adult-onset epilepsy could be personally understood as the result of the extreme – physical and emotional – stress (itself the result of medical negligence), this understanding was dismissed by professionals. It was important to her that we heard about the difficulties she and her family had faced prior to her first seizure, since her impairment had been boxed off elsewhere as a solely medical issue. This point is also often extremely pertinent for people experiencing mental distress.

Encompassing physical impairments and mental distress

That we included parents experiencing 'mental health impairments' in our sample, and that we used this term, rather than terms such as 'mental health problems' or 'mental health difficulties' throughout the book, reflects our belief in the importance and relevance of a social model approach to this group. In addition, mental distress can be experienced by people with physical impairments and may be considered a 'symptom' of impairment and/or rooted in social disablement. It has been argued more and more that the social model of disability, as applied to physical and sensory impairment, has an important resonance for the mental health service users' (or survivors') movement (Beresford, 2000; Johnstone, 2000; Sayce, 2000). It is important, too, for the development of 'holistic' mental health social work, which acknowledges damaging social responses to mental distress as well as the social (personal and structural) precursors of it. Tew (2002) highlights the importance of broadening an understanding of a social perspective in this way, since there is a tendency within social work to limit the social to practical issues such as benefits and housing. In contrast to the disability movement, the mental health users' movement has been focused on gaining reform within the mental health service system, rather than by directly challenging the system. This focus is not surprising, given the difficulties identified among our sample in accessing support from psychiatric and psychotherapeutic services, and the despondency expressed about psychiatric wards. This has had consequences for the development of a social model of distress:

> The mental health service users'/survivors' movement has not yet developed its own philosophy – the equivalent of the social model of disability – and has tended instead to accept implicitly a medicalised individual model of 'mental illness' relying on a range of euphemisms like 'mental health issues' and 'mental health problems' to try and distance itself from the illness construct. However, mental health service users/survivors are now beginning to explore a 'social model of madness and distress' located within the framework of the social model of disability. This is likely to have significant implications for the social model of disability as well as survivors' own conceptualisations and understandings of madness and distress. (Beresford et al, 2002, p 393)

The conceptualisation of impairment within the social model of disability has been a stumbling block to those writing from the mental health perspective. These writers reflect the feelings of many of those diagnosed with a 'mental illness' or using mental health services that their distress cannot (or at least cannot fully) be understood as a question of biological function. Plumb, for example, rejects this broadening of the social model of disability in order to encompass mental health:

> [I]n keeping with the perspective of Mental Health System Survivors ... I attribute my experiences not to chemical imbalances or aberrant genes (physical impairment) but to my life's experiences within the culture and social structure of society. (Plumb, 2002, p 118)

If we conceptualise mental distress not simply as illness, but either wholly or in part as a response to current socioeconomic and family difficulties, or to past hurt or trauma, a more subtle approach to the social causes of disability is crucial. This has a broader relevance, including psychiatric diagnoses:

> If one area of impairment is disputed as 'real', why should there not be a similar deconstruction of other medical categories within the impairment classificatory scheme. (Barnes et al, 1999, p 62, cited in Beresford and Wilson, 2002, p 551)

One barrier to the alignment of mental health service users with the disabled people's movement might be the extent to which people experiencing mental distress identify themselves as disabled. Beresford (2000) argues that, when disability theorists have tentatively included mental health service users within a definition of disabled people, they have done so in a way that simply medicalises their experiences of distress as illness. This is a direct result of the way in which the social model of disability is based on the distinction between impairment of the body and the disadvantage that results from social organisation. Individuals differ widely in the way in which they conceptualise their mental distress. For instance, dagnosis of 'mental illness' is often the trigger for psychiatric intervention, yet 'diagnosis' of a mental health condition is not the only way in which a need for support due to emotional pain or 'madness' can be understood. When understood as illness, this might be represented to some as an impairment that is distinguishable from the person's social relationships and personal history. However, within our sample we found that this is necessarily the case: people can have complex understandings of their impairments, and discuss both an 'illness' and previous experiences that were seen as contributing to it.

For example, one single mother described her 'psychotic depression' as a 'hidden disability', which she felt had not been identified early enough – indeed, she felt that it had already begun when she was a young child. Alongside this were personal events and difficulties throughout her life that, at the very least, exacerbated her depression. Long waiting lists for psychotherapy and the lack of social support, however, meant that the support she received was, in the main, medical, with little opportunity to develop a personal understanding of distress.

Not identifying oneself as 'disabled' may reflect a refusal to take on an additional identity that is perceived as negative. This may be particularly so in the case of those people already identified as 'mentally ill'. However, this refusal does not exclude an awareness of social barriers to full participation in family relationships or wider social life. For example, Tierney (2001) has drawn both on her own personal experience of anorexia and from her research with women who either defined themselves – or had been medically labelled – as 'anorexic'. She found a social model approach useful: while her respondents would not define themselves as 'disabled', they did highlight social barriers that impacted on their relationships (particularly in terms of the disabling attitudes of others). She also considered the different ways in which her specific experience had been understood by others, and the way in which mental distress is rarely understood in terms of the social barriers she faced, both as a result of others' responses to her body and the lack of accessibility of buildings:

> During the eight years I have been labelled 'anorexic', my situation has been referred to in various ways: madness, female hysteria, illness, attention seeking, brain disorder, hereditary, family problem, media created. However, 'disabled' is one definition society has declined from imposing on me, even though at one point I became reticent to leave the house because of hostile stares and I was sometimes unable to attend school because the [flight of] 'stairs' there also proved a barrier to my emaciated frame. (Tierney, 2001, p 749)

Parents in our study who experienced mental distress also highlighted these barriers. Perhaps it is unsurprising that mobility was an important issue to most of these parents who identified themselves as disabled, given the prominent campaigning around transport and access for people with physical and sensory impairments. We have already seen that, while three quarters of our respondents who had a primary physical impairment identified themselves as a disabled person, only one fifth of those experiencing mental distress did so (although two others said that they sometimes considered themselves to be disabled). These six respondents were two mothers in dual-parent families who had been diagnosed as having agoraphobia; a single mother and a married mother who were both experiencing chronic depression; and a mother and a father (both in dual-parent households) who had been diagnosed with manic depression. Both parents who experienced agoraphobia were clearly very restricted in terms of their mobility, which may in part explain their identification as a disabled person. The mother with manic depression also had a physical impairment (which she considered to be secondary to her manic depression) that could make it more difficult for her to use public transport. She felt, however, that her physical impairment was underrecognised by other family members who were irritated and embarrassed when she tried to get assistance (when travelling by train, for instance). A mother whose severe depression began suddenly following a traumatic experience had also become much more limited in her ability to get out and about, both locally (finding it difficult to talk to neighbours) and on public transport. Public transport was also a difficulty for the single mother with depression, who explained how she struggled getting the right money to pay the bus driver. Others experiencing mental distress with no physical impairment, and who did not identify themselves as disabled, also expressed their difficulties in getting out and about. In one sense, this might be understood as 'impairment as barrier'; however, there was also a clear absence of community-based support that might have increased people's confidence and reduced their distress.

The argument for a social model approach to disability that is inclusive of mental distress is strengthened further when we consider even more the experiences of some parents who have physical impairments. For example:

> Disabled people may feel negative and depressed about their situation because they have absorbed negative attitudes about disability both before and after becoming disabled, and much of the depression and anxiety they feel may be the result of other people's attitudes, poor access, non existent job prospects and poverty. (Finkelstein and French, 1993, p 31)

This corresponds to the way in which some parents with physical impairments in our study talked about mental distress; that is, not as an 'illness' or a direct consequence of impairment, but linked, rather, to the social difficulties they faced. Partners also mentioned the emotional difficulties they faced, often describing them in social rather than medical terms. For example, a single mother who had a physical impairment spoke of how a lack of support from her ex-husband, living on benefits, and only minimal home-care support was not conducive to her emotional wellbeing. However, a father in a dual-parent family did speak of his depression as being wrapped up in his physical impairment, but also talked of adjustments which he did not yet feel ready to make, such as using a wheelchair, and of *other people's* embarrassment (that is, the impact of others' attitudes) towards his impairment.

For Tew, social relations and interpersonal relationships are of paramount importance in his proposal for a social model of mental distress:

> [A] social model locates experience [of distress] within an understanding of social relations in which power plays a determining role, both in terms of 'macro' scale structural inequalities in relation to gender, 'race', class, age, sexual orientation, and so on, and in terms of the 'micro' scale dynamics of conflict, exclusion or abuse that may take place within families or other intimate social contexts. (Tew, 2002, p 147)

The perception of families as 'causal agents' of distress or disability has been a core component of psychiatric and psychotherapeutic approaches to 'mental illness' over the past century. This is a significant barrier to the inclusion of families within policy and practice in mental health, despite the fact that, as we have seen, families are often expected to be "the lynchpin of community care" (Jones, 2002, p 248). Tew (2002) argues that, in contrast to some medical and psychological approaches that can marginalise family members, a social model approach can support recognition of the distress that might also be experienced by them.

Pathologising parents and their relationships can in itself be a barrier to accessing support. Pertinent issues were raised by Tanner (2000) in her review of *Crossing bridges*, a Department of Health training pack for people working with 'mentally ill' people and their children. She finds that, while the department pays lip service to structural factors, the approach is in fact rooted in medical and family models that pathologise individuals and their relationships. Within our sample, one mother with physical impairments who also experienced depression told us that an attempt to label her with Muchausen's-by-Proxy formed part of her conflict with social services. Family members' experiences of illness, impairment, housing difficulties, economic difficulties and social isolation were thought to have been relegated to the bottom of social services' concerns. We also spoke to one mother whose long-term depression began after her father died, and she felt this was exacerbated by the birth of her son some years later. Her grief about her father's death had implications for her feelings towards son, and yet she had found this very difficult to articulate to her GP. Fear about conveying difficulties in parenting relationships can simply be fear about a child being taken into local authority care. While this was not the outcome in this case, the actual fear had meant that she had spent two years parenting while experiencing severe emotional difficulties with little external support.

There are differing views as to whether or not the social model of disability is (or should be) inclusive of those experiencing mental distress. We should not assume that a social model – developed largely out of the experiences of those with physical and sensory impairments – is fully able to include all of those who experience disability. However, we have found it an important tool in examining the barriers facing those parents with mental distress (with or without physical and/or sensory impairments). This is particularly the case with reference to access to social care and to social security benefits.

According to Beresford et al (2002), grouping together mental health service users and disabled people into one administrative category in order to deliver financial and social support is one good reason why the disability movement and mental health service users need to engage with one another. This is important, given the low level of disability benefit receipt and of social work or other formal support that we found among parents experiencing mental distress. Among the six respondents whose primary impairment related to their mental health, only three received any form of disability benefit, such as Disability Living Allowance (DLA) or Incapacity Benefit. (Perhaps this explains why they also identified themselves as disabled.)

Parents experiencing mental distress often dismissed disability benefits and home care support as irrelevant to them (or – if relevant – inaccessible), even when needs were identified. Formal service involvement in alleviating mental distress was often through individual medical and psychotherapeutic approaches, although other (usually unavailable) options were preferred.

> It's hard – I know [my daughter is] OK but I find it hard. Nobody else helps. I didn't like the way I was treated in hospital – I wanted a rest at home for a few days and someone to take responsibility for the cleaning so I could be with my daughter.
> *Mother (MHI), single-parent family*

Disability, then, *was recognised* by parents. And in order to qualify for other forms of support (such as benefits) that might reduce both their experience of disability and of distress, people accepted medical diagnoses and intervention (measurement and management of their 'impairment').

> Qualifying for disability benefits may also depend on the acceptance of medical explanations of madness and distress. It may also depend on taking or being injected with prescribed drugs that may have damaging and dangerous effects. (Beresford and Croft, 2001, p 19)

We have already considered how relationships between family members can be undermined when inappropriate labels (especially 'carer' or 'young carer') are applied. Families may privately resist the application and use of such labels, yet at the same time accept them in order to access public services or highlight the lack of formal support. Watson (2002) found that many people with physical impairments do not privately identify themselves as 'a disabled person', indicating a resistance to this public categorisation. He suggests that identifying oneself as disabled is hardly a positive step, given current social values that demean disabled people. When such identification does occur, it may be in part due to other problems in that person's life that come to be understood as resulting from, or linked to, impairment.

So, identification as a disabled person involves tensions between public and private experiences and understandings. We would argue that parenting throws these tensions into particularly sharp relief, given the intensely public and private aspects of that role.

Conclusions

When approaching parent's support needs from the basis of a social model of disability, then, the experience of mental distress in particular can represent something of a conundrum. While impairment might be identified as being that within the private body, and disability as originating from the social and cultural context, mental distress itself can be understood in biological, personal, interpersonal, social and sometimes even spiritual terms. The question, however, is not whether or not social disablement is relevant to parents experiencing mental distress (since it clearly is). Rather, what is required is the development of a social model of mental distress, as well as an examination of the shared experiences of exclusion with other disabled people.

It is a challenge, of course, to examine the complex social networks that span public and private worlds. However, it is absolutely necessary when considering the experiences of disabled parents. The challenge, then, is not only in terms of our understanding of the processes involved, but also in terms of service response. We have stressed throughout this chapter that an awareness of family relationships and roles can be instrumental in enabling parents to take part in a 'normal life' within the family and community. In addition, this suggests that disability is most clearly understood not only from a social perspective, but also that policies that focus on individual care needs are disabling both to people with impairments and those closest to them with whom they face barriers in achieving the 'normal' interdependent relationships of family life.

We are not arguing that ownership of the disabled parents' experience should be claimed by non-disabled family members. Rather, we are arguing that a social model approach can highlight how disability not only has an impact on individuals who have impairments, but also on those with whom they have close relationships where disability is a central part of their life experience. It also suggests that the divisiveness of publicly identifying people as belonging to certain administrative categories (for example, 'carer', 'disabled') can be challenged by bringing the private and personal experiences of family life into clearer focus.

We have argued in favour of a social model that gives greater space to a discussion of impairments, and the experience of impairments. The construction of disability as a purely social phenomenon, or as 'oversocialised' (Bury, 1996, p 35), will struggle to adequately encompass the experience of disabled parents, given the parallel nature of parenting as at once an intensely private yet profoundly public role.

Notes

[1] As a result of the fact that our sample included more disabled mothers than disabled fathers, our examples are more often than not fathers discussing their wives or partners.

[2] The portrayal of an experience of mental distress within a family context may also have been relevant here.

SEVEN

Conclusion

Introduction

This book began with a discussion of the invisibility of disabled parents in mainstream policy and practice concerning parenting and family support. This invisibility is sustained and reinforced by the common assumption that parents are – or, at least, should be – non-disabled. We hope this book, then, by sustaining throughout a focus on disabled parents, has contributed to the process of addressing this invisibility.

Our study has been concerned with the promotion and realisation of the equal opportunities of disabled people to establish families, and care for children. In contrast to much current research, furthermore, it has not been about the search for negative outcomes in children, nor for pathological failings in disabled people. We hope the result is a significant contribution to what is an exciting period in the development of a disabled parents' movement in the UK, and to a greater awareness on the part of policy makers and practitioners about the importance of parenting responsibilities for many disabled people.

There are limits, however, to our study. In particular, research with a larger sample is required so that data with greater explanatory power can be collected. However, a purely quantitative approach is inadequate, given the many complex and interacting factors that structure the environment in which disabled people parent. The quantitative data presented throughout this book stand, we argue, as a springboard for subsequent research, since they point to important factors in structuring the experience of disabled parents.

Our study has not been about service users, although many parents in our sample were using one or more of a variety of healthcare and social care services. In a sense, this is a weakness of our research: we have not been able to focus in greater depth, consequently, on the way in which a particular service (for instance, child and adult social-work teams) responds to the parenting of disabled people. However, in our defence, carrying out research with a group of people defined only by their status as disabled parents as we have done, and not by their receipt of a particular service, has many advantages. Firstly, it avoids a service-led approach. Secondly, it allows us to look at parenting and disability in a much more 'bottom-up' and 'normative' way. That is, it allows us to look at the parenting experience of a group of disabled people as it really is, and not filtered through administrative and welfare categories.

Challenges for disability theory, policy and practice

We have explored a wide range of important issues concerning disabled parents, such as education, employment, social and healthcare services, informal networks, poverty, housing, leisure and transport. In addition, we have tried consistently to view the experiences of disabled parents, and other family members, in ways that recognise the importance of change. In other words, both impairment and disability are not static; rather they change both in terms of severity and in terms of their impact on family life. Likewise, individuals and their relationships change – people get older, families develop, dissolve and reconstitute. The structural environment in which disabled people parent is also subject to change, for instance in employment patterns, benefit receipt, housing status, and so on.

Making support accessible for parents with fluctuating and unpredictable impairments is clearly a major challenge, then, although we also argue that the changing context in which parenting takes place can have significant implications for the parenting of disabled people with quite stable and predictable impairments. It is a challenge to the ability of services to respond adequately to disabled parents and their families. It is also, however, a challenge to our theoretical understanding of disability, and we have argued that a life-course perspective is crucial in understanding impairment and disability over time.

We have emphasised throughout our research findings the different ways in which disabled parents manage both their parenting role, and the disability they encounter. Disabled parents are an extremely varied group, as are non-disabled parents. This variation is reflected not only in the wide range of impairments that disabled parents experience, but also in parents' access to (and use of) formal and informal support and material resources, employment and housing status, their ethnicity and age, their children's age, and their political, practical and emotional response to disability and impairment. Disability is therefore only one of many factors that structure the experience of parenting for people with impairments. It intersects with other issues that are part of a broader, common experience of parenting. These include poverty and 'social exclusion', gender roles and family shape, employment choices, environmental stresses and supports, the nature of family relationships, and the active role of children themselves in shaping the parenting experience. Throughout the research, we did not seek out the single experience of disability and parenting, or the solution in terms of support. What we have done, rather, is to create a space in which a multitude of hitherto 'absent voices' – those of disabled parents – could be heard.

The design of our research enabled us to explore diversity and difference, not only in terms of the experience of disability and parenting for those in our sample, but also in terms of their political orientation to it. The social model of disability seeks to explain the experience of disability with reference to attitudinal and physical barriers to the inclusion of impaired people in society. Crucially, many researchers who have adopted and developed the social model approach to disability have worked hard to avoid integrating impairment into their theory, as part of a wholesale rejection of the medical model. However, we have argued – as do disabled writers, such as Liz Crow – that the social model can benefit from an attempt to integrate the experiences of impairment into a consideration of the way in which social barriers operate. In particular, we have argued that a neat separation between impairment (with its roots in the function and workings of the body) and disability (a social experience) is easier to sustain for people experiencing physical impairments than it is for those experiencing mental distress. Mental distress can have physical, biological *and* social origins and explanations; therefore what is required is a renewal of the social model to incorporate mental distress. This is particularly important given the location of parenting as both a private and public activity.

Towards more equal opportunities

Our work has pointed to the many ways in which disabled people face extra barriers in fulfilling their parental responsibilities. These include barriers to the use of formal and informal sources of support as well as those barriers that can be erected when the judgements of professionals restrict the options available to families in terms of assistance. Most important of all has been our argument that the kind of support that disabled people require in parenting their children is intrinsically no different from the kind of support that all parents need. This list is hardly exhaustive, but basic requirements surely include:

- an adequate income;
- housing that meets the needs of all family members;
- appropriate informal support;
- the opportunity to have a break from caring for children;
- the opportunity to take an active part in the education of children;
- the opportunity to get out and about as a family;
- the opportunity to deal with problems (for instance, bullying) that children face;
- the ability to access mainstream facilities in the public, private and voluntary sectors.

However, the barriers that disabled parents face in accessing some or all of these sources of support are of central importance, and we would argue that the focus must remain on dealing with the barriers that restrict disabled people from parenting on a level playing field. This, rather than the erection of new forms of welfare provision founded on the principle that disabled parents' support needs are 'special', should remain the central organising principle of interventions designed to support disabled parents.

This is particularly important in the context of current developments in social policy towards families and parenting, and in particular the centrality of 'ecological' perspectives on parenting in the *Framework for the assessment of children in need and their families* (DoH, DfEE and HO, 2000). In Chapter One, we argued that there are inherent tensions in this framework between a willingness to understand parenting that takes place within the structural parameters of poverty, social exclusion and so on, and an attachment to individual capacity as the key factor in assessing the quality of parenting on offer, and the likelihood for positive change. It remains to be seen how this tension is played out.

On the basis of our data, however, we argue that this persistent concentration on capacity within ecological perspectives on parenting can not be fully reconciled with an approach to disability grounded in a social model approach. We have also pointed to the ways in which disability intersects with other forms of exclusion and disadvantage in the parenting experience of disabled people. Indeed, disability itself can only have meaning when experienced through these other forms of exclusion. Socioeconomic disadvantage and gender are particularly powerful factors that mediate not only the experience of parenting, but also the way in which barriers are erected. This focus on disability as one of many factors that influence the equal opportunities of disabled people as parents requires that we acknowledge both the commonality of the experience of disabled parents as well as structural divisions in that experience. In other words, all disabled parents will share experiences based on physical and attitudinal barriers to their participation in parenting, but some disabled parents will have more in common with non-disabled parents. With these non-disabled parents they will share experiences based on gender, economic disadvantage, ethnicity and sexuality, for example, to a far greater extent than they can with disabled parents who are more removed from them in terms of these other experiences.

Children, parents and the meaning attached to domestic and 'caring' work

Although we have stressed that our sample is not necessarily representative of disabled parents generally, our data indicate that children are involved in generally low levels of domestic and 'caring' work. This low level of involvement is partially the result of a lack of need for assistance on the part of many disabled parents, but also of strategies devised by disabled parents and their partners in preventing the involvement of their children in what could be labelled 'caring' roles. This can be to the detriment of disabled parents' health and to the health of their partners, as we have seen, since they behave in ways that exacerbate impairments, or leave them with less energy to manage family life.

The data do not highlight any differences in the likelihood of boys and girls, or older and younger children, being labelled a 'young carer'. However, in response to a range of questions, both single parents and their children independently reported higher levels of involvement, and a greater degree of sole involvement and/or responsibility for providing assistance than was the case for dual-parent families. This should alert policy makers and practitioners to the additional support that single disabled parents may require in order not to have to rely inappropriately on their children. It also alerts us all to the importance of family breakdown (and the creation of a 'new' single parent) as a possible precursor to children being drawn into providing inappropriate levels of assistance.

From our discussion in Chapter Four, it is clear that the absence of alternative sources of support hinders parents' efforts to prevent their children from becoming 'young carers'. Assistance aimed at preventing the children of disabled parents from becoming 'young carers' must be based on a broader understanding of these factors:

- the meaning attached to domestic and caring work by family members;
- the place of 'caring for' parents as an aspect of *caring about* parents within family dynamics;
- the role of children themselves in adopting, negotiating and resisting caring roles.

In particular, our data point to the way in which the discursive framework for explaining and managing children's involvement in housework is entirely different when it is concerned with younger – as opposed to older – children. This is important, given that children as young as three or four years of age have been labelled as 'young carers' in the literature.

Future directions

Disabled parents have been talking about the barriers they face for some time now, often in publications that do not reach academic audiences. The increasing number of personal accounts has been complemented by an increase in publications looking at parenting from a social model perspective, and at aspects of women's experience of disability that necessarily deal with issues of childbearing and child rearing. However, high-quality research on disability and parenting that is grounded in social model thinking is still in its infancy.

What the current literature is sorely lacking are reliable and valid statistics on the numbers of disabled parents in the UK. Not only would these statistics give greater weight to the political process of getting disabled parents' issues higher on policy agendas, they would also provide an important backdrop to the more qualitative and evaluative work that has yet to be done.

What is also currently lacking is a research method that engages with both the actual and the potential development of innovative services for disabled parents. This would include work on the importance of – and access to – direct payments for disabled parents; the evaluation of service provision aimed at disabled parents; and the ways in which barriers to accessing mainstream services and facilities (across a wide spectrum of sectors) can be tackled.

The issue of 'access to parenthood' also requires far greater attention than it currently receives. By 'access to parenthood' we mean the extent to which young people who grow up disabled feel that parenthood is a role open to them, as well as the ways in which they manage transitions to adulthood and the opportunities (or lack of them) for partnering and parenting. There is already an extensive literature on the transitions of disabled people to adulthood for this work to build upon. However, we believe that it needs to extend the concept of transition to include choices around parenting. It would therefore include choices and barriers in fertility treatment, genetic counselling, access to fostering and adoption for prospective disabled parents, and so on.

Two other issues that we would have particularly liked to explore within this book are ethnicity and racism in the experience of parenting and disability. We would argue that research that examines the way in which barriers to parenting operate for disabled parents from minority ethnic communities is particularly needed.

Finally, our understanding of parenting and fatherhood is particularly underdeveloped. Studies of disabled parents, both from the medical model perspective of clinical studies and the social model perspective, have thus far focused almost exclusively on disabled mothers, and have uncritically allowed parenting and mothering to be seen as one and the same thing. We have pointed in this book to the barriers that disabled parents face to their parenting role. In particular, disability can often be used as a mechanism for denying custody of – and access to – children in the legal system, and disabled parents frequently talk about their concern about access to their children following separation and divorce. Of course, the other significant risk factor for being separated from, or denied access, to children is fatherhood and it is therefore particularly important that we develop an understanding of the particular barriers faced by disabled fathers in accessing parenting roles.

Methods

Introduction

In Chapter One, we argued that the literature on parenting and disability was dominated by medical, rather than social, model approaches. This appendix describes the methodological dilemmas we faced in attempting to address this absence, and the methods we used in response.

Key variables

This study was informed partly by concerns about the way in which policy, practice and research around 'young carers' had gained an almost hegemonic pre-eminence as a way of looking at parenting and disability. A key aim of our study, therefore, was to address the factors that might enable disabled parents to avoid dependence on their children for 'care'. However, it was important to address two particular issues that the 'young carer' literature had identified as significant: parental mental health impairments, and the presence of one or both parents.

The 'young carer' literature highlighted not only the significant number of children caring for parents with mental health impairments, but also the particular nature of that caring experience (Dearden and Becker, 1995, 1998). In addition, parental mental health impairments have featured strongly in research on, among other things, the incidence of child abuse (Sheppard, 1997), child protection procedures (Dartington Social Research Unit, 1995), and the characteristics of children 'looked after' (Bebbington and Miles, 1989). Consequently, we designed our study in a way that enabled us to compare the experiences of parents with mental health impairments with those of other disabled parents.

The 'young carer' literature also pointed to the likelihood that children of single disabled parents will be less protected from involvement in caring activity than those children who have two co-resident parents (the assumption being that the other, implicitly non-disabled, parent would act as a buffer between parental disability and child involvement). It was important for our study to be designed in such a way as to allow comparison between single-parent and dual-parent families. Our materials and analysis, and the data presented in this book, are therefore frequently couched in terms of these two variables, which we have termed *impairment group* and *family shape*.

We were also aware that an understanding of the experiences of disabled parents would be impossible without reflecting adequately the importance of change. Our focus, therefore, was also on the changing impairments and changing barriers that parents face, changes in the needs of children as they age and develop, changes in the socioeconomic circumstances of the family, and so on. A further, second stage, of the research was therefore devised, structuring our study in Stage One and Stage Two.

Stage One

Stage One was designed to provide a retrospective and descriptive survey of households containing a disabled parent (or two disabled parents) and one or more dependent children. It was important to gather quantitative data so that we could analyse our findings in terms of the two key variables, impairment group and family shape. However, we also wanted to capture the complex ways in which parental disability intersected with other important issues. We were aware that we would struggle to capture this complexity were we to use research instruments that were too closed. In addition, we felt it was important to gather the views of both parents *and* children. We decided to interview one child aged between seven and 18 years in each family[1].

Pilot work

We conducted preliminary pilot work in order to organise research tools in a sensible and coherent way, as well as to ensure that the content and structure of these tools were meaningful to disabled parents. Stage One, then, began with pilot interviews with seven families with a variety of parental physical and mental health impairments, encompassing both single-parent and dual-parent families. They were carried out, in most cases, with parents and children present, and the interviewees were recruited from a variety of sources, including a local organisation of disabled people, through word-of-mouth and personal contact, and following news items in local newspapers.

The pilot interviews were open-ended discussions about parenting and disability, and the discussions covered a wide range of issues. These interviews were recorded, transcribed and used to inform the design of the main Stage One questionnaires. We then returned to each family and reinterviewed them using these draft questionnaires, simultaneously seeking further feedback from family members and assessing the utility of each set of questions before producing final-draft questionnaires[2].

The parent questionnaire

Several writers have argued that research that does not recognise the essentially *social* nature of disablement is likely to enhance – rather than challenge – the oppression of disabled people (Morris, 1992; Barnes, 1996). This has led to calls for a fundamental rethinking of the social relations of research production (Oliver, 1992), and for research into disability that is grounded in a commitment to empowerment. In the development of the parent questionnaire, then, we grappled with several issues, particularly a commitment to working within a social model of disability.

We approached our research with a keen sensitivity to these debates. In particular, we sought to anchor our methods in a social model perspective that seeks to identify the barriers to participation in parenting facing disabled parents. However, our experience in the pilot stage told us that, in compiling the questionnaires, we would have to perform a balancing act between taking this approach and allowing space for parents to talk about the impact of their *impairments* on parenting. In other words, we had to devise research instruments that were sensitive to the fact that, in the real world, disabled people conceptualise disability in ways that reflect social *and* medical model thinking. Our questionnaires, then, reflected a social model approach that nonetheless allowed respondents to talk as freely as possible about disability and parenting. In other words, we were keen "to allow space for absent voices" (Morris, 1992, p 159).

Of particular significance was the way in which we decided to record and categorise parents in terms of impairment. Parents often found it difficult to specify a particular condition, diagnosis and point of onset. This was particularly the case for parents with multiple impairments, and for those who questioned their current diagnosis by an 'expert'. Most important of all, this was also the case for those reporting both physical and mental health impairments where the significance of each, and the relationship between them, were confused and/or intricate (for example, parents who had been diagnosed as suffering from depression for many years only for their symptoms to be rediagnosed as myalgic encephalomyelitis, or ME).

As our research developed, we found that any simplistic attempt to allocate families to discrete categories of impairment was problematic. In addition, placing parents in a series of groups based on single and multiple impairment groups would leave too few parents in too many boxes for meaningful analysis. We therefore decided to ask parents to describe their impairments and, if they could, to identify what they thought their 'primary condition' to be. This enabled us to analyse the data, where appropriate, in terms of a binary distinction between those parents who reported having primarily physical and/or sensory impairments and those who reported having primarily mental health impairments. This division in the sample is used frequently throughout this book in the presentation of quantitative data. In addition, we made a point of asking *all* parents whether they ever experienced any mental health impairments, whether diagnosed/treated or not. This enabled us to carry out further analysis comparing those reporting 'any' mental health impairments with those reporting 'none'.

The child questionnaire

Several authors have pointed to the way in which studies of children and childhood have traditionally been concerned with what kind of adults children will become, and what kind of adulthood they will enjoy, be it in terms of child development, or in terms of socialisation (see, for example, James and Prout, 1990).

> [T]he treatment of childhood phenomenon as notable primarily in terms of what children are supposed to become, rather than what they actually are, positions children as a passive or deficient social group, being relentlessly pushed towards full adult (and therefore social) status. (Mizen et al, 1999, p 426)

We recognised, then, the importance of including the views and experiences of children as social actors in their own right (Qvortrup, 1990) – it is important for children's voices to be heard. We recognised at the outset that it might be difficult for some children to talk about parental disability and that, despite our sensitivity to current 'good practice' in obtaining informed consent from children in social research (Alderson, 1995), many children might feel uncomfortable in taking part. Yet they feel obliged to do so given their parents' involvement. In Stage One especially, with no scope for introductory visits and the establishment of a longer-term rapport with children, it was important to design a questionnaire that was as non-threatening as possible. Consequently, it involved a relatively closed set of questions on family life, while at the same time providing space for further comments for those willing to share more. We asked about a range of issues that the literature, especially about 'young carers', had told us might be important for the children of disabled parents, including the extent of their free time, their contribution to domestic and caring work, their experience of bullying, and so on.

The children's questionnaire also allowed us to gather data on issues central to debates about 'young caring', by adapting Looking After Children (LAC) materials routinely used for assessing outcomes for children looked after in the UK (Ward, 1995). In particular, we saw an opportunity to engage with children on the issues of 'false maturity' and the performance of age-inappropriate domestic tasks and responsibilities. As part of their development, the original LAC schedules had been tested on a community sample of children in the late 1980s. We therefore wrote several of the questions on the child questionnaire in a way that would enable us to compare the experiences of the children of disabled parents in our sample with those in the original community sample (see Appendix Two of this book).

The adaptations necessary to use the LAC schedules had some important consequences. Firstly, the approach of the LAC materials is to assess the extent to which children have reached appropriate developmental milestones (for instance, their ability to do simple first-aid by the age of 12, or to deal with organisations such as the Department of Social Security by the age of 17, and so on). They do not assess whether children have learned, or are carrying out, tasks at *too early* an age. In addition, they do not assess the frequency with which children are carrying out particular tasks or roles, or the level of responsibility children have for these tasks. For instance, being able to cook a hot meal may be a valued developmental goal, but not necessarily for a child of eight, and not if it involves ongoing responsibility for hot meals within the family, both issues of importance in reflecting on debates about 'young caring'.

In order to address the issue of 'false maturity', we adapted the LAC schedules by drawing relevant questions from three of the age-banded assessment and action records (ages 5-9, 10-15, 16+) and addressing them to the children in our sample. However, in addition to being asked questions from their own age band, the seven- to nine-year-olds in our sample were also asked those questions drawn from the 10- to 15-year-old schedules. Similarly, the 10- to 15-year-olds in our sample were asked, in addition to their own, age-appropriate questions, those drawn from the age 16+ schedules. This enables us to say something not only about differences between the children in our sample and their age-matched peers in the community sample, but also about the extent to which the children in our sample were unusually young in their ability to carry them out. In order to address the problem of assessing frequency with which children are involved in domestic and self-care tasks, we devised a grid in which children were asked to list the range of things they did in the house, and the frequency of their involvement.

It is important to recognise the limitations involved in our adaptation of LAC materials. Firstly, the LAC schedules themselves were not designed to assess *problematic* levels of caring and domestic activity in the home. Rather, they are about ensuring that children are developing 'normally', and, for older children, that they are ready to leave care with a set of life skills that will promote independence. Indeed, Newman (2000) has pointed out that the LAC materials are somewhat ambiguous about the value and worth of children's involvement in work per se. Secondly, the first version of LAC schedules, used with the community sample, was administered jointly with parents and children up to the age of 15; for the under-10s, questions were addressed to parents rather than children (Moyers, pers. comm.). In this study, our approach was to interview children alone (or in the presence of a parent if requested to do so) and the questions were directed at children irrespective of their age. This limits the extent to which we can make concrete comparisons between the children in our sample and those in the original LAC community sample. As a consequence, we have interpreted the data cautiously when looking at them in Appendix Two.

The partner questionnaire

The emphasis in the partner questionnaire was on the way in which families had adopted different roles for spouses. The scope was inherently limited by our focus on *family shape* as a variable, and the need to recruit adequate numbers of single-parent families to make this viable. The parent questionnaire, therefore, had to cover all aspects of parenting and family life, leaving the partner questionnaire to concentrate on issues particular to dual-parent families.

Two particular issues were important in the design of the partner questionnaire.

First, we were aware that some partners would also be disabled. This allowed us to explore assumptions made in the 'young carer' literature about the importance of (implicitly non-disabled) partners as a buffer against children's overinvolvement in domestic and 'caring' activity. However, we had to decide how to 'allocate' which parent to which questionnaire. There were dangers in simply administering the parent questionnaire to the parent with the most severe impairments. In doing so, we would be adopting a medical model, by assuming that parenting issues are more likely to be 'driven' by the severity of impairments rather than the social roles adopted by the parents, the structural and social barriers faced, and so on. On the other hand, it was also important not simply to administer the main parent questionnaire to the 'most involved' parent, such as a stay-at-home mother, as this would risk excluding fathers from our sample. It would also hinder the exploration of issues for those disabled parents who were in employment. In the small number of families where both parents were disabled, we explained to parents the differences between the two questionnaires, and left them to choose who would adopt the role of 'parent' for the purposes of the research. The partner questionnaire was then designed so that those partners identifying themselves as disabled were asked a series of further questions about their own support needs and barriers to participation in parenting.

Second, we took the opportunity to centre the partner questionnaire on the issue of roles, and changing roles, with regard to parenting. Consequently, it contained questions that focused on the degree to which their involvement in parenting was a product of parental disability. We did this in order to avoid the pitfall of assuming that, for instance, a high level of partner responsibility for domestic tasks was inevitably the product of parental impairments. Instead, we were interested in whether parental disability led to a reorientation of partnership roles (for example, with the partner taking on some of the parenting tasks that, other things being equal, would be less likely to have been done by them). We were then able to explore how families managed such changed roles, for instance in regard to non-disabled partners feeling sole responsibility for the discipline of young children given mobility impairments in the disabled parent, or the complex issues involved, for instance, in fathers providing guidance on personal issues to teenage daughters. We were also interested in the role of the partner in pursuing support for the disabled parent and for the family. This enabled us to explore the way in which formal support (or the absence of it) promotes or undermines existing family relationships (an important theme that runs throughout this research).

Stage Two

The aim of Stage Two was to explore the experiences of a small number of families where a parent had recently experienced the onset of impairments. We envisaged that the disruption to family roles and responsibilities would be greatest at these times, given the likelihood of prolonged hospitalisation, uncertain prognosis, the sudden transformation of the world in terms of reduced accessibility, and so on. The aim was to speak to the families as soon as possible after the onset of impairment, and then again after nine months, allowing the development of key issues to be followed and critical incidents to be analysed.

We wanted to recruit 12 families, with four involving parental traumatic injury, four involving progressive conditions, and four involving severe mental health impairments. We planned to conduct initial interviews with the parents (jointly and separately), with follow-up interviews also involving one child in the household. Initial topic guides were developed covering key areas that we wanted each interview to address, although the emphasis was on families being able to highlight significant issues in a more open way. The topic guides were informed by 'critical incident' techniques, a well-established approach to social research involving the identification of key events and experiences (Flanagan, 1954)[3]. We did this by seeking to identify the key events on the horizon for family members at the first Stage Two interview. The responses to questions about these horizons would then form the basis for second interviews, with the aim of reflecting on the role of these key events in shaping the parenting experience of disabled people and the availability and suitability of formal and informal support.

Recruitment

Parents in Stage One were to be recruited from a variety of voluntary sector groups in Leicester and neighbouring areas, with various publicity activities carried out by ourselves. Stage Two families were to be recruited via acute and community NHS trusts locally, given the focus on recently impaired or diagnosed parents. Here we describe the recruitment strategies we used, and the changes we made in order to achieve meaningful samples in each stage.

Stage One

In Stage One we interviewed members of 67 families, recruited from Leicester, neighbouring areas and, occasionally, from other parts of England. The disabled parent was interviewed in each family. In most cases, we also interviewed a child and, in dual-parent families, the spouse. We adopted a randomised approach to selecting which child would be interviewed (in cases of there being more than one child aged between seven and 18). This was to avoid the danger of bias resulting from parents putting forward particular children as candidates for interview. We used a Kish grid, produced specifically for our randomisation process, although parents were entitled at all times to veto the participation of any individual child[4].

In a small number of families, partner and/or child interviews were not carried out. The reasons for this are varied, and included the unavailability or disinterest of the partner, and requests on ethical grounds that no child interview should take place. While this was disappointing at one level, it also meant that we were able to capture the experiences of parents for whom some of the issues were particularly difficult, and who would not have volunteered other than on the understanding that no children would be involved. We decided, therefore, to proceed with families so long as it was possible to conduct a parent interview, but not if the only option was to interview a partner and/or child.

Contact was made with organisations of – and for – disabled people, as well as day centres and other community facilities. Initial visits, at which we could discuss the aims of the project, were often followed by individuals in these organisations making informal enquiries on our behalf and distributing our literature to possible participants. (Other contact was made by telephone, and by providing newsletters.) We attempted to cover as many local and national organisations as possible, including general groups (guilds of disabled people, advocacy organisations, and so on) as well as impairment-specific groups.

As Stage One progressed, it became clear that it was proving difficult to recruit families with disabled fathers, single-parent families, and parents with mental health impairments. Given our commitment to an inclusive notion of parenting, and in recognition of the exclusion of fathers from much research on parenting, we subsequently made even greater efforts to indicate in our literature that we were interested in disabled fathers as well as mothers.

We also faced difficulties in recruiting parents with mental health impairments. This is reflected in the final sample, although the number of physically impaired parents who also talked about mental health impairments helped to redress the balance. Our request in the introductory literature to interview one child aged between seven and 18 may have been significant here. Despite our assurances that we were not connected to any formal or voluntary service, and that our research did not intend to pass judgement on the quality of respondents' parenting, some parents may have been anxious about our research. This reflects broader fears about family separation and the negative involvement of outside professionals.

Our response to ongoing difficulties in recruiting parents with mental health impairments was to intensify our contacts with voluntary organisations and to approach several general practices in Leicestershire with the aim of them helping us with recruitment. A large proportion of adults with mental health impairments are unlikely to receive secondary or inpatient care, and their main (perhaps only) point of contact with formal support is likely to be their GP (Meltzer et al, 1995), although we are aware that many will receive no formal medical support at all. We therefore received ethical approval for recruiting parents via general practice. It still proved difficult to recruit parents with mental health impairments, but the sheer volume of invitations to parents known to meet the criteria for inclusion, backed by a covering letter from their GP, enabled us at least partially to address the impairment group imbalance in the achieved sample.

Stage Two

Recruitment for Stage Two involved making contact with medical and nursing staff specialising in neurology, trauma and orthopaedics. In addition, we established contact with consultants in the local mental health services. Ethical approval for this stage was obtained. We devised the following inclusion criteria in Stage Two, with the aim of capturing a more longitudinal perspective on families where parents had experienced the recent onset of impairments:

- participants should have recently experienced a diagnosis of, or severe deterioration in, a neurological or psychiatric condition *or* have recently experienced a traumatic injury involving moderate to severe long-term impairments;
- participants should be parents, with at least one child between the ages of seven and 18 ordinarily resident with them (discounting any current period of hospitalisation).

It became increasingly clear that this approach was unlikely to yield the required 12 families. This was partly because of the inherent difficulty of recruiting families at a time of great disruption and difficulty. It was also partly because people experiencing traumatic injury are frequently transferred to specialist spinal and head injury units elsewhere, while our ethical approval extended to Leicestershire only. Consequently, we were limited to recruiting from Leicestershire Trusts.

We then adapted the inclusion criteria for Stage Two, in order to increase the chances of finding the required number of families, but also in the light of ongoing analysis of our Stage One questionnaires. Our interviews with parents in Stage One told us that impairment was only one factor among many others that structured the experience of parenting and family life. At least as important were the social, economic and environmental contexts in which parenting takes place. We therefore felt that a set of inclusion criteria for Stage Two that rested too heavily on diagnosis and severity of impairment risked ignoring this broader context and leant too heavily on the medical model. We made secondary contact with consultants and nursing staff who were helping us recruit for Stage Two, and asked them to reconsider including families where a diagnosis, deterioration or injury may or may not be recent, but for whom major life changes were either taking place, or were about to take place. This allowed them to include those parents whose impairments were long-standing and relatively stable, but who, for instance, were about to have a new baby, or who were divorcing.

In addition, we identified a number of families from Stage One interviews for whom significant changes were anticipated. For example, these included families who were on the point of having further children; had talked about impending significant changes in service use; or had particularly difficult short- and medium-term employment and financial issues to resolve. We then returned to these families and conducted semi-structured qualitative interviews exploring change in the same way as we had for those originally recruited as Stage Two families.

Data management and analysis

Our pilot work revealed the degree of complexity, change and variability with which disabled parents live. As Stage One interviews were progressing, it became apparent that what people were telling us *outside* the structured range of possible answers was often more illuminating than the data available from 'tick-this-box' answers. For instance, parents with fluctuating impairments found it difficult to answer our sections on support for parenting without distinguishing between spells when they saw themselves as 'ill' or 'well'.

Our pilot work allowed us to build as much flexibility into the questionnaires as possible, often involving complex, multi-layered grids, and asking parents to distinguish between times when the disabled parent was 'ill' or 'well'. However, it was still impossible to design questionnaires that could encompass neatly both the heterogeneity of the sample (in terms of impairment, as well as family shape and demographic characteristics) and the patterns of change and variability in the life of each family.

For these reasons, we thought it important to draw out the qualitative themes arising from each interview in a systematic fashion alongside the growing body of quantitative data. Following each interview, we wrote a short summary of the key issues identified by respondents. In addition, we carefully extracted all relevant themes from the questionnaire, and organised them into relatively coherent clusters. Each theme was entered in a grid that gave the basic characteristics of the family concerned, including number of children, gender of disabled parent, family income, the impairments of the disabled parent, and family shape. This enabled us, on subsequent analysis, to contextualise data in a manageable way. Once the process of compiling themes and data entry had been conducted, we were able to analyse the qualitative and quantitative data from Stage One in a more reciprocal and complementary way.

In Stage Two we analysed the transcripts for each interview[5]. In analysing these transcripts, we were aware that the families in the two stages were less distinct, in terms of recent onset, than we had originally intended. What distinguished Stage Two families was the scope and extent of change they were currently experiencing. We therefore decided to avoid analysing Stage Two transcripts for clusters of themes in quite the same way as we had for Stage One (we already had more than enough data from our 67 Stage One families). Instead, we analysed the transcripts around the central organising themes of change and complexity across a range of issues, including impairment, family shape, significant life events, service input, and so on.

Notes

[1] The age at which children are included in research is always a matter of judgement. We limited our interviews to children aged seven to 18, since they could articulate their experiences better than younger children, which would aid us in overcoming some of the subject matter's complexity.

[2] All research materials used are included as appendices in Olsen and Clarke (2001).

[3] The approach is often applied to research into the views of health service users and/or disabled people regarding formal and informal support available to them (Pryce-Jones, 1993; Kemppainen, 2000; Martensson et al, 2001; Muir and Ogden, 2001).

[4] A small number of parents took the opportunity to do so, mainly on grounds of a child's lack of knowledge about parental impairments, learning disabilities on the part of the child, or a concern that the child would find the interview too difficult.

[5] The exceptions to this were the six Stage Two families who had been followed up from Stage One. In these cases, we only had transcripts from our second visit.

Comparisons with the 'Looking After Children' (LAC) community sample

As discussed in Appendix One, we also collected data on children's abilities with regard to a range of self-care tasks and developmental skills. The questions were adapted from the Looking After Children (LAC) schedules, and allowed some degree of comparison between the children in our sample and those in a community sample on which the original LAC materials were tested (Ward, 1995). Table A.1 presents the data for the children in our Parenting and Disability (PANDD) study and compares them with those for the original LAC community sample (three children have been excluded because they were below the age of seven at the time of interview). The table is split into three broad columns representing the three age bands used in the LAC schedules and reproduced in our study (ages 7-9, 10-15 and 16+). Each age group is then subdivided (the data from our study have been left unshaded, and the data from the LAC shaded). The questions for each sample are then listed in italics. This enables the reader to compare the data for children in the same age band across the two studies. For instance, we can see that 76.9% of seven- to nine-year-olds in our study could get a drink or a snack for themselves, compared with a figure of 93.3% for those in the LAC sample. However, it also enables us to compare the children in our study with *older* children in the LAC sample, reflecting concerns about the 'false maturity' experienced by the children of disabled parents. For instance, 31.5% of young people aged 16+ in the LAC sample had filled in a claim form. In our sample, the figure was 44.4% for those of a similar age, but only 11.1% for those aged between 10 and 15.

We must be cautious when interpreting these data. Firstly, the numbers are small and valid percentages are given only as an indication of the breakdown of the sample in response to each question, rather than as an indication of statistical significance. Secondly, while the LAC sample questions for all children (up to and including those aged 15) were asked in the third person – that is, to professionals – all of our questions were directed at children themselves. Thirdly, the two samples are not matched in any respect other than age. Any difference may therefore be attributable to other factors distinguishing the groups, such as the likelihood that our sample of children experience greater poverty than children in a random population sample.

However, the samples seem to indicate two things. Firstly, the children in the PANDD sample appear to possess a range of self-care and developmental skills comparable to those of their age-matched peers in the wider community. There are no areas in which the children in our sample have a radically different profile of answers to those of their age-matched peers in the LAC sample. Secondly, it suggests that the children in our sample *are not* unusually advanced in their performance of the self-care skills covered. In general, there is a wide difference between the performance of self-care tasks in our sample, and the performance of those same tasks among older children, whether in our study or in the LAC community sample. For instance, 38% of children aged 10-15 in the LAC sample can undertake simple repairs unaided, such as changing a plug or fuse, with 39% unable to do so either with or without assistance. The corresponding figures for the 10-15 year olds in our sample are 30.5% and 41.7%. However, for seven- to nine-year-olds in our sample, the figures are very different: 7.7% are able to undertake repairs and 76.9% are unable to do so.

The one area that appears to indicate some degree of unusual maturity is using a launderette or doing the laundry. Those aged 16+ in our sample have much greater experience of this (albeit based on very small numbers), and the experience of 10- to 15-year-olds in our research mirrored that of those aged 16+ in the LAC sample (but once again, based on small numbers).

In summary, the data suggest that the children of disabled parents are likely to have similar levels of self-care development skills to their peers in the wider community, and are unlikely to have acquired self-care skills any earlier. However, more research (with greater numbers) is needed in order to verify these suggestions, to explore broader areas of self-care and other-care, and to include analysis of gender, social class, family shape and other potentially significant variables.

Table A.1: Comparison between the LAC community sample and PANDD sample for a range of self-care and developmental skills (valid % figures given in brackets)

	Children aged 7-9 years				Children aged 10-15 years				Children aged 16+ years			
	PANDD		LAC		PANDD		LAC		PANDD		LAC	
	Answer	N	Answer	N	Answer	N	Answer	N	Answer	N	Answer	N

Q1. Can the child get a drink or snack for him/herself?

	PANDD		LAC	
Yes	10	(76.9)	84	(93.3)
Learning	2	(15.4)	6	(6.7)
No	1	(7.7)	0	(0.0)
Total	13		90	

Q2. Can the child make their bed?

	PANDD		LAC	
Yes	9	(69.2)	69	(77.5)
Learning	2	(15.4)	13	(14.6)
No	2	(15.4)	7	(7.9)
Total	13		89	

Q3. Can the child answer the telephone?

	PANDD		LAC	
Yes	11	(84.6)	79	(95.2)
Learning	n/a		n/a	
No	2	(15.4)	4	(4.8)
Total	13		83	

Q4. Can the child make an emergency telephone call?

	PANDD		LAC	
Yes	10	(76.9)	74	(82.2)
Learning	0	(0)	7	(7.8)
No	3	(23.1)	9	(10.0)
Total	13		90	

Table A.1: Contd.../

	Children aged 7-9 years				Children aged 10-15 years				Children aged 16+ years			
	PANDD		LAC		PANDD		LAC		PANDD		LAC	
	Answer	N	Answer	N	Answer	N	Answer	N	Answer	N	Answer	N
Q5. Can the child cook a simple meal?												
	Yes	3 (23.1)			Yes	26 (72.2)	Yes	93 (93.0)				
	Learning	2 (15.4)			Learning	8 (22.2)	Learning	7 (7.0)				
	No	8 (61.5)			No	2 (5.6)	No	0 (0.0)				
	Total	13			Total	36	Total	100				
Q6. Can the child use a public telephone?												
	Yes	8 (61.5)			Yes	29 (80.6)	Yes	96 (96.0)				
	Learning	1 (7.7)			Learning	4 (11.1)	Learning	2 (2.0)				
	No	4 (30.8)			No	3 (8.3)	No	2 (2.0)				
	Total	13			Total	36	Total	100				
Q7. Can the child go to the shops or hairdressers alone?												
	Yes	8 (61.5)			Yes	35 (97.2)	Yes	99 (99.0)				
	Learning	n/a			Learning	N/a	Learning	n/a				
	No	5 (38.5)			No	1 (2.8)	No	1 (1.0)				
	Total	13			Total	36	Total	100				
Q8. Can the child do repairs such as changing a plug or a fuse or handling tools?												
	Yes	1 (7.7)			Yes	11 (30.5)	Yes	38 (38.0)				
	Learning	2 (15.4)			Learning	10 (27.8)	Learning	23 (23.0)				
	No	10 (76.9)			No	15 (41.7)	No	39 (39.0)				
	Total	13			Total	36	Total	100				

Table A.1: continued

	Children aged 7-9 years		Children aged 10-15 years		Children aged 16+ years	
	PANDD	LAC	PANDD	LAC	PANDD	LAC
	Answer N	Answer N	Answer N	Answer N	Answer N	Answer N
Q9. Can the child undertake simple first aid (such as putting a plaster on if you cut yourself)?						
	Yes 9 (69.2)		Yes 27 (75.0)	Yes 90 (90.0)		
	Learning 2 (15.4)		Learning 7 (19.4)	Learning 6 (6.0)		
	No 2 (15.4)		No 2 (5.6)	No 4 (4.0)		
	Total 13		Total 36	Total 100		
Q10. Has the child ever used the launderette or done the laundry?						
			Yes 19 (52.8)		Yes 7 (77.8)	Yes 46 (51.7)
			No 17 (47.2)		No 2 (22.2)	No 43 (48.3)
			Total 36		Total 9	Total 89
Q11. Has the child ever sewn on a button?						
			Yes 21 (58.3)		Yes 7 (77.8)	Yes 72 (81.8)
			No 15 (41.7)		No 2 (22.2)	No 16 (18.2)
			Total 36		Total 9	Total 88
Q12. Has the child ever filled in a claim form?						
			Yes 4 (11.1)		Yes 4 (44.4)	Yes 28 (31.5)
			No 32 (88.9)		No 5 (55.6)	No 61 (68.5)
			Total 36		Total 9	Total 89

Table A.1: continued

| | Children aged 7-9 years | | | | Children aged 10-15 years | | | | Children aged 16+ years | | | |
| | PANDD | | LAC | | PANDD | | LAC | | PANDD | | LAC | |
	Answer	N	Answer	N	Answer	N	Answer	N	Answer	N	Answer	N
Q13. Has the child had to negotiate with an organisation like a hospital or social security by him/herself?												
					Yes	8 (22.2)			Yes	4 (44.4)	Yes	18 (20.2)
					No	28 (78.8)			No	5 (55.6)	No	71 (79.8)
					Total	36			Total	9	Total	89
Q14. Has the child ever worked out how to read a bus or train timetable?												
					Yes	22 (61.1)			Yes	9 (100.0)	Yes	88 (98.9)
					No	14 (38.9)			No	0 (0.0)	No	1 (1.1)
					Total	36			Total	9	Total	89

References

Alderson, P. (1995) *Listening to children*, London: Barnardos.

Aldgate, J., Tunstill, J., McBeath, G. and Ozolins, R. (1994) *Implementing Section 17 of the Children Act – the first 18 months*, Leicester: Leicester University.

Aldridge, J. and Becker, S. (1993a) *Children who care: Inside the world of young carers*, Loughborough: Young Carers Research Group.

Aldridge, J. and Becker, S. (1993b) 'Children as carers', *Archives of Disease in Childhood*, vol 69, pp 459-62.

Aldridge, J. and Becker, S. (1993c) 'Punishing children for caring: the hidden cost of young carers', *Children and Society*, vol 7, no 4, pp 376-87.

Aldridge, J. and Becker, S. (1993d) 'Children who care', *Childright*, June, pp 13-14.

Aldridge, J. and Becker, S. (1994) *My child, my carer: The parent's perspective*, Loughborough: Young Carers Research Group.

Aldridge, J. and Becker, S. (1999) 'Children as carers: the impact of parental illness and disability on children's caring roles', *Journal of Family Therapy*, vol 21, no 3, pp 303-20.

Allan, J. (1994) 'Parenting education in Australia', *Children and Society*, vol 8, no 4, pp 344-59.

Andron, L. and Tymchuk, A. (1987) 'Parents who are mentally retarded', in A. Craft (ed) *Mental handicap and sexuality*, Tunbridge Wells: Costello, pp 238-62.

Appleby, L. and Dickens, C. (1993) 'Editorial: mothering skills of women with mental illness', *British Medical Journal*, vol 306, pp 348-49.

Barlow, J. (1999) 'What works in parent education programmes?', in E. Lloyd (ed) *Parenting matters: What works in parenting education?*, Ilford: Barnardos, pp 64-84.

Barnes, C. (1991) *Disabled people in Britain and discrimination: A case for anti-discrimination legislation*, London: Hurst and Co.

Barnes, C. (1996) 'Disability and the myth of the independent researcher', *Disability and Society*, vol 11, no 1, pp 107-10.

Barnes, C., Mercer, G. and Shakespeare, T. (1999) *Exploring disability: A sociological introduction*, Cambridge: Polity.

Barnett, B. and Parker, G. (1998) 'The parentified child: early competence or childhood deprivation?', *Child Psychology and Psychiatry Review*, vol 3, no 4, pp 146-55.

Barron, K. (1997) 'The bumpy road to womanhood', *Disability and Society*, vol 12, no 2, pp 223-39.

Bebbington, A. and Miles, J. (1989) 'The background of children who enter local authority care', *British Journal of Social Work*, vol 19, no 5, pp 349-68.

Beckett, C. and Wrighton, E. (2000)'"What matters to me is not what you're talking about": maintaining the social model of disability in "Public and Private" negotiations', *Disability and Society*, vol 15, no 7, pp 991-9.

Begum, N. (1996) 'General practitioners' role in shaping disabled women's lives', in C. Barnes and G. Mercer (eds) *Exploring the divide: Illness and disability*, Leeds: The Disability Press, pp 157-72.

Belsky, J., Robins, E. and Gamble, W. (1984) 'The determinants of parental competence: towards a contextual theory', in M. Lewis (ed) *Beyond the Dyad*, New York and London: Plenum Press, pp 251-79.

Beresford, P. (2000) 'What have madness and psychiatric system survivors got to do with disability and disability studies?', *Disability and Society*, vol 15, no 1, pp 167-72.

Beresford, P. and Croft, S. (2001) 'Mental health policy: a suitable case for treatment?', in C. Newnes, G. Holmes and C. Dunn (eds) *This is madness too: Critical perspectives on mental health services*, Ross-on-Wye: PCCS Books, pp 11-12.

Beresford, P., Harrison, C. and Wilson, A. (2002) 'Mental health service users and disability: implications for future strategies', *Policy & Politics*, vol 30, no 3, pp 387-96.

Beresford, P. and Wilson, A. (2002) 'Genes spell danger: mental health service users/survivors, bioethics and control', *Disability and Society*, vol 17, no 5, pp 541-53.

Bilsborrow, S. (1992) *'You grow up fast as well': Young carers on Merseyside* (3rd draft), Ilford: Barnardos.

Bird, G. and Ratcliff, B. (1990) 'Children's participation in family tasks: determinants of mothers' and fathers' reports', *Human Relations*, vol 43, no 6, pp 865-84.

Booth, T., and Booth, W. (1993a) 'Parenting with learning difficulties: lessons for practitioners', *British Journal of Social Work*, vol 23, pp 459-80.

Booth, T. and Booth, W. (1993b) 'Learning the hard way: practice issues in supporting parents with learning difficulties', *Social Work and Social Sciences Review*, vol 4, no 2, pp 148-62.

Booth, T. and Booth, W. (1994a) *Parenting under pressure: Mothers and fathers with learning difficulties*, Buckingham: Open University Press.

Booth, T. and Booth, W. (1994b) 'Parental adequacy, parenting failure and parents with learning difficulties', *Health and Social Care in the Community*, vol 2, no 3, pp 161-72.

Borsay, A. (1997) 'Personal trouble or public issue? Towards a model of policy for people with physical and mental disabilities' in L. Barton and M. Oliver (eds) *Disability studies: Past, present and future*, Leeds: The Disability Press, pp 115-37.

Bowlby, J. (1965) *Child care and the growth of love* (2nd edn), Harmondsworth: Penguin.

Brannen, J. (1992) 'British parenthood in the wake of the New Right: some contradictions and changes', in U. Bjornberg (ed) *European parents in the 1990s: Contradictions and comparisons*, New Brunswick and London: Transaction Publishers, pp 307-19.

Brindle, D. (1995) 'Two cats and a flat', *Search*, Spring, Joseph Rowntree Foundation, pp 8-11.

Bronfenbrenner, U. (1979) *The ecology of human development: Experiments by nature and design*, Cambridge, MA: Harvard University Press.

Burleigh, M. (1994) *Death and deliverance: 'Euthanasia' in Germany c1900-1945*, Cambridge: Cambridge University Press.

Bury, M. (1996) 'Defining and researching disability: challenges and responses', in C. Barnes and G. Mercer (eds) *Exploring the divide: Illness and disability*, Leeds: The Disability Press, pp 17-38.

Campion, M. (1995) *Who's fit to be a parent?*, London: Routledge.

Carlisle, D. (1998) 'Child friendly?', *Community Care*, 26 March-1 April, pp 18-19.

Coleman, R. and Cassell, D. (1994) 'Psychiatric patients and their families', *Health and Social Care in the Community*, vol 2, no 3, pp 187-9.

Cotson, D., Friend, J., Hollins, S. and James, H. (2001) 'Implementing the Framework for the Assessment of Children in Need and their Families when the parent has a learning disability', in J. Horwath (ed) *The child's world: Assessing children in need*, London: Jessica Kingsley Publishers, pp 287-302.

Cottrell, D. (1989) 'Family therapy influences on general adult psychiatry', *British Journal of Psychiatry*, vol 154, pp 473-7.

Crow, L. (1996) 'Including all of our lives: renewing the social model of disability', in C. Barnes and G. Mercer (eds) *Exploring the divide: Illness and disability*, Leeds: The Disability Press, pp 55-73.

Dartington Social Research Unit (1995) *Child protection: Messages from research*, London: HMSO.

Dearden, C. and Becker, S. (1995) *Young carers: The facts*, Loughborough: Young Carers Research Group.

Dearden, C. and Becker, S. (1998) *Young carers in the UK*, London: Carers National Association and Young Carers Research Group.

Dearden, C. and Becker, S. (2001) 'Young carers: needs, rights and assessments' in J. Horwath (ed) *The child's world: Assessing children in need*, London: Jessica Kingsley Publishers, pp 221-33.

Dearden, C., Becker, S. and Aldridge, J. (1994) *Partners in caring: A briefing for professionals about young carers*, Loughborough: Young Carers Research Group, Carers National Association and Crossroads UK.

De'Ath, E. (1989) 'Families and children', in B. Kahan (ed) *Child care research policy and practice*, London: Hodder and Stoughton, pp 30-54.

De Chillo, N., Matorin, S. and Hallahan, C. (1987) 'Children of psychiatric patients: rarely seen or heard', *Health and Social Work*, vol 3, pp 296-302.

DfEE (Department for Education and Employment) (1999) *From exclusion to inclusion: Final report of the Disability Rights Task Force*, London: The Stationery Office.

DoH (Department of Health) (1991a) *Care management and assessment: Managers' guide*, London: HMSO.

DoH (1991b) *Care management and assessment: Practitioners' guide*, London: HMSO.

DoH (1994) *Children Act report, 1993*, (Cmnd 2584), London: HMSO.

DoH (1996) *Community Care (Direct Payments) Act 1996: Policy and practice guidance*, London: Crown Copyright.

DoH (1998) *Crossing bridges: Training resources for working with mentally ill parents and their children*, Brighton: Pavilion.

DoH (2000a) *Caring about carers: A national strategy for carers*, London: Crown Copyright.

DoH (2000b) *A jigsaw of services: Inspection of services to support disabled adults in their parenting role*, London: SSI.

DoH (2001) *Valuing people: A new strategy for learning disability for the 21st century*, (CM 5086), London: The Stationery Office.

DoH (2002) *Fair access to care services: Guidance on eligibility criteria for adult social care* (LAC [2002] 13), London: DoH.

DoH, DfEE and HO (Department of Health, Department for Education and Employment, and Home Office) (2000) *Framework for the assessment of children in need and their families*, London: The Stationery Office.

Dowdney, L. and Skuse, D. (1993) 'Parenting provided by adults with mental retardation', *Journal of Child Psychology and Psychiatry*, vol 34, no 1, pp 25-47.

Drewett, A. (1999) 'Social rights and disability: the language of "rights" in community care policies', *Disability and Society*, vol 14, no 1, pp 115-28.

Edwards, J. (1995) '"Parenting skills": views of community health and social service providers about the needs of their "clients"', *Journal of Social Policy*, vol 24, pp 237-59.

Falkov, A. (1996) *Study of Working Together. Part 8: Reports: Fatal child abuse and parental psychiatric disorder: An analysis of 100 Area Child Protection Committee case reviews conducted under the terms of Part 8 of Working Together under the Children Act 1989*, London: DoH.

Fallon, K. (1990) 'An involuntary workforce', *Community Care*, 4 January, pp 12-13.

Ferri, E. and Smith, K. (1996) *Parenting in the 1990s*, London: Family Policy Studies Centre.

Finger, A. (1990) *Past due: A story of disability, pregnancy and birth*, London: The Women's Press.

Finkelstein, V. and French, S. (1993) 'Towards a psychology of disability', in J. Swain, V. Finkelstein, S. French and M. Oliver (eds) *Disabling barriers – Enabling environments*, London: Sage Publications, pp 26-33.

Flanagan, J. (1954) 'The critical incident technique', *Psychological Bulletin*, vol 5, pp 327-58.

Frank, J. (2002) *Making it work*, London: The Children's Society and the Princess Royal Trust for Carers.

Frank, J., Tatum, C. and Tucker, S. (1999) *On small shoulders: Learning from the experiences of former young carers*, London: The Children's Society.

French, S. (1993) 'Disability, impairment or something in between?', in J. Swain, V. Finkelstein, S. French and M. Oliver (eds) *Disabling barriers – Enabling environments*, London: Sage Publications, pp 17-25.

Gath, A. (1988) 'Mentally handicapped people as parents', *Journal of Child Psychology and Psychiatry*, vol 29, no 6, pp 739-44.

Gibbons, J., Thorpe, S. and Wilkinson, P. (1990) *Family support and prevention: Studies in local areas – Purposes and organisation of preventive work with families*, London: HMSO.

Gibbons, J., Conroy, S. and Bell, C. (1995) *Operating the child protection system*, London: HMSO.

Gilhool, T. and Gran, J. (1985) 'Legal rights of disabled parents', in S. Thurman (ed) *Children of handicapped parents: Research and clinical perspectives*, London: Academic Press, pp 11-34.

Goodman, M. (1994) *Mother's pride and others' prejudice: A survey of disabled mothers' experiences of maternity*, London: Maternity Alliance.

Green, R., Hyde, E., Katz, I., Mesie, J., Vincenti, O. and Worthing, D. (1997) *Long-term problems, short-term solutions: Parents in contact with mental health services*, London: NSPCC.

Greer, B. (1985) 'Children of physically disabled parents: some thoughts, facts and hypotheses', in S. Thurman (ed) *Children of handicapped parents: Research and clinical perspectives*, London: Academic Press, pp 131-44.

Griffiths, R. (1988) *Community care: Agenda for action*, London: HMSO.

Gross, D. (1989) 'Semprevivo; mentally ill mothers of young children', *Journal of Community Psychiatric Nursing*, vol 2, pp 105-9.

Hallett, C. (1991) 'The Children Act 1989 and community care: comparisons and contrasts', *Policy & Politics*, vol 19, no 4, pp 283-91.

Handley, C., Farrell, G., Josephs, A., Hanke, A. and Hazelton, M. (2001) 'The Tasmanian children's project: the needs of children with a parent/carer with a mental illness', *Australian and New Zealand Journal of Mental Health Nursing*, vol 10, no 4, pp 221-8.

Hardiker, P. (1996) 'The legal and social construction of significant harm', in M. Hill and J. Aldgate (eds) *Child welfare services: Developments in law, policy, practice and research*, London: Jessica Kingsley Publishers, pp 105-19.

Harding, L. (1996) *Family, state and social policy*, Basingstoke: Macmillan.

Hasler, F., Campbell, J. and Zarb, G. (1999) *Direct routes to independence: A guide to local authority implementation and management of direct payments*, London: Policy Studies Institute.

Hawes, V. and Cottrell, D. (1999) 'Disruption of children's lives by maternal psychiatric admission', *Psychiatric Bulletin*, vol 23, pp 153-6.

Henricson, C., Katz, I., Mesie, J., Sandison, M. and Tunstill, J. (2001) *National mapping of family services in England and Wales: A consultation document*, London: National Family and Parenting Institute.

Heslinga, K., Schellen, A. and Verkuyl, A. (1974) *Not made of stone: The sexual problems of handicapped people*, Springfield: Charles C. Thomas Publishing.

Hill, M. and Aldgate, J. (1996) 'The Children Act 1989 and recent developments in research in England and Wales', in M. Hill and J. Aldgate (eds) *Child welfare services: Developments in law, policy, practice and research*, London: Jessica Kingsley Publishers, pp 3-23.

Hirsch, B., Moos, R. and Reischl, T. (1985) 'Psychosocial adjustment of adolescent children of a depressed, arthritic, or normal parent', *Journal of Abnormal Psychology*, vol 94, no 2, pp 154-64.

Hughes, B. and Paterson, K. (1997) 'The social model of disability and the disappearing body: towards a sociology of impairment', *Disability and Society*, vol 12, no 3, pp 325-40.

Jack, G. (2001) 'Ecological perspectives in assessing children and families', in J. Horwath (ed) *The child's world:Assessing children in need*, London:Jessica Kingsley Publishers, pp 53-74.

James, G. (1994) *Department of Health discussion – Report for ACPC conference: Study of Working Together. Part 8: Reports*, London: DoH.

James, A. and Prout, A. (eds) (1990) *Constructing and reconstructing childhood: Contemporary issues in the sociological study of childhood*, London: Falmer Press.

Jamison, R. and Walker, L. (1992) 'Illness behaviour in children of chronic pain patients', *International Journal of Psychiatry in Medicine*, vol 22, no 4, pp 329-42.

Johnstone, L. (2000) *Users and abusers of psychiatry: A critical look at psychiatric practice* (2nd edn) London: Routledge.

Jones, D. (2002) 'Madness, the family and psychiatry', *Critical Social Policy*, vol 22, no 2, pp 247-72.

Kelley, S., Sikka, A. and Venkatesan, S. (1997) 'A review of research on parental disability: implications for research and counselling practice', *Rehabilitation Counselling Bulletin*, vol 41, no 2, pp 105-21.

Keith, L. and Morris, J. (1995) 'Easy targets: a disability rights perspective on the "children as carers" debate', *Critical Social Policy*, vol 45, pp 36-57.

Kemppainen, J. (2000) 'The critical incident technique and nursing care quality research', *Journal of Advanced Nursing*, vol 32, no 5, pp 1264-71.

Kestenbaum, A. (1993) *Making community care a reality: The Independent Living Fund 1988-1993*, London: Independent Living Fund.

LeClere, F. and Kowalewski, B. (1994) 'Disability in the family: the effects on children's well-being', *Journal of Marriage and the Family*, vol 56, pp 457-68.

Lloyd, E. (ed) (1999) *Parenting matters: What works in parenting education?*, Ilford: Barnardos.

Mahon, A. and Higgins, J. (1995) *'A life of our own'. Young carers: An evaluation of three RHA-funded projects in Merseyside*, Manchester: Health Services Management Unit.

Martensson, J., Dracup, K. and Fridlund, B. (2001) 'Decisive situations influencing spouses' support of patients with heart failure: a critical incident technique analysis', *Heart and Lung*, vol 30, no 5, pp 341-50.

Mason, M. (1992) 'A nineteen-parent family', in J. Morris (ed) *Alone together: Voices of single mothers*, London: Women's Press, pp 112-25.

Maternity Alliance (1994) *Listen to us for a change: A charter for disabled parents and parents-to-be*, London: Maternity Alliance.

Meltzer, H., Gill, B., Petticrew, M. and Hinds, K. (1995) *The prevalence of psychiatric morbidity among adults living in private households*, London: HMSO.

Meredith, H. (1992) *The young carers project: A report on achievements 1990-1992*, London: Carers National Association.

Mizen, P., Bolton, A. and Pole, C. (1999) 'School-age workers: the paid employment of children in Britain', *Work, Employment and Society*, vol 13, no 3, pp 423-38.

Morgan, P. (1995) *Farewell to the family? Public policy and family breakdown in Britain and the USA*, London: Institute of Economic Affairs.

Morris, J. (ed) (1989) *Able lives: Women's experience of paralysis*, London: Women's Press.

Morris, J. (1991) *Pride against prejudice: Transforming attitudes to disability*, London: Women's Press.

Morris, J. (1992) 'Personal and political: a feminist perspective on researching physical disability', *Disability and Society*, vol 7, no 2, pp 157-66.

Morris, J. (1993a) *Community care or independent living*, York: Joseph Rowntree Foundation.

Morris, J. (1993b) *Independent lives: Community care and disabled people*, Basingstoke: Macmillan.

Morris, J. (1997) 'A response to Aldridge and Becker – disability rights and the denial of young carers: the dangers of zero-sum arguments', *Critical Social Policy*, vol 17, no 2, pp 133-6.

Morrow, V. (1996) 'Rethinking childhood dependency: children's contributions to the domestic economy', *The Sociological Review*, vol 44, no 1, pp 58-77.

Mortley, E. (1998) *'Good enough parenting': The role of parenting education*, Social Work Monographs, no 170, Norwich: University of East Anglia.

Mowbray, C., Oyserman, D. and Ross, S. (1995) 'Parenting and the significance of children for women with a serious mental illness', *Journal of Mental Health Administration*, vol 22, no 2, pp 189-200.

Muir, E. and Ogden, J. (2001) 'Consultations involving people with congenital disabilities: factors that help or hinder giving care', *Family Practice*, vol 18, no 4, pp 419-24.

Munoz, N. (1998) *Young carers and their families in Westminster*, London: Westminster Carers Service.

Newbrough, J. (1985) 'The handicapped parent in the community: a synthesis and commentary', in S. Thurman (ed) *Children of handicapped parents: Research and clinical perspectives*, London: Academic Press, pp 181-93.

Newman, T. (2000) 'Workers and helpers: perspectives on children's labour 1899-1999', *British Journal of Social Work*, vol 30, pp 323-38.

Newman, T. and Roberts, H. (1999) 'Assessing effectiveness', in E. Lloyd (ed) *Parenting matters: What works in parenting education?*, Ilford: Barnardos, pp 39-63.

Oakley, A. (1976) *Housewife*, Harmondsworth: Penguin.

Oakley, A., Mauthner, M., Rajan, L. and Turner, H. (1995) 'Supporting vulnerable families: an evaluation of NEWPIN', *Health Visitor*, vol 68, pp 188-91.

Oakley, A., Rajan, L. and Turner, H. (1998) 'Evaluating parent support initiatives: lessons from two case studies', *Health and Social Care in the Community*, vol 6, no 5, pp 318-30.

Oliver, M. (1990) *The politics of disablement*, Basingstoke: Macmillan Educational.

Oliver, M. (1992) 'Changing the social relations of research production?', *Disability, Handicap and Society*, vol 7, no 2, pp 101-14.

Oliver, M. and Sapey, B. (1999) *Social work with disabled people* (2nd edn), Basingstoke: Macmillan.

Olsen, R. (1996) 'Young carers: challenging the facts and politics of research into children and caring', *Disability and Society*, vol 11, no 1, pp 41-54.

Olsen, R. (2000) 'Families under the microscope: parallels between the "young carers" debate of the 1990s and the removal of children from the industrial labour force in the 19th century', *Children and Society*, vol 14, pp 384-94.

Olsen, R. and Clarke, H. (2001) *Parenting and disability: The role of formal and informal networks* (DoH90 RO/HC), Leicester: Nuffield Community Care Studies Unit.

Olsen, R. and Parker, G. (1997) 'A response to Aldridge and Becker – disability rights and the denial of young carers: the dangers of zero-sum arguments', *Critical Social Policy*, vol 17, no 1, pp 125-34.

O'Neil, A. and Platt, C. (1992) *Towards a strategy for carers: Young carers*, Tameside: Tameside Metropolitan Borough Council.

Oyserman, D., Mowbray, C. and Zemencuk, J. (1994) 'Resources and supports for mothers with severe mental illness', *Health and Social Work*, vol 19, no 2, pp 132-42.

Packman, J., Randall, J. and Jacques, N. (1986) *Who needs care? Social work decisions about children*, Oxford: Blackwell.

Page, R. (1988) *Report on the initial survey investigating the number of young carers in Sandwell secondary schools*, Sandwell: Sandwell Metropolitan Borough Council.

Parker, G. (1993) *With this body: Caring and disability in marriage*, Buckingham: Open University Press.

Parker, G. and Clarke, H. (2002) 'Making the ends meet: do carers and disabled people have a common agenda?', *Policy & Politics* vol 30, no 3, pp 347-59.

Parker, G. and Olsen, R. (1995a) *A sideways glance at young carers*, Working Paper WP36 9/95 GP.RO, Leicester: Nuffield Community Care Studies Unit.

Parker, G. and Olsen, R. (1995b) 'A plea to practitioners', *Community Care*, 14-20 September, p 21.

Parton, N. (1991) *Governing the family: Child care, child protection and the state*, Basingstoke: Macmillan.

Parton, N. (1997) 'Child protection and family support: current debates and future prospects', in N. Parton (ed) *Child protection and family support*, London: Routledge, pp 1-24.

Patel, N. and Fatimilehin, I. (1999) 'Racism and mental health', in C. Newnes, G. Holmes and C. Dunn (eds) *This is madness: A critical look at psychiatry and the future of mental health services*, Ross-on-Wye: PCCS Books, pp 51-73.

Plumb, A. (2002) 'Review article of Liz Sayce [2000] *From psychiatric patient to citizen: overcoming discrimination and social exclusion*', *Social Work Education*, vol 21, no 1, pp 117-23

Priestley, M. (1998) *Disability politics and community care*, London and Philadelphia: Jessica Kingsley Publishers.

Priestley, M. (2000) 'Adults only: disability, social policy and the life course', *Journal of Social Policy*, vol 29, no 3, pp 421-39.

Pryce-Jones, M. (1993) 'Critical incident technique as a method of assessing patient satisfaction', in R. Fitzpatrick and A. Hopkins (eds) *Measurement of patients' satisfaction with their care*, London: Royal College of Physicians, pp 87-98.

Qvortrup, J. (1990) 'A voice for children in statistical and social accounting: a plea for children's right to be heard', in A. James and A. Prout (eds) *Constructing and reconstructing childhood: Contemporary issues in the sociological study of childhood*, London: Falmer Press, pp 78-98.

Radke-Yarrow, M. (1991) *Attachment patterns in children of depressed mothers*, London: Routledge.

Reder, P. and Lucey, C. (eds) (1995) *Assessment of parenting: Psychiatric and psychological contributions*, London: Routledge.

Reder, P. and Duncan, S. (1997) 'Adult psychiatry – a missing link in the child protection network: comment on Falkov's *Fatal child abuse and parental psychiatric disorder*', *Child Abuse Review*, vol 6, issue 1, pp 35-40.

Reder, P. and Duncan, S. (1999) 'Auditing mental health aspects of child protection', *Child Abuse Review*, vol 8, issue 3, pp 147-51.

Roker, D. and Coleman, J. (1998) 'Parenting teenagers' programmes: a UK perspective', *Children and Society*, vol 12, issue 5, pp 359-72.

Rutter, M. (1966) *Children of sick parents: An environmental and psychiatric study*, London: Oxford University Press.

Rutter, M. (1981) *Maternal deprivation reassessed* (2nd edn), Harmondsworth: Penguin.

Rutter, M. and Madge, N. (1976) *Cycles of disadvantage: A review of research*, London: Heinemann.

Rutter, M., Quinton, D. and Yule, B. (1976) *Family pathology and disorder in children*, Chichester: John Wiley.

Sayce, L. (1999) 'Parenting as a civil right: supporting service users who choose to have children', in A. Weir and A. Douglas (eds) *Child protection and adult mental health: Conflict of interest?*, Oxford: Butterworth-Heinemann, pp 28-48.

Sayce, L. (2000) *From psychiatric patient to citizen: Overcoming discrimination and social exclusion*, London: Macmillan.

Shah, R. and Hatton, C. (1999) *Caring alone: Young carers in south Asian communities*, Ilford: Barnardos.

Shakespeare, T. and Watson, N. (1997) 'Defending the social model', in L. Barton and M. Oliver (eds) *Disability studies: Past, present and future*, Leeds: The Disability Press, pp 263-73.

Sheppard, M. (1997) 'Double jeopardy: the link between child abuse and maternal depression in child and family social work', *Child and Family Social Work*, vol 2, no 2, pp 91-107.

Sheppard, M. (2002) 'Depressed mothers' experience of partnership in child and family care', *British Journal of Social Work*, vol 32, issue 1, pp 93-112.

Siddall, R. (1994) 'Lost childhood', *Community Care*, 9-15 June, pp 14-15.

Smith, C. (1997) *Developing parenting programmes*, London: National Children's Bureau/Joseph Rowntree Foundation.

Stanley, N. and Penhale, B. (1999) 'The mental health problems of mothers experiencing the child protection system: identifying needs and appropriate responses', *Child Abuse Review*, vol 8, issue 1, pp 34-45.

Tanner, D. (2000) 'Crossing bridges over troubled waters? Working with children of parents experiencing mental distress', *Social Work Education*, vol 19, no 3, pp 287-97.

Tew, J. (2002) 'Going social: championing a holistic model of mental distress within professional education', *Social Work Education*, vol 21, no 2, pp 143-55.

Thoburn, J., Lewis, A. and Schemmings, D. (1995) *Paternalism or partnership? Family involvement in the child protection process*, London: HMSO.

Tierney, S (2001) 'A reluctance to be defined "disabled": how can the social model of disability enhance understanding of anorexia?', *Disability and Society*, vol 16, no 5, pp 749-64.

Tisdall, E. (1997) *The Children (Scotland) Act 1995: Developing policy and law for Scotland's children*, Edinburgh: The Stationery Office.

Tunstill, J. (1996) 'Family support: past, present and future challenges', *Child and Family Social Work*, vol 1, pp 151-8.

Tunstill, J. (1997) 'Implementing the family support clauses of the 1989 Children Act', in N. Parton (ed) *Child protection and family support*, London: Routledge, pp 39-58.

Twigg, J. and Atkin, K. (1995) 'Carers and service: factors mediating service provision', *Journal of Social Policy*, vol 24, no 1, pp 5-30.

UPIAS (Union of the Physically Impaired Against Segregation) (1976) *Fundamental principles of disability*, London: UPIAS.

Vondra, J. and Belsky, J. (1993) 'Developmental origins of parenting: personality and relationship factors', in T. Luster and L. Okagaki (eds) *Parenting: An ecological perspective*, Hillsdale, NJ: Lawrence Erlbaum Associates, pp 1-33.

Walker, A. (1996) *Young carers and their families*, London: The Stationery Office.

Wang, A. and Goldschmidt, V. (1994) 'Interviews of psychiatric inpatients about their family situation and young children', *Acta Psychiatrica Scandinavica*, vol 90, pp 459-65.

Ward, H. (ed) (1995) *Looking after children: Research into practice (The second report to the Department of Health on assessing outcomes in child care)*, London: HMSO.

Wates, M. (1997) *Disabled parents: Dispelling the myths*, London: National Childbirth Trust and Radcliffe Medical Press.

Wates, M. (2002) *Supporting disabled adults in their parenting role*, York: Joseph Rowntree Foundation.

Wates, M. and Jade, R. (1999) *Bigger than the sky: Disabled women on parenting*, London: The Women's Press.

Wates, M. and Olsen, R. (2003, forthcoming) *Disabled parents: Examining research assumptions*, Research Review, no 6, Sheffield: Research in Practice.

Watson, N. (2002) 'Well I know this is going to sound very strange to you, but I don't see myself as a disabled person: identity and disability', *Disability and Society*, vol 17, no 5, pp 509-27.

Webster-Stratton, C. (1999) 'Researching the impact of parent training programmes on child conduct problems', in E. Lloyd (ed) *Parenting matters: What works in parenting education?*, Ilford: Barnardos, pp 85-114.

White, C. and Barrowclough, C. (1998) 'Depressed and non-depressed mothers with problematic pre-schoolers: attributions for child behaviours', *British Journal of Clinical Psychology*, vol 37, no 4, pp 385-98.

White, C., Nicholson, J., Fisher, W. and Geller, J. (1995) 'Mothers with severe mental illness caring for children', *Journal of Nervous and Mental Disease*, vol 183, no 6, pp 398-403.

White, S. (1996) 'Regulating mental health and motherhood in contemporary welfare services: anxious attachments or attachment anxiety?', *Critical Social Policy*, vol 16, no 1, pp 67-94.

Wing, J., Curtis, R. and Beevor, A. (1996) *Health of the nation outcome scales: Report on practice and development, July 1993-December 1995*, London: Royal College of Psychiatrists.

Wing, J., Curtis, R. and Beevor, A. (1996) *Health of the nation outcome scales: Report on practice and development, July 1993-December 1995*, London: Royal College of Psychiatrists.

Winnicott, D. (1964) *The child, the family and the outside world*, Harmondsworth: Penguin.

Zarb, G. and Nadash, P. (1994) *Direct payments for personal assistance*, Social Policy Research 64, November, Joseph Rowntree Foundation.

Zeitz, M. (1995) 'The mothers' project; a clinical case-management system', *Psychiatric Rehabilitation Journal*, vol 19, no 1, pp 55-62.

Zill, N. and Peterson, J. (1982) 'Learning to do things without help', in L. Laosa and I. Sigel (eds) *Families as learning environments for children*, New York: Plenum Press, pp 343-67.

Index

Page references for tables are in *italics*; those for notes are followed by n.

Also available from The Policy Press

Children caring for parents with mental illness
Perspectives of young carers, parents and professionals
Jo Aldridge and Saul Becker
Paperback £19.99 US$29.95
ISBN 1 86134 399 X
Hardback £50.00 US$59.95
ISBN 1 86134 400 7
234 x 156mm 224 pages
March 2003

Mental health services and child protection
Responding effectively to the needs of families
Nicky Stanley, Bridget Penhale, Denise Riordan, Rosaline Barbour and Sue Holden
Paperback £15.99 US$25.00
ISBN 1 86134 427 9
234 x 156mm 128 pages tbc
September 2003

Children, family and the state
Decision-making and child participation
Nigel Thomas
Paperback £18.99 US$29.95
ISBN 1 86134 448 1
234 x 156mm 256 pages
October 2002

Disabled people and European human rights
A review of the implications of the 1998 Human Rights Act for disabled children and adults in the UK
Luke Clements and Janet Read
Paperback £15.99 US$25.00
ISBN 1 86134 425 2
234 x 156mm 144 pages
February 2003

Child welfare
Historical dimensions, contemporary debate
Harry Hendrick
Paperback £18.99 US$29.95
ISBN 1 86134 477 5
Hardback £55.00 US$59.95
ISBN 1 86134 478 3
234 x 156mm 304 pages
February 2003

For further information about these and other titles published by The Policy Press, please visit our website at:
www.policypress.org.uk

To order titles, please contact:
Marston Book Services
PO Box 269 • Abingdon
Oxon OX14 4YN • UK
Tel: +44 (0)1235 465500
Fax: +44 (0)1235 465556
E-mail: direct.orders@marston.co.uk